Reader's Comments

I really, really enjoyed reading this [Part 1], and I'm so thankful that I did when I did. My mother has never shared anything with me about that part of her life, and it would be so much help to me if she did. I can testify that God has already used these words He has given you to speak (to me). I was shown things in my life that are or were not pleasing to God. It seemed as though many of the struggles written about were my very own.

[I felt relieved] that God was faithful, and that I could relate; I wasn't alone. [I was encouraged] by the fact that God remained with you and even spoke to you when you thought He never would.

I am so thankful that God has given you these words, and I only wish that someone had addressed this topic sooner. The only place that I hear this topic talked about is with friends or in media, and the picture these resources paint is not the picture God would paint. Now I pray that God would give me the *strength* to take what I've learned and the ... *courage* to apply it.

—C.W. (age 20)

You are very frank. Praise the Lord for your honesty and courage describing [the] path from [the] world to toddling steps of Christianity to maturity in Christ. You have done a great job so far, Nancy, and are to be admired for your "no mask" approach. Rarely are Christians this honest. This book will have far more impact and ministry because of your total honesty.

—B.C. (age 70)

I felt the stories melded well with the teaching. Thank you for being so transparent and vulnerable. [I was] amused: You have a real way with words! [I was] encouraged, to know I'm not the only one who has struggled in this whole area.... [Was it] helpful? Yes, only I wish I had read this about ten years ago. I can see where this would have been very helpful then. [And I felt] sympathetic: I could relate to your continuous struggles.

Nancy, I can't wait to read the rest! This book is going to help a lot of women, especially young women and new Christians, but I also think it will minister to older Christians who are afraid to admit they struggle with their past at different times. Way to go! God will have a bride without spot or wrinkle.

—S.A. (age 42)

Overall, I really enjoyed reading this—it is a real page-turner! I was horribly disappointed when I got to the end [of Part 1] and didn't get to read the part about when things started going right for you! You must either have a phenomenal memory or else very good journals—the narratives were very immediate and detailed, and grounded the teachings very well. I thought there was a very good mix of story vs. abstract thought/teaching.

I also appreciated the tone of your writing. Your conviction is evident, but for the most part you avoid being preachy or condemning. I appreciated your honesty—admitting your inward struggles, although others would probably have called your behaviour blameless. A lot of the thought patterns you describe resonated with me and my experience. I identified with the struggle, the difficulty in discerning the "grey"—which is partly why I was disappointed when I realized I only had the first half of the book.... I think reading about how God did eventually bless you and reward you will be very encouraging to girls who are just now struggling to believe that His grace is sufficient in seemingly endless temptations and confusion.

On the other hand, I truly appreciated your faith in God, His grace, and His good plan for your life during these "Chasing Mr. Wrong" years. You make it evident that, for you, He *was* enough; He was gentle, compassionate, and firm in guiding you in the paths of righteousness. It is very interesting to read about someone else's experience, to get a glimpse of shared and different insights that you had, compared to my own life.

—E.B. (age 26)

When I read this chapter, I felt so strongly to everything that you said (wrote) ☺.... I love the fact that you *understand*. It is so comforting to know someone who can relate to the many struggles of youth today. I was thinking to myself, "Wow, if I was so moved by this *one* chapter, how am I gonna feel about the *whole book*!" LOL

I am *very much* looking forward to reading it! Thank you for the privilege of getting to read a bit of it ahead of time!... Also, I hope that somewhere in your book, you talk about "losing your virginity"—to the point of when, with who, and really just the whole stupid concept of it! Everybody has a different opinion on the subject, and I'm just really curious and interested in what your point of view is and what you have to say about it.

—K.K. (age 17)

I am *so* glad you are writing this book!

—L.S. (age 49)

First I must say what a gift God has given you for story-telling. You use your own life experiences, these raw and passionate emotions, that are so relatable to other young women's feelings, and use them, with the Word, to help us learn from your experiences.... I find your writing very refreshing and pragmatic. You are telling things the way that they are, but managing to never cross a line to offend.... Every word that you wrote had a purpose.

I myself am relatively new along my walk with Him. I only became a Christian a little over a year ago, and I cannot say that I have not already made some major slips and falls, especially in that wonderful department we call relationships. When you talked about your battles with lust and loneliness, your words about liking the power that your sexuality gave you, I could not help but relate to that. Yet knowing that God does not want you to abuse that, but be modest and humble, it can be so difficult to try and change your ways. I pray for courage and strength to act as the Lord wants me to.

—A.R. (age 18)

Nancy, you are a gifted writer! Your writing just flows and your words captivate. I honestly could not put your story [Part 1] down once I started reading it. I appreciate your openness on this subject; it allowed me to be more honest with myself regarding choices I had made when I was younger.

Your message is powerful and thought-provoking. A message that definitely needs to be present in our world today!...I found myself...more cognizant of the messages "our world" is sending re: sexual issues (T.V., movies, internet, etc.) and how important it is for parents, teachers, church leaders, etc. to provide the truth.

I wish that I had been exposed to this message when I was a teenager. As a happily married woman, I've asked [God] for forgiveness for choices I made as a youth, but every once in a while I face this "old guilt" again.

Thank you, Nancy, for allowing me to have a "sneak preview." You definitely left me wanting more!

—C.F. (age 38)

Made in Heaven
FLESHED OUT ON EARTH

Made in Heaven
FLESHED OUT ON EARTH

one woman's journey into
wholeness in marital intimacy

Nancy Fowler Christenson

Tate Publishing & *Enterprises*

Made in Heaven, Fleshed Out on Earth
Copyright © 2009 by Nancy Fowler Christenson. All rights reserved.

No part of this publication may be reproduced, stored in a retrieval system or transmitted in any way by any means, electronic, mechanical, photocopy, recording or otherwise without the prior permission of the author except as provided by USA copyright law.

Scripture quotations marked "KJV" are taken from the Holy Bible, King James Version, Cambridge, 1769. Used by permission. All rights reserved.

Scripture quotations marked "NKJV" are taken from The New King James Version / Thomas Nelson Publishers, Nashville: Thomas Nelson Publishers. Copyright © 1982. Used by permission. All rights reserved.

Scripture quotations marked "TAB" are taken from The Amplified Bible, Old Testament, Copyright © 1965, 1987 by the Zondervan Corporation and The Amplified New Testament, Copyright © 1958, 1987 by The Lockman Foundation. Used by permission. All rights reserved.

Scripture quotations marked "MSG" are taken from The Message, Copyright © 1993, 1994, 1995, 1996, 2000, 2001, 2002. Used by permission of NavPress Publishing Group. All rights reserved.

Scripture quotations marked "NIV" are taken from the Holy Bible, New International Version®, Copyright © 1973, 1978, 1984 by International Bible Society. Used by permission of Zondervan Publishing House. All rights reserved.

Scripture quotations marked "NAS" are taken from the New American Standard Bible®, Copyright © 1960, 1962, 1963, 1968, 1971, 1972, 1973, 1975, 1977, 1995 by The Lockman Foundation. Used by permission. All rights reserved.

Scripture quotations marked "NLT" are taken from the Holy Bible, New Living Translation, Copyright © 1996. Used by permission of Tyndale House Publishers, Inc. All rights reserved.

The opinions expressed by the author are not necessarily those of Tate Publishing, LLC.

Published by Tate Publishing & Enterprises, LLC
127 E. Trade Center Terrace | Mustang, Oklahoma 73064 USA
1.888.361.9473 | www.tatepublishing.com

Tate Publishing is committed to excellence in the publishing industry. The company reflects the philosophy established by the founders, based on Psalm 68:11,
"The Lord gave the word and great was the company of those who published it."

Book design copyright © 2009 by Tate Publishing, LLC. All rights reserved.
Cover design by Lance Waldrop
Interior design by Joey Garrett
Author Photo, back cover, Melissa Christenson, 2008

Published in the United States of America
ISBN: 978-1-60696-394-4
1. Biography & Autobiography / Personal Memoirs
2. Religion / Christian Life / Love & Marriage
09.02.26

Dedication

This book is first of all dedicated to my husband, Greg—

I love you! I am so grateful to God that He put us together. I'm thankful for your commitment to the Lord and for your love for me—for the way you respect me, honour me, cherish me, and really listen to me. It is my deepest desire, my fondest hope, and my most earnest prayer that our sons would become—and our daughters would find—the kind of husbands their father has been.

And so I also dedicate this book

to Ben—

to Lindsay—

to Melissa—

to Rachel—

May each of you "know the love of Christ which surpasses knowledge,"[1] for wrapped up in that knowledge, in that Relationship, is the culmination of all truth and beauty, all knowledge and wisdom, all happiness and fulfilment. Subsequent to this—for upon the former the latter relies—is the fervent hope that each of you would find the spouse of God's own choosing, that you might know the joy, the fulfillment, the adventure, and the comfort that your father and I have known in this great sacrament of God.

May each of you find a marriage within which God can reveal to you, in day-to-day living, the mystery of the love that the Bridegroom desires to lavish upon His Bride.

And finally, this book is dedicated to you, the "unknown" reader. You are unknown to me but intimately known and dearly loved by God. I pray that my story might be a catalyst for growth in your life. May you find hope where there has been discouragement and even despair, and healing where there has been brokenness. May you be encouraged to look to God, because all the answers are in Him.

Acknowledgements

My thanks go out to the many friends who have encouraged me in my writings in general and in this project in particular, especially those at the little community church that we call Lifegate.

A special thanks to those women of all ages who read portions of the manuscript and gave me feedback.

Thanks also to the team at Tate Publishing. What a privilege to work with such professional, warm, and courteous people! The whole process has been a very positive experience.

Last but most important, thanks to my husband, Greg, for sharing my desire to tell this story; for the endless hours of talking that shaped my understanding of what I was writing; for the astute, sensitive, and discerning comments on the manuscript. I could not have done this without you.

Table of Contents

Foreword — 17

A Note from the Author — 19

Part 1: Chasing Mr. Wrong — 25

Paperback Romance — 27

The Search for Love and Acceptance — 37

Dream or Delusion? — 45

The Young and the Restless — 55

Fleeing Youthful Lusts — 65

A Flame and a Funeral — 73

Re-Enter the Doctor — 79

Go East, Young Woman — 87

Delightful Delinquent — 93

Charming a Snake — 101

Progress of a Pilgrim — 113

Letting Go — 123

A Prophecy — 129

Part 2: Finding Mr. Right — 131

A Date with Destiny — 133

God Has Some Fun	145
A Valentine's Letter	153
The First Date	161
Facing My Fears	171
Lots of Letters	183
Needs and Expectations	199
The Breakaway Letters	207
Home Again	215
The Second Date	223
Old Things Become New	237
Wife-in-Waiting	251
Giving Up Control	261
The Final Countdown	275

Part 3: Ever After 285

Is the Honeymoon Over Yet?	287
What Is Wrong With Me?	299
Babies and Kisses	309
Healing Finally Comes	319
Happy Ever After	329
Endnotes	345
Other Works by the Author/Contact Info	353

Songs and Poems

He's Twenty-Nine; He's an Animal Doctor	33
Babysitting the Telephone	35
I Found the Love of Jesus (one verse only)	42
Heathen vs. Christian	46
Sinnerman	57
Prayer of Repentance	63
Heavenly Father	66
Lonely and Blue Blues	69
Prayer for Hartley	76
The Lord's Got Me Tight in His Loving Arms	82
Revelation at Rockford	89
Lord, Hear My Prayer, Hear My Song	98
What Will I Do for an Encore?	106
First Love	109
It's Still Coming Up Weeds	118
Let Go	123
It Amazes Me	128
How Would You Feel?	139
I Never Knew	174
As I Lay Me Down to Sleep	199
How Many Times?	224
The Ballad of Nancy and Greg	275
Love Song	287

Foreword

> "The things we have done
> and the places we have gone
> remain a part of who we are forever."
> —Nancy Christenson

Settle down with a hot cup of coffee or tea; you are about to be introduced to a very honest and bold fellow-sojourner of the faith.

We have been friends with Nancy since the pre-Greg era, and we participated in the adventure of newfound faith together. That was oh-so-long ago. We remember the day that we first heard about this man Greg, and we have continued in the kind of friendship that lasts throughout the decades of raising our children in two different parts of the world. Every time we are together, we enjoy the privilege of picking up where we left off, and that warm, familiar sense that comes from a lifelong friendship.

That Nancy is such a credible communicator is no surprise to us. It is her profound honesty in this writing that catches the breath. She dares to be honest where most of us would be tempted to hide the truth. And that Greg is so willing to have his story paraded for the masses shows the heart of this wonderful couple. They seem to say, "We'll do whatever we are asked to do if it helps further the story of Christ in us"—this is the very posture with which they confront life.

This is not a book of "how-tos" or a manual of sorts; rather, it is a real-life story of "who to turn to" with the everyday and sometimes unique challenges of life. This is a story told with an honesty and openness that is rare if not nonexistent in this world of ours, which demands that we dress up even the most unpleasant of inner struggles.

This is a story of connecting the inner issues of life with a God that truly crafts miraculous outcomes, ones that are often surprises and very different from what we expect. This is an invitation of sorts, to enter into the process and to enjoy a loving God going about the business of fully forming the person He intended you to be. This is a process that is available to us all.

We know the people of this story. We know the author and have marvelled at the work of her Creator—not only in her, but in our lives as well. This is a story that will give you hope for your own inner struggles and will encourage you to be honest with yourself.

We truly wish that you could meet Nancy and her husband, Greg. However, after reading this book, you will know them very well. There is something very poignant about their ability to take the matters of the heart and wisely, creatively, with a special touch from the Lord, bring an understanding that causes that inner person to say, "Yes, that is exactly how I would describe my experience." In that, there comes this remarkable healing of our souls. For this reason, Nancy and Greg are a true gift.

Whether you are single, newly married, or well down that path, there is value in hearing this story. If you are someone who is sorting through the issues of intimacy in relationship, then you will enjoy the fact that you are not alone.

Whatever your perspective, sit back, relax, and read, but prepare to be challenged to gaze inwardly, and accept the invitation to be refined and re-formed in your most intimate of thoughts and emotions.

Kevin and Shawna Walker
Victoria, B.C.

A Note from the Author

Several years ago I was asked to speak at a women's retreat. Because I was heavily immersed in this manuscript at the time, I decide to spend one session doing an encapsulated version of the story line: the lost years of chasing all the wrong guys; the adventure of meeting the wonderful man who was to become my husband; our courtship and wedding; the sudden and surprising shutdown of all my passion; and finally, God's gracious and enduring healing. At the end of the session, the retreat director opened the microphone for women who wanted to share how the evening had impacted them. The words of one woman in particular touched me deeply:

"I've been married for thirty-eight years," she said, "and I've never liked sex. My husband is a good man, and he has been very faithful and patient with me, but I've just never liked sex. Tonight is the first time it has ever occurred to me that I could bring this problem to God."

That was all, and then she sat down. But I felt assured that a process had been set in motion with her admission; that God was beginning a work in her.

This is my desire for this book, to see God's work set in motion in this very personal area of people's lives; to see young people cautioned from conforming to this world's casual approach to relationships and sex; to see them inspired to seek God's best; to see marriages healed and restored to true intimacy; to see the fires of godly passion rekindled to burn for a lifetime.

Perhaps the best way to introduce this book is to share some of the correspondence that was flowing during its early stages. When I began to write on this subject, the story of my journey into wholeness and holiness in the area of sexual intimacy, I found myself nervous about the very frank approach I wanted to take. I wondered if Christian readership would be offended by my forthrightness. So as I finished the first draft of Part 1, "Chasing Mr. Wrong," I sent out copies to a number of friends and acquaintances, women ranging in age from seventeen to seventy. Most of the responses were enthusiastic. But one, from a gal I'd been close to twenty-five years earlier, set me right back on my heels.

"Well, I began reading your manuscript when I got it..." she wrote, "put it down for a week to think about it, and then read through it cover to cover. Guess I need to know some of the ground rules for it. Is it supposed to be a sex-capades autobiography about you, or is it supposed to be a teaching tool for Christian sisters...as they date?"

She went on from there, but that was enough already to seriously rattle my cage. After some thought, I e-mailed her back:

Hi Mary Kaye,

Thanks for your response. Honestly, you're the first person who hasn't been extremely enthused about the transparency of the story. I gather you must have felt that I was glamorizing my sin somewhat—or rubbing people's noses in it. That's certainly not my intent.

I guess what has been striking a chord with most women reading this is that my writing frankly admits the way that too many of us think, feel, and behave—in dating relationships. It seems to be a relief to them to be able to say, "She's just like me. Or she was just like I was." The same people tend to say, "Thank you for saying it like it is. We've had too much of people in the church skirting around issues."

But if I end up being titillating (do you think I am?)—or being flippant about what is really very serious stuff, I at least need right now to take a hard and prayerful look. Not that that necessarily means I would change it. I have to go with my heart—unless of course almost every person that I love and respect (as I do you) feels about it the way you do.

What I am doing in Part 1 is saying, "This is what I was like, as a Christian newly saved from a hedonistic lifestyle; I thought I was cleaned up a lot, but I wasn't. I was looking for companionship and marriage in all the wrong places—'Chasing (wrong ideas, wrong ways, all the wrong people) Mr. Wrong.'"

Maybe it helps your perspective if you understand something—which happens to be the whole reason I have a desire to share my story:

Who I was—or should I say, how I behaved—back then, as an unbeliever and then as a new Christian—greatly impacted my marriage. Once Greg and I were married, I found myself unable to respond to him sexually. It took ten years for God to heal me, not only of the spin-offs from the irreverent attitude I once had about sexuality, but of something that went much deeper and that I was unaware of—a fear and revulsion regarding sex.

Many marriages would not have survived. Many others would have gone into a state of emotional divorce—and I see people like that all around me. Many people do not enjoy the kind of intimacy that God designed for marriage. I want to give them hope that God can and will bring complete healing and complete purity in this area.

In Part 2 there is a complete shift in attitude from the portion you read, as God brings Greg into my life. Much of this part ("Finding Mr. Right") is our letters, which chronicle some of the struggle about both of our attitudes toward intimacy, as messed up by "the world." At that stage there were only the slightest hints (that I did not notice at the time) of the trauma that I would feel once we were married.

Part 3 ("Ever After") covers our married life and everything related to our difficulties—and the eventual healing of them.

Yes, I hoped that this would be a teaching tool for young Christians—and even for some of the searching "unsaved." Your comments shake my confidence in that hope! But you know, I'm just thinking, the other women our age who have been reading it not only know something of my struggles in my early marriage, they also were hearing things about my intent for this book long before I began to write it.

However, I sent the manuscript off to you with no introduction to give you any hint of where I was coming from. At the very least, I think this is something I need to address in the introduction—and maybe allude to at times in the text of Part 1. Otherwise I may lose some of my readers before they ever get to the "good part"—they'll be wondering, like you did, "What is the point of this—this is not very edifying!"

Does this explanation change your perspective at all?

Please be in touch.

Thanks,
Nancy

Hi Nancy:

Well, I failed at my first attempt to be "honest and gentle" with my advice on your manuscript. I apologize. I should have explained more thoroughly what I was concerned about. And yes, I did not understand the basis for the desire to share your story—to express how God blessed your relationship with Greg despite your worldly experiences.

What I was trying to say was that the message was good about your "hedonistic" Christian dating practices and how your inward spirit had changed but your outward actions were projecting another message to men. I was making an assumption that you would have photos in your book, which would demonstrate [that] you were an eye-catcher to men as a non-Christian and new Christian. You had beautiful waist-length hair, good figure, and you wore stylish clothes—that you often made yourself—to accent your figure's best qualities.

Maybe I was reading into the story too much emphasis on your attempts to get a guy's attention and get their hormones running high—which was [the] truth. But I guess I wanted to read more words about [how] wrong it is for Christian women to play these movie- and magazine-driven sexual games with men—both Christian and non-Christian men—as Satan is lying to them that they won't get caught. Maybe I felt you stopped too short with just a sentence or two of advice and Scripture when I was wondering why...you didn't explain to women what it does to men's testosterone levels when they [lie] next to them in a bed or on a couch, or get a back massage—how men are hormonally different [from] women, with physical contact—and how men perceive women who play these cat-and-mouse games—and worse yet, what it does to women's purity by playing seductive games.

But maybe that is just what I would write, and it isn't my book. My desire would be to give some Christian women a verbal slap in the face to shake them up with how foolish they are and how deceived they are by listening to the world's messages about sex and relationships with men. You and I know how they are selling themselves short by not wanting God's sexual best for themselves and choosing to settle for a low-level, temporary sexual thrill with the opposite sex because romance novels and movies tell them "that is all there is" and "go for the gusto of it."

Anyway, I am just about writing [a book] here myself, with this long explanation.

So I am sorry if I hurt your feelings about your manuscript. I would not want to do that. I know you are baring yourself to the world about your life's mistakes, and I respect you for that. I realize also that I may have known you well as a sister in Christ [back then] and a few years afterwards, but after you got married, we were not so close, so I did not know of the spiritual challenges you faced as a married woman. So I did not know the complete perspective you were trying to present in your manuscript.

Mary Kaye

"A match made in heaven." That's what everybody says about a good marriage. And so they should—the union is made by God, not just the good ones, but every marriage. His Word says, "So then, they are no longer two but one flesh. Therefore what God has joined together, let not man separate."[1]

But what God has *Made in Heaven* must then be *Fleshed Out on Earth*. "Fleshed out" is an idiomatic expression meaning "to add substance and detail to something"[2] or "to complete; to create details from a basic outline or structure...."[3] We have the privilege of working with the heavenly blueprint, with the help of the Master Builder Himself.

It is my prayer that, in these pages, men will learn to honour their girlfriends, understand and cherish their wives, and minister to their daughters, and that women will find inspiration, correction, hope, and healing.

Nancy Christenson

# Part 1

Chasing Mr. Wrong

Paperback Romance

The phone rang. It was my good friend Carole Chatt, telling me that Neil (her boyfriend) was expecting a visit from four old college friends, now all medical doctors. They were coming up from the coast to ski for the weekend.

"We're all going down to the Stomp at Heffley Creek this Saturday night, and we're going to need some extra ladies to dance with all these guys. Can you come?"

It sounded pretty good to me.

It was March of 1978. I was a new Christian, hanging out at Tod Mountain (now called Sun Peaks), doing a little skiing with old friends, and house-sitting down in the valley for Jack and Velma Brady, an elderly couple, while they were off in Hawaii. This phone call brought the promise of some social action into my quiet life.

Saturday evening I put on a long-sleeved black leotard, a wrap-around denim skirt, and a funky patchwork vest that I'd sewn out of scraps from old blue-jeans. I brushed my hair out long and zipped on a pair of high, black suede boots. I felt pretty fine as I drove down to Heffley, wondering what adventure of romance might be waiting. I was not to be disappointed.

When I arrived, people were milling around on the dance floor, waiting for the band to fire up. I spotted Neil and Carole standing in a group with four young men, all of them in their late twenties, and as my song would later say:

> When I saw this one
> Well, son of a gun!
> I couldn't believe my eyes

I was introduced to all four fellows, but I never even saw the other three. Duncan Collins, ERP (Emergency Room Physician), was a knockout and a very entertaining guy to boot. I always was a sucker for a good sense of humour, never mind tall, dark-haired, and handsome. I felt like I had fallen into the middle of a paperback romance. The only thing missing was a dramatic accident and rescue, but then the story wasn't over yet either.

He and I danced the entire evening together. He was dazzling on the dance floor. I had never considered myself to be much of a dancer, but he made me look great. The evening swept by in a whirl of jiving and laughing.

Neil's guests, bachelors all, were bent on a weekend of partying, sweet respite from the responsibilities of their practices. A good time was the order of the day. Neil even commandeered the microphone from the band's lead singer at one point and ground out a rockin' rendition of Elvis's "Blue Suede Shoes."

When the dance finally shut down, we all went back to Neil and Carole's to visit into the wee hours. Duncan tried to teach me to play backgammon, and we played for several hours. It was difficult to make sense of any of it, though; I was in such a swoon that I couldn't think straight.

His friend Bruce sat watching us play, intermittently reading a newspaper and making rude comments, even long after the rest of the household had wandered off to get some sleep. I had the distinct impression that Bruce was staying there to irritate his buddy, to foil any plans Duncan might have of making a move on this young lady.

The young lady did not mind the presence of the third party at all. As a new Christian, I was trying to be very careful about the situations I allowed myself to get into. If this had been a year earlier, it would have been a different story entirely: I would have been heading for the nearest available bedroom with some serious making out in mind, even if I would have refrained from full-blown sex the first night. As it was, when Bruce finally did leave, there was a bit of a pass from Duncan, but you might say that it fell to the ground and rolled out of bounds. I bowed out gracefully and found a place to sleep in a spare room with one of the other girls who had been partying with us.

The next morning was an early start for one last day of spring skiing before the two-vehicle cavalcade of doctors had to return to the coast. I spent the day skiing with Duncan and Bruce, especially relishing the time on the double chairlift when I could chat alone with Duncan.

I so clearly recall that last ride up, high above the bald face of the "Chief." I remember what I said:

"You know, Duncan, I was really blown away when I found out that you were an emergency doctor, because I've always had these romantic fantasies about doctors and accidents and rescues."

Sometimes my sense of humour is a little bit weird and people have trouble catching on that it's a joke. This was one of those times.

"Yeah, well, actually, for that reason I really don't like people to know that I'm a doctor when they first meet me, because a lot of people actually react that way." (He probably meant, "A lot of *women* actually react that way.")

Now I was embarrassed: he seemed to think I was serious, which left me looking like a real bimbo. We had reached the Top of the World now, and I didn't bother to try to explain. Better to just ski hard and leave the embarrassment behind.

We stopped two-thirds of the way down to survey a nasty part just ahead: the big Caterpillar had been grooming this section of the run and had chopped up the huge, icy moguls. The terrain was flat now, but covered with three- to six-inch chunks of ice.

"This is horrible," the guys said.

"No problem," I said. "Just set your edges hard; do big, wide, high-speed GS turns; and muscle your way through it." Smart aleck.

And off I went, doing big, wide, high-speed giant slalom-type turns and muscling my way through the "Cat crud." Everything was going fine, except that my speed was increasing steadily. And even that was okay, if I could just ski it out to the bottom. But suddenly I ran out of groomed terrain and was surprised by huge, unforgiving moguls of ice. Big, with deep valleys, and very close together. I had no chance to check my speed. I hit the first one and got some air that I really didn't want to get. Then I came down off-balance and hit another one, this time doing some unplanned aerobatics in the air. I came down head first, taking the icy blow directly on the top of my right shoulder, and bounced a few times. And then I lay very still, because the pain was awful.

Duncan and Bruce skied up moments later with a harsh *whoosh* of metal edges on ice. (They told me afterward that it had appeared from up the hill that I'd landed on the back of my neck. The fact that I had then lain so still had scared the wits out of them.) Duncan's skis were off in a flash, and he knelt down beside me, his aqua eyes searching my face.

"Can you feel your legs?" he asked. The intensity and the import of the question burned through the haze of the shock.

"I'm not paralysed. My legs are fine," I said. "It's my shoulder."

He sat back, his face relaxing. He lapsed now into comic relief. "Have you got your health-care card on you?" he asked.

"No, I don't."

"Well, in that case, I'll have to get the ski patrol to look after you. Come on, Bruce, let's go," and he reached as though to put his skis back on.

I started to laugh, but it hurt too much. The laugh petered out into a little moan.

He reached inside my ski jacket and felt around the shoulder.

"Well, this is farther than you got the other night, isn't it?" I mocked him.

Bruce seemed delighted with my comment.

"I think you have an A-C joint sprain," Duncan ventured, "but I'll have to wait till I examine you thoroughly before I can be sure."

"Examine me thoroughly?" I queried nervously.

"Oh, yes," he smiled wickedly, rubbing his hands together. "Once I get you down to the patrol shack, we're going to get all your clothes off and examine you thoroughly."

(If this seems to the reader a little shocking, remember that such is the humour of the world. It was really all very funny.)

By now the patrol had arrived with a toboggan. They loaded me on and skied me down: an experience all in itself.

A number of patrol members were in the hut, and most of them were close friends of mine, as I'd been working and skiing at this mountain off and on for the past four years. They, along with my two new doctor companions, made me comfortable on a cot. Then they began the painful process of getting my clothes off.

It was painful in more ways than one. The patrol members knew me from my pre-Christian party days, when modesty was moot and propriety was a joke. They couldn't have begun to understand how I felt as a new Christian. Furthermore, professionalism had kicked in: they had a job to do.

I was mortified. I was going to be stripped to my underwear, at least from the waist up, not only in front of all these male friends, but in front of this handsome doctor with whom I was head-over-heels infatuated. I closed my eyes and began to pray silently. Maybe I could lean into God so closely that I wouldn't really be aware of what was happening. *Lord God, Lord God, help me!*

I heard Duncan's voice suddenly cut through my prayer. He was speaking to the two female patrollers who were present. "You ladies get her undressed and covered up," he said. "Come on, guys, let's go get a coffee." And he led them all out of the patrol shack. What a guy! An ERP, tall, good-looking, funny—and sensitive. I was toast.

It was late when Duncan, Bruce, and I left Emergency at the Royal Inland Hospital in Kamloops and headed for Jack and Velma's. The guys had long since given up on the possibility of heading back to the coast that night. Besides, I would need some help with the evening chores. My arm was in a snug sling to support my shoulder, and I had been given some stout pain medication. Not a good time to try to throw a bale of hay over the fence.

I remember pulling into Jack and Velma's driveway. I was squashed in the front seat between the two of them. Duncan braked his Jeep to a stop and turned toward me. "Why do you wear a cross?" he asked. He sounded curious, perhaps with a tinge of hostility.

"Because I'm a Christian."

The two of them exchanged a look. "Well, we're Christians too," he said, shrugging slightly.

I could tell that he didn't understand what I meant—that we were operating on two different definitions of the word "Christian." I tried to share with them how I had come to know the Lord, how it was not just a case of White Anglo-Saxon Protestant with a mental assent about the existence of God. But the words did not flow, probably because they were not being received. The subject went on hold, left hanging in the air.

The two guys helped me with the chores and supper; then they broke open the case of beer they'd picked up in town and returned to the mode of Young, Over-Worked Doctors On A Much-Needed, Pull-Out-The-Stops Vacation. In a word, they got crazy. I sat on the couch, cradling my arm in its sling, thoroughly enjoying their jokes and foolish antics.

Later, after I was settled in bed, Duncan came in quietly and crawled in with me. I hopped right out, supporting my arm carefully, and went to find another place to sleep. I greatly desired to be with him, but even more I desired to do things God's way so that this relationship, as it grew, would be built on a solid foundation.

I gave no explanation as I left the room, and I knew that he didn't understand: it was obvious that I was crazy about him, and in "the world" there are certain things that are a natural matter of course. Under God's rule and reign, however, things are different. (At least, dear reader, they're supposed to be.)

In the morning he and his buddy headed out on their return trip, Bruce to Vancouver, Duncan to Victoria, to their respective practices. But not without first a warm embrace from Duncan and a promise to keep in touch.

And then I was left alone. Alone to daydream about this wonderful beginning and where it would go from here.

It had been almost a year since God had got a hold on me, convicted me, forgiven me, and begun to clean up my life. I felt so changed, so pure. My life now seemed so righteous to me, because it was such a far cry from what it had been in my "heathen" days. I was *so* ready for marriage, or so I thought. I felt sure that God must have Mr. Right waiting just around the next corner. I didn't know that I still had a long way to go, and that I would make a lot of mistakes along the way.

So although I told God that I was ready for a husband, He thought differently. He had a lot more work to do in my life first. He was busy with that while I was busy trying to help Him find me that special someone. But already nine months had slipped by with nothing interesting happening—until now, that is.

I'd never felt before what I felt for this man. No, he wasn't a Christian: in spite of what he had said, it was as clear as his blue-green eyes that he was unregenerate. But I was sure that God would reveal the whole Truth to him, that he would see and embrace the Lord as easily as I had, and that then we would marry and live happily ever after. And what a wonderful story to tell, for all that "ever after," of how I met the man of my dreams. My mother had often said that I should marry a veterinarian, because of my love of animals and the outdoor life. Well, this guy wasn't an animal doctor, but he was a doctor—and he was an animal!

I went to a dance down at Heffley Creek
Just the other Saturday night
Neil said some old friends of his would be there—
If I'd like to join them. I said, "All right!"
So I walked over to that group standing there
To get introduced to these guys
And when I saw this one
Well, son of a gun!
I couldn't believe my eyes

Oh, he's twenty-nine, he's an animal doctor
And Mother will be so pleased
He's not a vet but he's the closest yet
So she can set her mind at ease
Sakes alive, I'm twenty-five—
I'm not a spring chicken no more
I don't know if it's love, but Lord above!
Mom caught a man when she was twenty-four

We got inflamed
With a backgammon game
His friend sat there looking bored
He read a newspaper and made rude remarks
Which the two of us ignored
Yeah, Bruce looked on
The whole evening long
Of all the unmitigated gall

Then when he finally left
To catch a little rest
He didn't miss anything at all

He's twenty-nine, he's an animal doctor
And you should have seen him dance
He looked like a hot dang in his lumberjack shirt
And he was looking for romance
And he was taller than me, which was nice for a change
But like a friend of mine once said:
"He's got a pretty, pretty face and a mighty fine body
But try to get a look inside his head."

I was a damsel in distress and you rescued me—
It was silly, but it was sweet
And only twenty minutes after I'd been telling you
How you'd swept me off my feet
I said, "Moonlight dances, Harlequin Romances,
Doctors, accidents, and drama too"
I couldn't have been bolder
Then I crunched my shoulder
Just to get a little attention from you

Oh, he's twenty-nine, he's a doctor, he's an animal
And oh! how that man could jive!
And I couldn't really tell you what he made me feel
Except he made me feel alive
Hey there, Ms. Chatt, don't look at me like that
I've been through this before—I'm going to be all right
'Twas just a typical romp
At a typical stomp
At Heffley, on a Saturday night

Shades of McMurray
And romantic flurry—
Hey there now, Carole, I'm going to be all right
'Twas just a typical romp
At a Heffley Stomp
On a Saturday, Saturday night

The days and the weeks crept slowly by. There was another Heffley Creek Stomp coming up soon. I wrote a letter to Duncan, asking him if he would fly up for it.

Each day blurred into the next. I didn't do a whole lot, except that I continued to do a whole lot of fantasizing. I sat around, played my guitar, waited for my shoulder to heal, and twice a day I wrestled a bale of hay over the fence to Jack's horses. Mostly, although I wouldn't have wanted anyone to know, I was just waiting for the phone to ring. It was driving me crazy, waiting like this. Duncan would be glad to know that—to listen to him talk, it seemed that his fondest goal in life was to get all his friends committed to mental institutions.

Sitting here all alone
Babysitting the telephone
I'd die if anyone saw me
Sitting waiting for you to call me
Yes, I'd die if anyone saw
Me waiting for you to call

'Twas a long week ago I wrote you a letter
I s'pose I was taking a bit of a chance
Asking you to fly four hundred miles
Just to take me to a country dance
Now I know you don't know when I'm serious
When you think I'm joking, I'm not
A couple of hours was all we had together
And now memories is all I've got

So I'm sitting here, trying to concentrate on singing
Wondering why that phone ain't ringing
I'd die if anyone could see
What kind of wreck you're making of me
Yes, I s'pose before this story ends
I'll be committed like the rest of your friends

Gee, I liked the way you danced
Gee, you know, I even kind of liked your friend

Gee, I liked the way it all started
I hope this isn't where it'll end

So I'm sitting here all alone
Babysitting the telephone
I'd die if anyone saw me
Sitting waiting for you to call me
Yes, I'd die if anyone saw
Me waiting for you to call

    Finally one evening he phoned. No, he wouldn't be flying up for the dance, but would I consider coming down for a visit?
    I didn't want to act too eager, but he didn't have to ask me twice. It would soon be time to return to Douglas Lake Cattle Company for my fourth season as cow-camp cook. Once I got started there again, it would be difficult to get away: Sunday was my only official day off there, and usually I worked, unofficially, that day the same as every other. The time to go to Victoria was now. I made a plan: I would leave as soon as Jack and Velma got back.

The Search for Love and Acceptance

Romance is important to most women. And it's more important to some than to others. One would never have guessed how important it was to me: the persona I had adopted as a young (pre-Christian) adult was rough and tough and almost masculine. I was so busy pretending I didn't need anyone that half the time I even had myself convinced. I didn't want to be a typical woman, not in any way. I didn't want to become a nurse or a secretary or a schoolteacher. Even worse was the thought of getting married at eighteen or nineteen and having a bunch of babies. I despised that kind of tameness and predictability; especially I despised that kind of dependence on men. I liked challenge and adventure and independence.

During a TV interview about my book *Yes, I Really Was a Cowgirl*, I was asked this question: "Why did you feel like you had to have that tough spirit about you, to where a woman that was a homemaker looked weak to you?"[1] Initially the question threw me for a loop. I had never before asked myself that particular "why." For a split second, with the awful tension of cameras rolling, I wondered how to answer. But God (I believe it was He) brought a quick flash of understanding to me, enabling me to answer with barely a pause: "Maybe it was because until I knew God, I had to be strong enough for myself; I couldn't lean on anybody." Yes, I realized with sudden clarity, I had been afraid that no one else was strong enough for me to lean on.

I have thought about that old bravado a lot since that interview. I think that I was afraid of life and that my tough-girl persona was how I dealt with my fear. The best defence is a good offence.

As a young girl of nine or ten, I remember being worried about what life would be like as an adult. I asked my father, "Who will look after me when I grow up and move away from you and Mom?"

"Well," he answered, "then your husband will look after you."

I nodded, but it wasn't an adequate answer for me; it did not comfort me. From my perspective as a child, my parents were big and knowledgeable and powerful. They made me feel secure in terms of the emotional and physical needs of a child. Though we were not what you would call an openly demonstrative family, my parents' love for us children and their commitment to each other undergirded our lives and gave us a solid foundation. And I am grateful for that background.

But somehow I innately sensed that any future husband would be more of a peer—an equal. He wouldn't be much bigger or stronger or smarter than I, so he wouldn't be powerful enough to make me feel safe from all the unknown challenges of life in the grown-ups' huge world. I perceived, even then, that life in an adult world was going to be more challenging than any mortal could adequately help me with.

Perhaps I wondered whether any man would be reliable enough for me to depend on; maybe I would only be let down, betrayed. Perhaps I feared that no man would ever love me enough to let me really lean on him. Looking back now on that time in my childhood, I think that was the first time my heart expressed its need of God: I wanted to know that there was someone big enough to protect me and comfort me in the challenges I instinctively knew would be part and parcel of the adult world.

But since I didn't know God (I was raised with some basic religion but with no understanding of the real relationship that is available with Him through His Son), as I grew up I came to this conclusion: Nobody was big enough to look after me, so I would have to look after myself. I had to be tough—on the outside. And I was. I even believed it myself.

This brave exterior, as it developed, helped me to tackle life courageously and head-on. But at the same time, it also masked a very deep insecurity and uncertainty about who I was as an individual. It is only as I have got older that I've come to see and understand this insecurity, how it came to be, and how it caused this "tough girl," paradoxically, to crave romance.

My father was a doctor, a good provider of temporal, material needs, but as I see now, he was unable to deliver to his children on an emotional level. I blame his British heritage. In my books, the Brits are, generally speaking, sadly out of touch in the emotions department. Their "stiff upper lip" is a contagion that has spread its malady to the heart.

I know now that Dad did not receive demonstrative love from his own father; neither did he receive affirmation for simply being who he was—his unique abilities, his particular personality. And he was unable to pass on what he hadn't been given.

He would never have dreamed of taking any one of his teenage daughters on his knee and telling her that she was beautiful, that she was special. I think it was this deficiency that left me very unsure of myself, so lacking in confidence on the inside—with (as I have described elsewhere) "kind of a blank spot where my self-image should have been." I had no sense whatsoever of what I looked like or of how people perceived me.

You might say, "Well, you should have looked in the mirror, and you would have figured it out." Not so. A mirror doesn't speak nearly so loudly as Daddy does, and if Daddy isn't speaking, neither is the mirror. Or if it is, the message is distorted.

I remember going on a band trip, a long bus ride from Castlegar to Vancouver, when I was in Grade Ten or Eleven. Sometimes interesting things happen in the dark at the back of those buses, and not always the kinds of things you think of immediately. I was sitting with a guy a year older than I, and as the hour got late, kids got tired and inhibitions relaxed. This young man sat with his arm around my shoulders and talked in a very personal way. He told me that I was pretty, that in fact he figured I was just about the most beautiful girl in the whole school.

I simply could not process this opinion. It's not that I thought I was ugly; it's just that I was a blank. Nothing.

Sometime later I sneaked (underage) into the bar with this same fellow, along with a friend of his. This time it was the beer that lowered the inhibitions, and some disturbing things came at me in the conversation. His friend told me that I was vain and a snob to boot. This confused me. I thought that to be vain and snobbish, one first had to be beautiful. I didn't think I was beautiful at all.

The reason he had this opinion, as he explained, was that when he passed me in the hallways at school and tried to say hello to me, I wouldn't even look at him.

I knew the real answer here, but I didn't tell them. Without my glasses, I could hardly see past the end of my nose. Yet I felt so unattractive wearing them that I reserved them for classroom use, picking them up off my desk and peering through them only when I had to see something on the board. Walking down the hallways, I felt plenty insecure already, but given that I couldn't see who was coming toward me and whether they were looking at me with a friendly countenance, I was forever glancing down and away from the approaching stream of students. Hence, I guess some perceived me as snobbish.

Life is hard for teens. Not only do they have a lot of raw fear of rejection, but they have peers—other rejection-sensitive teenagers—bad-mouthing them because of their own misconceptions and insecurities.

It was around this time that guys began to ask me out. I discovered my sexuality. Initially I kept things quite firmly in hand, but then little by little, I slowly gave up ground. I gave it up deliberately; it was never taken from me against my will.

It was worth giving up part of my self. I had found a wonderful thing in return: I had power, through my sexuality, over young men. I had the power to make them desire me. It made me believe that I was beautiful; I was wanted. It was like being given sparkling, cold water when I hadn't even perceived that I was thirsty. I began to feel like I was somebody. I had an identity. I was desirable.

Sexual excitement, all by itself, is a heady narcotic. Mix it with the elixir of acceptance and affirmation, and you have a powerful concoction indeed. Easy to swallow. Dynamite in its effects. Extremely addictive.

God has wired women to love romance, so that was part of my natural, generic wiring. But beyond that, I had a specific weakness for romantic attention from attractive young men. I craved it, because it filled in me a need that had never before been met. Romance was great, for its own sake, but much more than that, it filled the aching hollowness of longing to be loved. Although that abyss was never quite satiated, relationships were the thing that most quieted the cry inside. So life for me became a continuous string of emotional attachments, some of them overlapping with one another.

In the two years that I spent at university, I felt lost and frightened. At the end of my first year there, as I contemplated finding a job for the summer and making my way in the wide world alone, I remember how I lay on my bed and wailed as my current boyfriend sat on a chair and watched me with consternation.

"I'm so afraid of life," I cried.

It was at university that I really began to project a tomboyish image and an attitude of self-reliance. I had to act tough, because I realized somehow that as an adult now, I had to look after myself. "Fake it till you make it" was an adage that I claimed as my own. After I dropped out of school—only halfway to a degree, I moved from job to job, outwardly seeking adventure, inwardly longing for security. By the time I was in my early twenties, I found myself living the illustrious life of a camp-cook and cowgirl. Although on the surface I prided myself more and more on my independence and confidence, subliminally I still had a fierce need to be romantically attached to someone or other at all times, and there was always sex involved, to one degree or another. My feelings about my escapades then were mixed. Sexual desire and sexual experiences brought feelings both good and bad, all twisted up together. I had no means of deciding which was the right feeling and no one to tell me.

Sometimes I had several fellows on a string at the same time—so much the better. I was rarely the one to get hurt in a relationship. My heart was safely hidden—and completely out of touch, cocooned down deep under my self-reliance and autonomy.

Then I met the Lord. I discovered that it was all right to be weak after all, that I could lean hard on Him. I wrote a new song to proclaim what had happened to me: "I Found the Love of Jesus." One verse in particular reflects the change in the mainspring of my being:

I was always so independent
Liked to rely only on myself
I never would have admitted
I really needed anyone else
It took a long time for me to realize
I was really not that strong
And now that I've found the strength of Jesus
Don't know how I used to get along

It felt good, very good, to know that He loved me and would always be there for me. He gave me a security that I simply could not have found anywhere else, because He *is* Love, and He is eternal, immutable, and omnipotent (forever unchanging and all-powerful—how comforting!). Nothing and no one else that we try to lean on has these qualities.

As He weaned me from my outward independence, He also began, though ever so slowly, to reveal to me my inner dependence on affirmation from men. Even though many things changed overnight when I found the Lord, deep down I still had this drive in me, this need to be romantically attached, because I still drew a huge part of who I was from the way the opposite sex responded to me. Romance had become an addiction, one that would not easily be broken.

Regarding the psychological impact of an emotionally absent father on a young girl, I do not consider myself an expert in such matters—but I have read a bit about what the experts say, and it fits with what I experienced. I speak not, as it were, as a cartographer, but as a traveller. The cartographer stands on a high place and surveys the lay of the land from an objective position, then draws a map to give the traveller guidance. I was just a traveller, and I had no map. I wandered the foot trails, one step at a time, without a clue as to where I was or where I was headed or what the hazards might be along the way.

Now I read the maps (the books by the experts), and I look back on the journey, and I say, yes, it is as they say. I see now the territory that I traversed from a more objective perspective: I see now why that particular bit was so difficult; there really is quite a climb there. I see that this other part was actually very dangerous: there is a precipice right there, near to where I stumbled and fell. I could have gone right off the edge. It was bad enough that I gouged my knees and scraped my shins and that I still carry the scars, but my word!—I could have been utterly destroyed.

There are many other travellers who have not been so fortunate as I. They walked a similar road, with similar challenges, but they fared in the end far worse than I. Often I find cause to give heartfelt thanks to God for His protection, which was there long before I recognized it. I look at others and say, "There, but for the grace of God, go I."

In some difficult places, His grace kept me from harm; in others, where I was not so "lucky," He afterward extended His grace to heal me.

> God knows—and plans—the circumstances where we have to live
> And with each peculiar trial a special grace will give[2]

It is not for us to question why God keeps some people relatively safe from harm whereas others seem to have to plumb the depths of the pit; but it is for us to learn—to embrace with confidence—the certainty that the grace that might have preserved us from danger is the same grace that will pull us from the pit and heal our wounds.

Because I was driven by my hunger to be loved, I was self-centred in my relationships. I was most interested in having my needs met, and while I appreciated these various beaux as unique individuals and usually formed deep and lasting friendships with them, within the romantic context I was oblivious to their feelings, their needs, and their hurts. Most often I was not in love with the young man of the moment so much as in love with the idea of being in love, happy to be attached, and enamoured, most of all, by someone loving me.

Now I had met this good-looking doctor, and this time it was different. Even this early in the game, I cared for Duncan more than I cared about myself. And I was on my way to Victoria to visit him.

Dream or Delusion?

It seemed that Duncan led an enviable life, as far as material things were concerned. He lived in an exquisite old house in a ritzy area of Victoria, sharing it with two other single doctors. There was a swimming pool in the backyard, surrounded by beautiful grounds kept by a gardener. In the driveway was the Jeep wagon that had become a familiar sight in my continual fantasizing. The vehicle wasn't fancy; it hardly reflected his standard of living, but that was okay: it spoke to me of rugged quality, practicality, a love of the outdoors, a healthy lifestyle.

I'd had no way of knowing that he had a second car, but as Duncan finished showing me through the house, he led me through the basement, and there, what a sight!—was an older model Mercedes convertible. It was a real honey—baby blue, in mint condition. It was soon to be carrying us around town, ragtop down, celebrating the sunshine.

On my third or fourth evening there, he took me for a tour of the city in the Mercedes, sun low in a clear sky, wind blowing through our hair. We parked high up on a viewpoint with a sweeping view of the city, and he pointed out his favourite landmarks.

"That's Eric Martin over there," he said, gesturing toward a large building in the distance. "It's the mental institution. There are a lot of Christians in there." This was becoming a recurring theme in his humour, taking little digs at my faith. I laughed.

Later at dinner, though, he told me that in his late teens, when it had come to choosing a vocation, it had been a toss-up between medicine and the ministry. My heart leapt with surprise and hope.

I learned some other things that night about his views on God.

And of course, I tried to share my faith with him. The conversation could have been entitled "Heathen vs. Christian."

When I first met you, we got along fine
Till I told you I was a Christian and I blew your mind
You pointed out to me all the mental institutions
And you told me they were full of Christians

Now, I appreciate your sense of humour
But that won't win you rapture wings to fly
And I know you're a real nice guy
But that isn't going to get you by

You've got to believe in the name of Jesus
Ask and receive forgiveness from Jesus
Turn your life over to Jesus

You tried, you really tried, to believe when you were young
God wouldn't show Himself then, or so you insist
Now you're angry, so angry—you don't believe at all
Can you be angry at God if He doesn't exist?

And then you say that probably when you're older
You'll want to turn to Him, but you don't need Him right now
Well, what makes you so very sure
You'll be here tomorrow, anyhow?

Now is the time to believe in Jesus
Repent and receive forgiveness from Jesus
Turn your life over to Jesus

You can't understand so you won't believe
Well, I'll tell you—He wasn't always real to me
The world says, "Let me see and then I'll believe"
But God says, "Believe and then you'll see"

And if you had to meet the Lord tomorrow
You'd say you did the best you could—you deserve that heavenly place
But it's not by our righteousness we're justified
But by His grace—and through our faith in that grace

The only way to the Father is through Jesus
Our only righteousness is faith in Jesus
So turn your life over to Jesus

Later that night, back at the house, he turned on the stereo in the living room and danced with me. I had showered and changed into a nightie that I had just finished making: white flannelette with light blue smocking across the bodice. The ruffle at the bottom swept the floor gracefully. The skinny little straps left my shoulders bare, but in the interest of modesty I also wore a lightweight blue and green Indian cotton robe that opened all the way down the front. I felt very feminine and beautiful in it. Not sexy in a provocative way—just beautiful, like a princess. And the way he danced me and twirled me that night, I thought I would faint with the heady, romantic joy of it all.

Then we slow-danced to a song that he said he really liked.

"See if you can guess what my favourite part is," he said.

I listened closely as we danced, and when I heard it, I knew it.

I know I'm not your only man
But you make me feel I am[1]

I sensed that he was asking me to make it a little clearer where he stood in my life. I realized then, all at once, that I had chatted incessantly to him about my friend Terry back at the Ranch, just because my adventurous life there was wrapped up with his on a day-to-day basis. We had become almost inseparable during my three seasons there. A physical relationship had developed in the beginning, but when I gave my life to the Lord, Terry had followed suit shortly thereafter, and God had been steadily reworking our friendship ever since. Terry was just a good friend now.

But for some reason, I felt no need to clarify to Duncan what the nature of that other relationship was. I did not even let on to him that I knew what line in the song he was talking about. Strange, that. I guess I thought that my exclusive feelings for him were obvious. After all, hadn't I made the long trip down to spend a week with him?

Time out, ladies: Some of you, the ones who are serious about serving God, are wondering about my going to visit this guy and staying in his house. My only explanation is this: Given the set of morals I had come to embrace before meeting the Lord, this was a natural thing to do. God had changed me a lot in the year that I had known Him, but I was such a mess in the morality department that He still had a whole pile to do. I had not yet even come across the Scripture that admonishes, "Abstain from all appearance of evil,"[2] or the ones that caution us about minding our behaviour and protecting our reputation for God's sake: "For the name of God is blasphemed among the Gentiles through you,"[3] and "Teach the young women... to be discreet... that the word of God be not blasphemed."[4] I really thought that as long as I wasn't having sex, my behaviour was above reproach. And I had the counsel of a Christian girlfriend to back me up. She was a friend from back at the Ranch who had helped to mentor me in the Faith. Speaking of morality in the context of her own courtship, she had told me this: "I didn't 'sleep' with my husband before we got married, but face it, there's a whole lot you can do without actually having intercourse with the guy."

This philosophy reflects a misconception to which I had been prey since way back in my teens. I understood from my parents (implicitly, not explicitly) that I should be a virgin when I got married: "Nice girls don't" was pretty much the sum total of my sex education. So I somehow came to understand that one could still be pure while partaking of anything and everything shy of actual intercourse. (Now I couldn't disagree more.)

And the values with which I was raised didn't protect me long, once I left home. With the godless influence of the people I met at university, I soon became convinced that surely I had been raised wrong and that all the rest of my immediate world was right.

I remember a fellow student telling me that she had turned eighteen the week before.

"I didn't even know," I protested. "We should have celebrated."

"Aw, naw," she said. "Your eighteenth birthday is just something you kind of want to get over with. Kind of like your virginity."

At this bastion of higher education, not only did I not know anybody else who wasn't sleeping around, but heterosexuality was deemed to be only one option and a narrow-minded one at that. It was considered by the intellectual, arts-faculty crowd with whom I ran that the sex of a person was as irrelevant as the colour of his or her eyes when it came to falling in love, and that, naturally, if you were in love, you would sleep with him or her. And then again, being in love wasn't necessarily a part of the equation either. Pretty confusing stuff for a small-town girl.

Eventually, after a couple more years of wrestling with my own sense of morality, I gave in to peer influence. I don't mean peer pressure; no one could ever pressure me into doing something with which I disagreed. I valued a clear conscience too much. But the gradual influence of being surrounded by a culture that implied incessantly that virginity was obsolete took its toll. I rationalized this "new morality," cogitating it in my mind until I could freely justify it all. My conscience was finally laid to rest—yes, dead—with a little tombstone saying "Rest in Peace," and I embraced a new so-called freedom. I didn't know that this "freedom" was putting me into bondage that would take years to break.

Now that I was a Christian, God had convinced me that sex was wrong for the unmarried. Nobody had come along and beaten me over the head with a Bible, saying, "Now that you're saved, you mustn't do this or this or this"; God Himself had done a work deep in my heart. The things that had once brought pleasure now filled me with uneasiness and sadness. I was not about to persist in behaviour that made me unhappy. So sex, or at least intercourse, would have to wait for marriage. And I hoped that that would be soon.

However, I still laboured under the misconception that although intercourse was taboo for now, certainly it was all right to carry things up to a point. Surely it was a good testimony, to shut things down just shy of intercourse? Do you think so?

What on earth was I doing, staying with this young man in his home, in his room, initially on the floor in my sleeping bag, to his great exasperation and confusion, and then finally, now that it was later in the visit, right in his bed? This is one of the ways in which women "defraud" men. We mislead them; we send mixed messages; we are unclear as to our intent.

"Defraud" is defined by Oxford as "to cheat by fraud." Fraud is defined, in part, thus: "the use of false representations to gain an unjust advantage; a person not fulfilling what is claimed or expected of [her]."

The word "defraud" is used once in the Bible in a sexual context: In 1 Corinthians 7:5 (KJV), it is used in a caution to husbands and wives not to withhold themselves from one another sexually except under certain, very temporary, conditions: "Defraud ye not one the other, except it be with consent for a time...." (Most other versions use the word "deprive.")

But although this admonition is to the married, there is also a whole lot of defrauding that goes on among unmarried Christians. In marriage, defrauding is withholding sex when you should not; among singles, it is withholding in the end what you had no right to pretend to offer in the first place.

God meant foreplay to be a physical and emotional prelude to intercourse—not an end in itself, aborted mid-process with frustration abounding. He wired us for sex; He knows how hard it is to have expectations built up and then to have them unmet. Women are often guilty of this kind of "cheating"—or teasing, as it's called; I certainly was. I frequently gave a false representation of what my intent was, failing to fulfill what I seemed to be claiming or promising. The reason? I wanted to feel wanted.

This is what I did with Duncan. I led him to have sexual expectations but had no intention of following through. I participated up to a point; then I sweetly demurred in the name of God. I'm sure it didn't cause him to think any more kindly toward my faith.

Neither did he understand, not even for a moment, what was wrong with having sex; his philosophy was right where mine had been a scant year before. He could not fathom that any harm would come of consummating this relationship.

"Look," he said, frustrated with me, "all that's going to happen if you sleep with me is that you're going to have a good time."

I asked him if he had any references that I could call.

The last day of my visit came warm and sunny. Duncan had the morning off. He took me for a long drive. "I want to show you something," he said.

Out of the city now, a winding road took us to a beautiful wooded area. We got out and hiked, climbing steadily for some minutes, then turned around to take in a pastoral panorama.

"This is a piece of land that I'm thinking of buying," he said. "It's a ten-acre parcel. I think the house should go right here, with a view of all this. What do you think?"

I kept my countenance nonchalant, but my heart was racing. Why was he asking *me* where the house should go? Was he thinking what I thought he was thinking? Aloud I said, "I think it's a really nice place for a house." Neutral. Non-committal.

He told me the price of the property. "If I take on this commitment," he said, "I won't be able to just go here and there, taking holidays, going skiing whenever I please." He was looking at me intently. Again he seemed to be waiting for a response from me. And again, I tried to be as enthusiastic as I could without being presumptuous about his drift. But really, why else would he bring me here and ask me these things unless he was seeing me as part of his future?

He was on call that afternoon, and I was left alone in that gorgeous house. It seemed so natural, to be waiting there at home for him, while he was at the hospital. It was so easy to imagine myself married to him. I decided to call my mother and have a chat with her.

"How are you?" she asked.

"I think there's something wrong with me," I answered.

"Oh?" She sounded concerned.

"Yeah. I can't eat and I can't sleep and I feel really weird."

"What's the matter, dear?"

"I think I'm in love," I told her.

The concerned tone disappeared into a laugh, and we had a long talk about everything that was happening. I really thought this was it. Wedding bells were clanging in my head.

Once I returned to the Ranch for another season in cow-camp, I found that my heart was divided concerning my life there. I still loved it, but now all I could think about was accumulating time off so that I could go visit Duncan again. Time moved slowly; it soon seemed like forever since I'd seen him.

I finally talked to my boss about taking a week off. It would have to coincide with a stretch of time when the crew would be busy on another part of the Ranch and wouldn't really need me. After waiting interminably, I was able to set a date. I drove from the log cookshack at Courtenay Lake, where the cattle operation was centred in June, out to a little roadside café on the Merritt-Princeton highway. There I asked to borrow the phone.

It was the middle of the day. Would I be able to reach him?

The phone rang and rang. And then suddenly, there was his voice on the line.

"Hi, Duncan," I said, trying to breathe normally. "It's Nancy."

"Nancy who?" he answered.

Well, ladies, that should have been the end of it right there. But somehow the fairer sex has a way of being obtuse when matters of the heart are not moving in the direction we have envisioned. I blithely continued the conversation and persisted in arranging my holiday itinerary with Duncan, proceeding as planned.

There were many things about that visit that did not measure up to the first. The writing was all over the wall, scrawled in great, big, ugly letters, but I was blinded by my infatuation. I did not want to see.

Perhaps the most blatant symbol, which would come into focus more clearly as time went on, was that instead of buying that beautiful piece of property, he had opted to pool his resources with several other bachelors and buy a big sailboat.

Yet, back at the Ranch again, even though part of me was reluctantly becoming aware that he had cooled off, I was convinced that he was the one for me and that as soon as he yielded himself to God, everything would be wonderful.

Of course, in order for God to put this relationship together (or so I reasoned), I would have to be in Victoria, ready and available. So as the season grew old and the gathering began for the big cattle drives back to the Home Ranch in late November, I quietly confirmed my plans to chase this good-looking doctor out to Vancouver Island.

I settled in Sooke, three-quarters of an hour from the city of Victoria, at the invitation of Pop and Lorna Smith, the parents of one of the cowboys on my Douglas Lake crew. Lorna was small in stature, but in the Spirit, she was a force to be reckoned with. She quickly became a trusted confidante and prayer partner.

She heard a lot about Duncan over the next few months, bless her patience forever! But in spite of all my talk, I never did call to let him know that I was around. God simply would not give me peace about it, and in spite of being wilfully deluded about the future of this relationship, I really was trying to obey the Lord. He honoured that obedience and gave me grace to wait and wait. And wait.

The Young and the Restless

Time went by. I moved into Victoria so that I could get a job. I found work as a cook in an old-folks' home and got more involved with the church that Lorna Smith had introduced me to. I joined the choir and took part in the youth group activities, even though I was, at the age of twenty-six, older than most of the others. They were a great bunch of young people who loved the Lord—and we had opportunity to sit under terrific teaching.

There were some interesting fellows in the youth group. And some nice-looking ladies. And although this group was passionate about God, there were other passions in the wind as well. Such a struggle, to live in a godly way! "The spirit indeed is willing, but the flesh is weak."[1] Sometimes it would be more accurate to turn it around and say that the spirit is just too weak and the flesh is way too willing—willing to detour off the straight and narrow.

There was one young man, Allen, whom I viewed from a distance. He had a long, lean frame, a roguish grin, and a charming arrogance. I would have liked to have taken a closer look, but there were a lot of other gals in the way, girls who were much closer to his age than I.

Some of the young ladies got involved with some of the fellows (including Allen) in ways that they shouldn't have. Not that these young people were sleeping together—they all knew better than that. At least I hoped they did. But still, there would be some degree of intimacy, and then the young ladies would come looking to talk to me, because I had a few years of maturity on them and, one would hope, a little more wisdom. They would want me to listen to their struggles and pray for their redemption.

I tried to hand out wise counsel. It was always firm, pointing to the narrow Way. Repentance. Consecration. Purity. It felt good to be able to help, and I felt rather motherly and protective toward these younger sisters in the Lord. But I felt something else too: I felt jealousy. I was envious that they were having a little fun on the side and getting away with it.

Of course, none of us really "gets away with" anything. All of our experiences, all our choices, stay with us for a lifetime. Even though sexual exploits happen in secret, in the dark, and usually no one knows beyond the people involved, these events are written in a person's history, indelibly. They never go away—it's all there, piling up in our hearts.

Maybe that's why, in spite of my envy, I was trying to give matters sexual a wide berth. I already had enough history, enough baggage, from the years before I knew God. I had brought all of these incidents to Him, one by one, as He had convicted me, and I understood that He had forgiven me.

Sometimes I would be troubled again with guilt from an old memory, and I would confess it once more, claim His forgiveness again. As yet I had no clue that God was going to have to delve much more deeply into my past with His searching, healing light; nor could I have guessed how and when He would do it.

Meanwhile, I was surrounded by the antics of the young and the restless, and it was bugging me. The sad truth was that my body and soul were yearning for the physical and emotional comfort of a nice male body, and yet as the love of Christ constrained me so effectively, I could not easily go looking for comfort in this direction. A part of me carried resentment at the pleasure these girls were indulging in, and along with this resentment was an indignant sort of judgement, which I hid from both them and myself with an understanding smile.

Mostly though, I ached for them, genuinely. I feared for them. And I prayed for them. I would find myself thinking of the old traditional spiritual "Sinnerman," and I wrote a song of the same name, echoing, in the refrain, some of the same trepidation.

Lord God, there's something tearing me apart
Lord, I've got to pray, but I don't know where to start
But Lord, I know you know, and it must break your heart

All around me, Lord, I see my sisters crying
My brothers say they're doing fine, but they're lying
The enemy has deceived them without even trying

Oh, Sinnerman, where will you run to
When the door is closed as in the day of the Flood?[2]
Oh, Sinnerman, will you be ready
In the day the sun is darkened and the moon turns to blood?[3]

I think, Lord, of Samson in the days of old
How he flirted with sin until he grew too bold
Then the Holy Spirit left him and the enemy took hold[4]

Oh, Sinnerman, what are you doing?
Whatever would you do if the Holy Spirit leaves?
Oh, Sinnerman, how can you do that?
You just keep laughing while the Holy Spirit grieves[5]

My sister, I see pain underneath your smile
My brother, I love you; I don't envy you this trial
But give Satan just one inch, and he'll take a mile

Oh, Sinnerman, where will you run to
When the door is closed as in the day of the Flood?
Oh, Sinnerman, will you be ready
In the day the sun is darkened and the moon turns to blood?

Oh, Sinnerman, it's you who bring discredit
To your Lord and Saviour and to His Holy Name
Oh, Sinnerman, you crucify the Son of Glory
On the Cross a second time, put Him to an open shame[6]

 Then, for a time, the attentions of this sexy young man Allen turned to me, and before long I had opportunity to experience, just like my younger girlfriends, that fleeting pleasure and lingering guilt.

It started innocently enough, or so I told myself. A back massage on the floor in front of a crackling fire. The lights turned down low. Warm, yellow-orange light from the fire, dancing with shadows in the room.

Yeah, that's exactly how it was—the Light, dancing with shadows.

I, of all people, should have been able to tell myself the truth about back massages. At Tod Mountain, where I had worked and skied as a pre-Christian, it was one of the favourite pick-up moves. You'd be walking back to staff quarters with a guy after a late-night drink, and he'd suddenly wince and reach around to some supposedly sore muscles that really wanted a good rub, and you knew that if you were interested in this fellow at all, here was your invitation.

Excuse me for being cynical, dear young reader, but a back massage between Christians is, most often, really only an excuse to get very physical, very intimate, whilst all the while pretending that there is absolutely nothing going on.

So it started with a back massage, and it wandered toward the wilderness. We had a few dates, which culminated in some kissing and some passionate writhing. Nothing much really, not compared to where I had come from. But it was way too much for where I was heading—supposedly pressing toward the mark for the prize of the high calling of God in Christ Jesus.[7] Furthermore, I now found myself ravaged with lust, longing for more intimacy, and preoccupied with my loneliness more than ever before. "Wine only makes you drier, though it satisfies at first."[8]

Deep inside, things were in turmoil about this involvement, but I remained flippant on the surface. I remember being in church with Allen one Sunday. I was coming back from taking communion; the congregation was singing that well-loved chorus based on Psalm 51:

> Create in me a clean heart, O God
> And renew a right spirit within me
> Cast me not away from thy presence, O Lord
> And take not thy Holy Spirit from me
> Restore unto me the joy of thy salvation
> And renew a right spirit within me[9]

As I returned to my place, I found my young beau leaning forward in his chair, his head bowed in a prayerful attitude. I came up behind him, put my hands on his shoulders, and leaned down with my head close to his. "Hey, Allen," I said lightly, "they're playing our song."

He lifted his head and looked at me, and I was instantly sobered: his eyes were wet with tears. He really did have a tender heart toward God, and he was in agony over his stumbling.

"Oh, God," he whispered, and then he quoted from the end of the sad story of Samson (Judges 16), whose life and ministry was ruined by his weakness for women: "He wist not that the Lord was departed from him." In effect Allen was saying, "Oh, Father, don't let that happen to me, that your Spirit should depart from me and yet that I should be so deceived and hard-hearted that I don't even realize He's gone."

My own heart had become somewhat hardened by my disobedience, but seeing this young man openly vilifying his weakness helped to put some of the healthy fear of God back into me. The Holy Spirit was using Allen's remorse to bring conviction to my soul, graciously continuing to woo me even as I flirted with earthly lovers. *Even if you are faithless,* He seemed to whisper, *I remain faithful.*[10] He had shown me in His Word that what I was struggling with was nothing new: it was a temptation as old as history itself. He promised that He would never allow me to be tempted beyond what I could resist, and that He would always give me a way out. "There hath no temptation taken you but such as is common to man: but God is faithful, who will not suffer you to be tempted above that ye are able; but will with the temptation also make a way to escape, that ye may be able to bear it."[11]

There was a circumstance that exemplifies God's incredible faithfulness to reach out to me, in the midst of temptation, and to provide a way of escape so clear that even I could not miss it.

One night some of us had been hanging out downtown, sharing our faith with any street kids who would listen. Afterwards Allen invited me up to his apartment. Now, accepting an invitation like this is not a wise thing to do for a young woman who is trying to be serious about a right relationship with God. I knew by now that His advice was to flee away from immorality.[12] But I had an excellent rationalization for why I should make an exception in this case, and this is how it went: I had a speaking/singing engagement coming up. One of the songs I was intending to sing made several references to "fences," and I had been wanting to find out if there were any Scriptures about fences that I could tie in to what I planned to talk about. Allen had a really good concordance, whereas as I didn't own one of any description.

But as the reader may easily guess, I was deceiving myself. This guy's concordance was not really what I was interested in.

As we walked from his car to the apartment building, there was a fragment of Scripture resounding loudly in my heart: *As an ox goeth to the slaughter... as an ox goeth to the slaughter.*[13] *Like a big, dumb ox being led to the slaughterhouse, ignorant of his pending doom,* I thought to myself.

But on another level, I pretended that I couldn't hear the warning and reminded myself about the opportunity to do some research with a good concordance.

Shortly after we entered the apartment, the phone rang. It quickly became clear to me by his end of the conversation that it was an ex-girlfriend. I felt jealous, but I denied the clenched feeling in my gut, feigning serenity inside and out.

Something deep inside was trying to tell me that this was a good time to leave. I ignored the prompting and opened the *Strong's Exhaustive Concordance* on the coffee table. I quickly found the word "fence." Hmm. Only one reference to the word "fence" in the whole Bible. Picking up the big King James that lay nearby, I eagerly looked up Psalm 62:3.

I never even got to the part about the fence. The verse began with a pointed question that stopped me dead in my tracks: "How long will ye imagine mischief against a man?"

As I grabbed my coat and purse, Allen was mouthing mute protests from the phone. With my hand on the doorknob, I gave him a bland smile and a wave. Then I closed the door behind me and fled.

Thank God for providing that way of escape! But we must be willing to take the escape route when it shows itself. The trouble is, too often, when the flesh is warring against the spirit,[14] we are not willing to take the way out of a situation when God gives the opportunity. Then the door closes, and we find ourselves entrapped. Enticed by our own lust and drawn away."[15]

I wish I could say that that was the last time I ventured into Allen's lair. It was not. Another night after sharing among Victoria's homeless into the wee small hours, we again went to his apartment and got cozy in front of the TV. Inadvertently we both dozed off, descending into a deep sleep. When I finally awoke, dawn's light was, to my dismay, invading the apartment. When I roused Allen, he was distraught. This looked really bad for a couple of Christians.

At the time I was living with a senior woman, a friend of Lorna Smith's. She was a God-fearing woman who had offered me dirt-cheap room and board for the Lord's sake. I couldn't go sneaking back there as the sun crept into the sky. And I wouldn't dream of lying to her.

I headed for my friend Pam's house. She was an old party pal from my Tod Mountain days. She had recently moved to Victoria, and I had had the pleasure and privilege of leading her to the Lord. She would understand. I'd catch a few more hours of sleep, then go home and tell my landlady that I'd "slept at Pam's." That wouldn't really be a lie.

After a short drive, I pulled into her driveway and knocked cautiously at her door. It was very, very early. Surprise registered on her face as she opened the door and saw me. Then the lights seemed to come on, and she answered her own question: "Oh, Nancy—you've been out witnessing all night!" Her eyes shone with admiration.

She opened the door wide, welcomed me in, and put on the kettle. Over a pot of tea, I straightened her out: no, I hadn't exactly been witnessing all night. Shamefacedly I confessed where I had been, then I crashed on her couch and she crawled back into bed.

Sometime thereafter, our church held a week of evangelistic meetings. The speaker spent one entire evening on the subject of unclean spirits. So thorough was his teaching, and so convicting, that at the close, when he gave an altar call for deliverance, about half of the congregation mobbed the front.

I stayed in my seat. I pretended that this sermon had not applied to me. I pretended because I did not want anyone else to guess what I was struggling with; and I pretended because I did not want to admit to myself what I was struggling with.

Before the evangelist left the microphone to begin praying for people, he said, almost like an afterthought, "And all those of you who want prayer for something else, you come and stand over here at the side."

I got up and joined this second, much smaller group. "Boy," I said, speaking to the woman next to me and nodding toward the larger group, "there sure are a lot of people here with unclean spirits, aren't there?" *Just look at all the nasty people over there!*

Now the evangelist spoke into the mike again: "You people who are left in your seats," he said, "I want you to come and pray for these people who have unclean spirits."

There was much rattling of chairs again as this third exodus moved forward and merged with the first group. We in the second group were left to wait for now.

But not all of us. It seemed that the Lord wanted someone to pray for me, right then, because from out of nowhere came a young lady, one of the very ones against whom I'd held such harsh judgement for their wanton ways, making a beeline right toward me. As she reached me, she hesitated for a moment, seeming suddenly unsure of herself.

"I know you don't have an unclean spirit," she began.

Of course not! I thought. *Look at the group I'm standing with.*

"But the Lord told me to come and pray for you anyway."

By the sovereign power of God, conviction hit me like a wave, and I threw my arms in the air, crying out—with absolutely no forethought, "I forgive them, Lord! I forgive them all!"

The buxom blonde had no idea what I was talking about; she just gathered me lovingly into her perfumy bosom and prayed like a house on fire while I wept.

Later the Lord put an interesting spin on a Scripture to show me what had happened to me: "Whose soever sins ye remit, they are remitted unto them; and whose soever sins ye retain, they are retained."[16] *Forgive people for their sins,* He was telling me, *and it will help them to receive my forgiveness and cleansing. But hold their sins against them, and you yourself will retain the same weaknesses.* He taught me a hard lesson that day, and I've never forgotten it.

I repented of my lust—for now—and resolved to flee temptation. I would try to draw closer to God in my loneliness.

Lord God, here I am, Lord—I've fallen again
I'm sorry, Lord, I'm sorry; I feel so ashamed
I'm only a sheep and sometimes I'm so dumb
But Lord, I want to be walking in the light when You come[17]

But sometimes, Lord, I get so lonely, I don't know what to do
I forget that loneliness cannot exist close to You
So teach me, Lord, so the next time I'll know what to do
Take all of my loneliness and draw closer to You

There is no temptation but such is common to man[18]
And temptation is not sin, but it will lead you there if it can
So give me strength, Lord, and wisdom to know what to do
Walk away from temptation and draw closer to You[19]

If we say we have no sin, we deceive ourselves
And the truth—the truth is not in us
But if we confess our sins to Him, He is faithful and just
To forgive us and cleanse us from all unrighteousness[20]

Lord, this body is Your temple;[21] I never want You to leave
But if I sin, Lord, I know it makes Your Holy Spirit grieve[22]
So teach me, Lord, so the next time, I'll do what I must do
Flee away from temptation[23] and draw closer to You

Lord God, please forgive me—I've stumbled again
I'm sorry, Lord, I'm humbled, and I'm, oh! so ashamed
Lord, I'm only a sheep and sometimes I'm so dumb
But Lord, I want to be walking in the light when You come
I want to be walking in the light when You come

A little sidebar here: Twice this song mentions feeling "so ashamed." Let me qualify this: Guilt and shame are natural for the Christian who has gone against her conscience and transgressed God's laws. They will, quite rightfully, remain while she refuses to repent. Although they are very negative and destructive emotions and can be used by the enemy to torment her, they can be a helpful part of conviction in motivating her to turn to God. As with all of the enemy's devices, he intends them for evil; but God can employ them for good.

Once the Christian repents, however, shame and guilt should absolutely evaporate; this is part of her birthright in Christ. If these feelings do not disappear, this likely indicates an inadequate understanding—and a lack of appropriation—of grace.

I was back on the straight and narrow for now, but I was still aware of covert shenanigans continuing here and there in the youth group. I grieved for their struggles, and much more, I sensed that the Holy Spirit grieved.

One Sunday evening after church, a bunch of us youth went to a restaurant for coffee. One of the young ladies had to leave early. Allen had his eye on her (he had his eye on many), and so he offered her a ride home. When he returned sometime later, he slipped into the booth where I now sat alone, looked across at me intensely, and asked a question:

"What is fornication?"

"Fornication is when you have sex with someone you're not married to."

He brushed off my definition impatiently: "I *know* that; I *know* that. But what is it really? Is *kissing* fornication?"

I wondered what he had just been up to.

I thought for a moment about his question; then answered: "It's the same spirit."

He pondered my statement briefly; then agreed. "Yeah, it is." He sighed, like someone who has the weight of the world on his shoulders—or maybe like someone who has the burden of sin on his back. He leaned back in the booth, lost in contemplation, while I sat thinking about what I had just said.

Fleeing Youthful Lusts

In our secular culture, serious commitments aside, sex is treated like the world's all-time favourite indoor sport. The "winner" is the one who scores with the most partners, who experiences the most passion and the most orgasms, while safely avoiding the hazards of emotional hang-ups, pregnancy, and disease. This is the spirit of fornication.

(In God's design, emotions are not a hang-up, pregnancy is not a curse, and sexually transmitted diseases are non-existent.)

As an unbeliever, I had finally, at the age of twenty, been seduced by the world's love affair with fornication, and for the next four years I freely embraced its philosophy. It had come as quite a surprise to me when, just a couple of weeks into my new life with God, He began to convict me about my cavalier attitude toward sex.

Now, two years later, I was seeing that God wanted me to treat even kissing as very serious business. Hey, it doesn't always lead to intercourse, any more than smoking pot always leads to crack, but in either case you're playing with fire. Kissing is the first step in sexual intimacy. Those who are wise will treat it with great caution, great respect, great sobriety. To indulge lightly in kissing with various partners is to use it (*and* your temporary partner) as a passing source of selfish pleasure. When it is used this way, it is part of the spirit of fornication. As such, it breeds and multiplies lust.

In a song I would later write, I refer to Christians taking part in this kind of kissing as "humming a tune that the worldly world sings."

I remember a sermon that Ted Follows, one of our pastors at the Church of the Way in Victoria, preached one Sunday. He talked about the fact that the English words "breath" and "spirit" are one and the same word in the Greek: *pneuma*.

As I recall, he made reference to these two verses:

"And the Lord God formed man of the dust of the ground, and breathed into his nostrils the breath of life; and man became a living soul,"[1] and "[Jesus] breathed on them, and saith unto them, Receive ye the Holy Ghost."[2] Then Ted made a thought-provoking statement: "I believe we need to be very careful about whom we kiss on the mouth."

His point was that in the exchange of a kiss, there is also the exchange of breath, as we are mouth to mouth and nose to nose. Just as in the two verses above there is reference to a mysterious impartation of life from the breath—or spirit—of God, so, Ted speculated, there is a transfer of the very spirit of one person to the other in a kiss.

God was teaching me deeply through these times. Back when I had been saved for just a couple of months, I thought that I was ready for marriage. It was now clear to me that I had been mistaken. There was much God wanted to show me first.

He was teaching me that there was a lot more to intimate relationship than the selfish passion to which I had reduced it back in my pre-Christian days. He was giving me glimpses of holy mysteries, even as I wrestled with my lust and my loneliness. Sometimes I wanted to run away and hide from the responsibility of this new knowledge, but mostly I wanted God to take me higher, to completely have His way in me.

Heavenly Father, I don't know what's going on
I'm feeling feelings I've kept buried for so long
I need You more than ever before, walking every step at my side
Take me right through this valley, Lord; don't let me run away and hide

Your ways, Lord, are so much higher than mine[3]
You say I'm more precious than gold and the fire just comes to refine[4]
Lord, help me to trust, and help me to obey
I see dimly through a glass now, but I'll see it all someday[5]

Lord Jesus, come, purge me with Your fire
I want to grow in You—Lord Jesus, take me higher
No, it's not easy, Lord, but You never said it would be
But I want to go all the way with You, so work Your work in me

Your ways, Lord, are so much higher than mine
You say I'm more precious than gold and the fire just comes to refine
When I go my own way, Lord, it causes me such pain
I want to die and bury myself in You so You'll raise me up again[6]

Lord Jesus, come, now baptize me with Your fire[7]
I want to grow in You—Lord Jesus, take me higher
No, it's not easy, Lord, but You never said it would be
Still, I want to go all the way with You, so work Your will in me

What was God's will for me regarding love and sex and marriage? Simply that I come to appreciate His perspective on it so that I could fully repent of my wayward attitudes and behaviours and thereby fully receive His forgiveness and His cleansing. That way, one day, in His time, He could bless me with all of the abundance that He designed love and marriage and sex to bring into our lives.

Fornication indulges in pleasures that God intended to be enjoyed only within a committed, lifelong relationship. The sad thing about the world's casual approach to sex is that it fails to appreciate or consider the long-term implications. Bonds are formed in lovemaking—bonds that no person can sever. "What God has joined together," He says, "let not man put asunder." As I have come to understand, mankind *cannot* put this union asunder. Only God can sever what He has joined, and He has determined that He will only break this tie at death. We can argue and rationalize all we want, but if God has said it, this is simply the way it is. We may disregard His counsel and go merrily off sleeping with whomever we desire, whenever the mood strikes, and then we may externally break off these liaisons, but there is something at a deep level that simply does not break off, and we may find ourselves, as the years go by, still entangled with and ever more troubled by lovers we really thought we had put behind us.

By this time, in my later mid-twenties and saved for about two and a half years, I clearly understood that fornication was wrong, even if it had been fun. I had not yet begun to understand how deeply it had damaged me. I only knew that it had made me feel desirable and that it had (though only ever temporarily) assuaged the awful loneliness inside.

I continued to think of the incident in that restaurant with Allen, where I had heard a response come out of my mouth concerning kissing, a response that surprised me because it was beyond the understanding that I actually had at the time. I had recognized then that God was speaking through those words. He was trying to teach me that this casual sexual involvement among Christians was of the same spirit that had captured me in the past: fornication. I was feeding the same lust, soothing the same loneliness.

"It's a form of idolatry: turning to sex to meet my deep, emotional needs—instead of to the love of the Father."[8]

Since that night at the crusade, I was managing, most of the time, to keep a reign on my lust, but the struggle against loneliness was harder. My efforts to "flee youthful lusts" meant that, necessarily, I was alone more, and sometimes the sense of isolation was overwhelming.

I remember late one afternoon sitting in my bedroom with the sun streaming in. I was in an agony of loneliness. I began to talk to God about it.

"Lord, You say that You meet all my needs. You say that Your grace is sufficient for me. But sometimes, I'm afraid You're just not real enough for me. Sometimes I just want 'somebody with skin on.' You say that You're a very present help in trouble. I can't go on anymore, being lonely like this. I need You to be 'very present.'"

I put my pillow on the floor beside my bed and knelt down on it. *I might be here for a while—I had better be comfortable.* "Lord, I need You to comfort me, in a real way. I'm not leaving until You do. I don't care if I have to kneel here for two days—I'm waiting until You touch me."

I buried my face in my hands on the bed and waited, quietly whispering my need to Him, determined that I would not move until something changed.

It seemed that a long time went by. Then I felt it: a feeling like a Hand on the back of my head, slowly stroking my hair down to the nape of my neck. It was so tender—like a mother, like a father—

even like a lover. I wept softly, holding very still, not wanting to interrupt the caress.

I knew for sure, in that special moment, that I was profoundly loved; I knew that I was completely accepted. I also knew now that God would make Himself real to me, in any way that I needed Him to, as long as I would take the time to come to Him, and as long as I would gear myself to His time frame and not my own. Through faith and patience we receive His manifest promises.[9] For those of us who have welcomed the living presence of Christ into our lives, we have an unfathomable and virtually untapped resource dwelling inside of us: the Mighty God of the universe living right in our hearts. Of course His grace is sufficient!

Lord Jesus, I'm feeling kind of lonely
Lord Jesus, I'm feeling kind of blue
Remind me, I need You only
Lord Jesus, I only need You

But sometimes, Lord, I get so weary
Though still I hear Your voice, I start to disagree
Then my spiritual sight gets kind of blurry
Bring me back, Lord, let me be just what You've called me to be

Sometimes, Lord, it seems
My troubles are all I can see
Remind me, Your Word says
That Your grace is sufficient for me

So when you're feeling lonely
And your loneliness threatens to tear you apart
Remember this one thing and this thing only
The Mighty God of the universe is living right in your heart

So, Jesus, when I feel lonely
And I get my eyes off You and onto me (poor old me!)
Let me trust in Your Word only
'Cause it tells me Your grace is sufficient[10]
You tell me Your grace is sufficient
And I believe that Your grace is sufficient for me

In the middle of my long trek through the desert of lust and loneliness, there was one friendship that was like an oasis for me. There was a fellow in the church, Kent, who took me out now and then, in between casually dating a number of other girls. He was different from the other guys I had known.

Kent had grown up in a nice home, although it was not a Christian home. During his high school years, a girlfriend had invited him to church. It wasn't long before he had come to know the Saviour and had begun to draw the rest of his family in as well. Then his parents' marriage fell apart, due to a long-standing infidelity that was suddenly exposed.

I wonder, in retrospect, how much this trauma affected Kent's attitude toward relationships and dating. Whatever the reason, he seemed to have his hormones much more firmly in check than anyone else I'd ever dated.

He'd take me out for dinner; we'd have a comfortable, intelligent conversation mixed with a lot of laughs; and then he'd drive me home. He would come around to my side and open the door, help me out of the car, and chat a few moments. Then he'd grin and say, "Well, Nance?" and he'd open his arms up wide. I'd step into his embrace, a firm, warm hug; then he'd say "Good night" and leave.

It was obvious that he enjoyed my company. I think he found me attractive. But there was a line he wouldn't cross, a line that he wouldn't even approach.

I had a long-standing crush on him, and I had occasional dates with him over a period of several years. There were a lot of things about him that would make him a good catch, but the most attractive thing about him to me was this quality of self-discipline. It spoke (in a way that mere words never can) about commitment to God and reverence for intimacy. Because of that, just being with him made me feel special. I felt respected, and I felt safe.

Mind you, not all of me wanted to feel safe. Part of me wanted to feel passion. Once or twice I gave him a back rub, and that served to make me yearn for something more. (Refer back to the previous chapter for my opinion on back massages among the young and restless.) But if it had the same effect on him—and it very likely did—he never let on.

Then one night, when he was bidding me farewell, saying how tired he was, he gave me his customary hug, but this time I held the embrace in a way that I hadn't before. I didn't want to let him go. I wanted to elicit more of a response from him.

He took me gently but firmly by the shoulders and stepped back a little so that he could see my face, and he just said, kind of humorously, "Nance, are you trying to wake me up?" Then he gave me another brotherly hug, said "Good night," and that was that.

I felt embarrassed. I felt slightly humiliated. I'd made a pass and I'd been rejected. I don't think that had ever happened before in my whole life.

But I also felt good. I was glad that Kent was so steady in his convictions. This was right; this was how single Christians ought to handle their relationships. And you know, Kent never treated me any differently, and so after a very short time, those feelings of shame and embarrassment vanished without a trace, because they had nothing to which to attach themselves; and they were replaced with gratitude for the renewed hope that there really were some godly young men out there.

A Flame and a Funeral

Early in 1980 I was approached by a fellow in our church who was a member of the board of Victoria's fledgling chapter of Youth for Christ International. The new organization needed a secretary, he said, and he would like to see me apply. So I got all dressed up and put my hair in a bun and went to an interview. Although my qualifications in the secretarial department were not very impressive (an understatement), I was hired.

In March, YFC gave me a two-week break from my new office job to honour an earlier commitment: house-sitting once again for Jack and Velma up in the Heffley Valley. It was a long and pleasant drive back to that very different world. Life on their small ranch was quiet—a nice change from Victoria; and a short drive took me to Tod Mountain for some skiing with friends of an earlier era.

I was overjoyed to see an old flame, Mike Hartley, again. Ever since I'd met him early in '74, I'd had a serious soft spot for "the little fella" (as some of his taller friends affectionately called him). The time and distance that had passed between us since then had not changed my feelings—or his either, from what I could tell. He agreed to join me for dinner at Jack and Velma's place one evening during my stay.

I don't remember what we ate that night, but I do remember that the old chemistry hung between us in the air, throwing a pleasurable tension into the evening. But I, three years old in the Lord now, and a little wiser for some of my recent stumbling, was being very careful to keep things right, both for my sake and for the sake of my "testimony."

After dinner we went and sat on the living room couch, side by side. The conversation wandered comfortably here and there. Then abruptly, Hartley, never one to mince words, got personal:

"So, Fowler, when's the last time you slept with anyone?" (We always called each other by our last names.)

I answered him as straight as he'd asked: "Almost three years."

"You're lying," he responded. "'Cause I know you, Fowler, and you've got to be lying." He sounded suddenly hostile.

I sat quietly. "It's true," was all I said.

He seemed agitated. "So how come?"

I was not about to leap in with a dissertation on the four spiritual laws. "I'm waiting for the right person to come along."

"Oh, so now if anyone asks me what Nancy's up to, I should tell them she's waiting for Mr. Right?"

I smiled and shrugged, noncommittal in the face of his sarcasm.

"So how come all of a sudden you're waiting for Mr. Right?"

I was not going to take the bait unless I had to. "Because I believe in marriage now."

"You never used to believe in marriage, Fowler. How come you believe in marriage now?"

I took a deep breath and let it out slowly. He wasn't going to back off. "I believe in marriage now because marriage is God's institution and I believe in God now."

"Ha!" he cried triumphantly. "I heard you were religious, Fowler. I just wanted to hear you say it with your own mouth."

The atmosphere was confrontational now, as it so often is when Christian and non-Christian air their views. But I wasn't going to enter into a sparring match—"witnessing," as we poorly defined it back then. I sat quietly and let the storm blow over for a bit.

He calmed down after a while and became relaxed and conversational again. "So now that you're religious," he said, mocking me gently, "what's different?"

I knew that he really wanted to know.

"Well, always before, I had this lost, restless feeling, sort of like feeling homesick when you don't even know that you're away from home. When I came to know the Lord, I had peace inside for the first time ever. I felt like I'd come home."

He mulled this over in silence. Then he said, "I've always felt restless inside." He paused. "I guess maybe I just have to accept that I'm always going to feel this way."

I said nothing, even though it might have looked (to the zealous young Christian that I was) like the ideal opening to tell him that God loved him and had a wonderful plan for his life. He was a sharp guy. It wasn't lost on him that he had just echoed my own past condition and complaint. He hadn't missed what I'd said about the cure. He could connect the dots for himself.

The mood lightened as we drew the evening to a close. "When do you head back to Victoria?" he asked.

"Tomorrow. Jack and Velma are coming back."

"But isn't tomorrow your birthday?"

"Yeah." I was surprised and pleased that he had remembered.

"Fowler, you can't leave on your birthday. I need to take you out for dinner."

So I decided to make arrangements to stay the extra night with friends in Kamloops, and I warned Hartley: "I'm going to wear a dress." He had never seen me in anything but ski clothes or blue jeans. Now he might be in for a bit of shock, because the Lord had been helping me get in touch with my femininity.

I felt like a million bucks when he came to pick me up that evening, in a chocolate brown dress and low heels, with my waist-length hair brushed out loose.

He looked me up and down and said, "Holy crow, Fowler, you really did put on a dress, didn't you!" He immediately assumed the role of fumbling, bumbling escort, doting on me with a feigned and exaggerated nervousness. It was funny—and very charming.

I had thought that maybe he wanted to discuss spiritual things at greater length, and I was ready for anything that might come, but he was just light, humorous, and endearing Hartley—bent on showing me a good time on my birthday. I could tell that my response the previous night to his questions about my love life had impacted him deeply; I could tell that he liked the change he saw. And he had seen that I didn't want to preach at him, and that had disarmed him again. We had a special evening.

I never dreamed that it would be the last time I saw him alive. A year later I viewed his still form in a coffin. I had arrived early at the tiny funeral parlour in a small town in B.C.; no one else was around. I was glad: I wasn't sure what other people would have thought of my speaking to a corpse.

"You finally managed to grow yourself a decent moustache, didn't you, Hartley?" I laughed sadly. He looked so handsome. Twenty-six years old, just graduated from nursing, with his whole life ahead of him. Returning from a cross-Canada motorcycle trip with a friend, his engine had seized, locking the wheels, putting the bike into a skid, and throwing him into the path of his buddy's bike.

It was heart-rending, yet at the reception that followed the funeral service, God in His goodness showed me, through conversations with other friends of Hartley's, signs of the spiritual stirrings that had come in his life before his accident. I also found out that my last encounter with him, along with the occasional letters I had sent since, had left a lasting impression.

How I hoped that he had opened his heart to God! With his death, heaven and hell were suddenly so imminent, so immediate. I knew that it was either one or the other for my dear friend. Yet I almost wanted to deny the Truth that I had come to know. I didn't want it to be so cut and dried.

I wrestled with it all and finally came to rest in the immutable righteousness, love, and mercy of God. A couple of days after I got back from the funeral, I wrote a "Prayer for Hartley."

Lord, I know that my fruit should be peace and joy[1]
But I've lost someone I very much loved
When he stood before your throne
Did he stand there all alone
Or was he covered, was he covered by Your blood?[2]

Lord, I did try to tell him, but I really don't know
If the message of your saving grace got through
Oh, Lord, before he died,
Did he lay down his pride?[3]
Did he turn, turn it all over to You?

You tell me that Your Word does not return void
But will prosper in the thing you sent it to do[4]

And Lord, I'd ask nothing more
But that this friend gone before
Would be safe, safe in glory with You

But why, why would anyone wait?
Hear the truth and just walk away?
Don't you know tomorrow may be too late?
The day of salvation is today.[5]

Lord, I know You know him better than anyone
Still I'd like to recommend him to You
He was so cute, Lord, so kind
So funny, so fine
I'm sure You'd want him right there with You

Well, no, he wasn't very holy; he wasn't very pure
He was a scoundrel and a bit of a knave
But I know You, my God
Your mercies are sure
And if he called on Your Name, he was saved[6]

I want to know, Lord—did he call on Your Name?
Sweet green eyes and dark shining hair
I don't quite know how to say this, Lord
It may sound kind of strange
But it wouldn't be heaven if he wasn't there

Now, Lord, restore to me the joy;[7] leave with me Your peace[8]
Let it descend on me like a dove
I believe that in the end
You reached out to my friend
Lord, I trust in your mercy and love[9]

Re-Enter the Doctor

Meanwhile back at Youth for Christ, it was becoming more evident with each day, as I struggled with the electric typewriter, wasting reams of expensive letterhead, that secretarial work was not in line with my spiritual giftings.

Now that the YFC office was established, they needed ministry staff. One of the main areas of identified need in Victoria was for ministry to troubled youth. While the executive director was trying, unsuccessfully, to hire "Youth Guidance" staff, I was unofficially following up phone calls from distraught parents and concerned neighbours, tracking down wayward youth, meeting them for coffee, and finding wide-open doors to speak into their lives.

One day Doug Perkins, my boss, called me into his office and, once I was seated, said, "For months I've been trying to hire ministry staff, and I've finally realized that she's been sitting right under my nose."

So they found another secretary, a good one, and I changed job descriptions. God had made no mistake in leading them to hire me; it just took us all a little while to tune in to His plan. Late nights found me roaming the downtown area again, talking with street kids, like I had done with Allen; but now it was in my new official capacity of Youth Guidance counsellor. Daytimes, when I wasn't in the office, I might be having coffee with someone who needed to talk or visiting the kids at the Juvenile Detention Centre.

One day Lorna Smith called me at the office. A young girl she knew had been in a car accident. Lorna was concerned about her spiritual condition; perhaps I could go with her to the hospital and try to talk to this teenager?

Lorna and I met in the hospital lobby and, after enquiring at the nurses' station, made our way up the elevator and down a hallway. We found the girl's room busy with family members. Lorna told them we'd go have a cup of tea and come back a little later.

We rode the elevator to the basement and took our place at the end of the long line in the cafeteria. And who should be immediately in front of us in that line-up but Dr. Duncan Collins himself!

I casually performed introductions, glad that I was dressed for the office and looking none too shabby. As Lorna and I got our tea, Duncan caught the attention of a nurse from emergency: "If anyone up there is looking for me, tell them I'm down here having coffee." Then he joined us at a table. I was thrilled.

The three of us chatted for quite some time, a fact that I found flattering in view of his busy schedule. At length he excused himself.

I turned back to my older friend. Lorna had this way of looking at you when she wanted to make a point—sort of like a border collie staring down a sheep. She was looking at me that way now.

"You don't want to marry that guy," she said, mincing no words. "He doesn't think about anything but himself. He's completely self-centred. He didn't hear a thing you said."

The fantasy sustained another deathblow.

But it wasn't ready to die just yet. I had been under some teaching that told me I could have anything I wanted from God if I just trusted Him hard enough for it. The Holy Spirit had quickened a passage of Scripture to me that I believed was God's take on Duncan's spiritual status—and His promise for the future—our future.

> "For I will not contend for ever, neither will I be always wroth: for the spirit should fail before me, and the souls which I have made. For the iniquity of his covetousness was I wroth, and smote him: I hid me, and was wroth, and he went on frowardly in the way of his heart. I have seen his ways, and will heal him: I will lead him also, and restore comforts unto him and to his mourners."
>
> Isaiah 57:16–18, KJV

God was angry at the sin of Duncan's self-centredness and his unbelief (or so I understood this to be saying); consequently, He had punished him by withdrawing from him, letting him go on wilfully in the way of his own heart. But God would not strive with him forever, neither would He stay angry. If He did, a mortal man could not bear it. This soul, whom God had created and whom He loved, would be consumed in His presence if God did not put away His wrath. Yes, God had seen his wilful ways, but He would cause him to mend them. God would lead him too, and restore comfort and bring peace and blessing both to him and to the one who mourned for him—namely, me.

I went for long walks on the streets of Victoria, quoting this passage in King James English over and over and over again. If I just had enough faith, I thought, if I just confessed the promise enough, surely one day I would possess it. I really, really wanted to marry this guy.

I no longer have the same take on this so-called "word of faith" teaching. Faith here might be described as the power to get what you want from God, a concept that can be misleading and even harmful, especially to immature believers. When we are young in the Faith, we often have not wrestled enough with the laying down of our own will. We haven't yet come to rest in the knowledge that God really does have our best interest at heart and that He knows what He's doing. We perhaps haven't yet learned to hear His voice, to really discern His will.

As we mature in faith, we learn to trust Him more, and we are quicker to yield to His will. I don't recall who gave the following definition of faith, but I believe it's one of the better ones: "discerning what God intends to do." On the basis of this discernment, we make our stand, sometimes praying, sometimes battling the enemy, sometimes just waiting in confidence on God. We have reached the place where we don't want to be too quick to tell God what we think He should do for us.

Do you realize that sometimes God will answer a prayer if we plead hard enough, even if it's not really what He would choose for us? Remember the story of the Israelites in the wilderness, tiring of the miraculous manna that God sent every morning to feed them, grumbling and crying out to God for some nice fresh fowl?[1] He finally gave them what they asked for, but then "the anger of the Lord burned against the people, and he struck them with a severe plague."[2] It's not that there was anything so wrong with some nice succulent quail; it's that they refused to trust God to provide, His way and in His time. They didn't believe that God had their best interest at heart. They were ungrateful and unbelieving. "You have rejected the Lord, who is among you, and have wailed before him, saying, 'Why did we ever leave Egypt?'"[3]

A brief summary of this episode appears in the Psalms, and it has always struck a holy fear in my heart: "And he gave them their request; *but sent leanness into their soul.*"[4] Another version puts it like this: "He gave them exactly what they asked for—but along with it they got an empty heart."[5] I don't want leanness in my soul; I want it to "delight itself in fatness," in "the profuseness of spiritual joy."[6] It makes me want to be careful what I pray for. Makes me want to submit everything to Him. He really does know what's best.

Fast-forward to the present, where I have been happily married for well over twenty years: Sometimes I think back to the hours that I spent pacing around Victoria's streets, confessing Scripture and trying to get God to give me Dr. Duncan Collins for a husband. If God had given me what I really, *really* wanted back then, I wouldn't be married to the wonderful man I have today. I am grateful every day of my life that God turned a deaf ear to all my pleading back then.

Duncan was rich in the things of this world, but he was spiritually bankrupt. For the longest time I held out the hope that God would change him. But the words of a song were finally starting to sink in, a song that I'd actually written way back in cow-camp, just a few months after I first met Duncan. Funny how long it can take to come to terms with something that you really do know, deep down in your heart.

I thought that you were going to be my "forever and ever"
In a way, maybe you always will
And it still could be if you'd accept the Lord
But certainly not until
'Cause Christ comes first in my life right now
And that's the way it's always going to be
To be unequally yoked[7]
Would be a sad, sad joke
So, babe, there's nothing—nothing for you and me

But should you ever decide you can't go it alone
And you want the Lord at your side
Just call His name; you've got a world to gain
And nothing, nothing to lose but your pride
But until that day, it's good-bye, good-bye:
That means "God be with you," you know—
And I'll be praying
That He'll be staying
Right beside you, wherever you go

And I'm sorry—baby, I'm sorry
More sorry than you'll ever know
But the Lord's got me tight in His loving arms
And He's the Way—the only way to go

Oh, should your mansion burn up, should your pool go dry
Should your pretty little car break down
Should your sailboat sink, your squash game slip
And the whole world you love just comes a-tumbling down
Should you ever decide that you need more of a god
Than the one you claim to be
Just call—He'll come to you, sure as His promise is true
He's going to make Himself real like He did to me
But until that day, it's good-bye, good-bye:
That means "God be with you," you know[8]
And I'll be praying
That He'll be staying
Right beside you, wherever you go

And I'm sorry, oh baby, I'm sorry
But I really don't hurt that bad
'Cause the Lord's got me tight in His loving arms
And it's the best love I've ever, ever had

    I did have a couple of other chance meetings with Duncan. On one of those occasions, I asked him if we could get together sometime soon, just to talk. The truth is, I wanted an opportunity to ask him point blank if I was as special to him as he was to me.
    (You, dear reader, are thinking that I must be a little slow on

the uptake. I'm sure you've never in your life been so stubbornly obtuse.)

So we set a date to meet at my favourite restaurant for supper and a chat.

I spent a long time getting ready that evening, and I was shaky with anticipation and nervousness.

And he stood me up. I sat alone a long time at the little "table for two" before I finally ordered. I ate a small meal, alone. Then I drove slowly around the city, crying out to the Lord: "God, I want to see him. I really want to see him."

No, you don't.

"Yes, I do, Lord; I really want to see him."

Suddenly, all alone on an otherwise empty downtown street, there sat the old Jeep wagon. Funny thing, it was parked right in front of the first restaurant he'd taken me to, more than two years before.

I was ecstatic. "Thank You, Lord!" I parked my little car right behind the Jeep and swept into the restaurant, right past the hostess and her "Please Wait To Be Seated" sign. I spotted him right away. And I also spotted a young lady seated across from him.

I had enough momentum that I wasn't going to be able to stop and turn and leave gracefully. He had seen me anyway.

"Hi!" I jumped right in. A good offence is the best defence. "I recognized your Jeep out front and thought I'd stop and say hi. How are you?"

He acknowledged my greeting and then introduced his young lady friend. I was smiling so broadly that I could hardly see straight, but she appeared to be quite lovely.

He gave me an appraising glance up and down and remarked, "You're looking all dressed up tonight. What are you up to?"

"I have a date." It wasn't really a lie. I had *thought* I had a date. Past tense.

I wished them a good evening, excused myself, and swept back out, my long coat swooping around the chairs and tables.

Back in my car, I drove the lonely, rainy way back home. The wiper blades flopped back and forth, trying to keep the rain off the windshield. My eyelids kept time with them, trying to clear the tears from my eyes. "You were right, Lord," I kept saying over and over, banging my hands on the steering wheel. "I didn't want to see him."

There was only one other time I saw him. A couple of years later, Youth for Christ took a bunch of kids on a ski trip to the huge Whistler/Blackcomb development. Amidst the many lifts and runs and amongst thousands of people spread out over miles of terrain, I saw him four different times that day. The last time, I finally made myself known and said hello. We chatted for a few minutes. Then:

"Are you still serving the Lord?" he asked me, light mockery in his voice.

"I sure am."

"Well, I'm still serving the devil." He flashed a big smile and skied away. I haven't seen him since.

Duncan Collins was the only man who had ever seriously made me think "Marriage!" But regardless of how infatuated I was with that good-looking young Emergency Room Physician, I knew the relationship shouldn't and couldn't and wouldn't go anywhere unless and until he submitted himself to God.

So if the spiritual dimension was missing, what was the attraction? Everything else: his looks, his personality, his profession, his income, his humour, his toys, his lifestyle—all of which, outside of God, added up to a big, fat zero.

As I slowly came to grips with the painful realization that this was not the man for me, I realized how shallow our relationship really had been. In the final analysis, I actually spent very little time with him. Our conversations were entertaining but, with the rare exception, quite superficial. Not that he was shallow; he just didn't want to delve beneath the surface, at least not with me.

Continual and meaningful communication is vital to any enduring relationship, challenging and stimulating all the reaches of the soul—the mind, the will, and the emotions. I had experienced this depth of communication in various friendships but never really with the addition of the romantic element. That combination was something I believe I had always yearned for, consciously or not. And now that God was a big part of my life, I longed also for the depth that I knew the spiritual dimension would add.

I had been so enamoured with everything about Duncan and his life, but I was beginning to understand that even without all of those "perks," as long as both parties were pursuing God, and if they had His approval on their relationship, they would have everything they needed for a great marriage.

God was trying to teach me not to look on externals. He Himself looks much deeper. I'll never forget how, during those years that I prayed so longingly for a husband, He spoke to me one day out of His Word: "Look not on his countenance, or on the height of his stature...for the Lord seeth not as man seeth; for man looketh on the outward appearance, but the Lord looketh on the heart."[9] And I thought, *Oh, great! God's preparing me for a pygmy with acne.*

Sadly, I was quick to malign God's intent, so quick to believe that if I wanted spiritual blessings, I would be cut off from natural, temporal blessings. I didn't comprehend how fully He desired to bless me. As His Word says, "Eye has not seen, ear has not heard, neither has it entered into the heart of mankind, what God has prepared for those that love him."[10] Meanwhile, it seemed that I was bent on finding another Mr. Wrong to chase. You see, there wasn't just one Mr. Wrong. There were many of them. I chased them from about age sixteen to age twenty-nine, searching for a nameless, faceless ideal. You, dear reader, have already seen how I managed to find a couple of them with whom to pacify myself, even while I was sorting out the truth about my Paperback Romance.

Go East, Young Woman

In the summer of 1981, I attended Youth for Christ's School of Ministry in Rockford, Illinois: three intense weeks of training for my work as a Youth Guidance counsellor. What a wonderful time, staying in residence with a group of six hundred like-minded people, many of them young, all of them zealous for God, most of them leadership material. It wasn't long before I noticed, and was noticed by, some very eligible young men.

One of them was from Alaska. His name was Lucas, and he was such a character. And he'd been bodybuilding and consequently had an awesome build, pretty hard to miss in the silky synthetic muscle shirts he favoured.

I enjoyed horsing around with him, and I spent more time than I should have on the men's floor, learning judo from him. I had always enjoyed getting physical; I liked to wrestle and fight with guys, and I frequently took the upper hand. Now, to get some real instruction in some of the martial arts was a blast, and it would give me an edge in the future that I hadn't enjoyed before.

I felt a warm affection for Lucas, and I ignored the knowledge that underneath that affection was a smouldering hotbed of lust. Truth be told, that's why I enjoyed the judo instruction so much— it was a legitimate excuse to get up-close and personal and yet I could still pretend that I was behaving myself. This was, I believe, the subliminal energy behind all my wrestling and play-fighting with guys over the years. Similar to back massages, it was a way to embrace and yet refrain from embracing. It was another way of deceiving myself; another way of getting a cheap thrill without admitting it.

There was an internal struggle that built continually during my stay there: God was trying to convict me of my lust, but if

I couldn't even admit to myself that I was lusting after this guy, then how could I repent of the lust? *It's just affection,* I kept telling myself. *I just feel a lot of affection for him.* "Affection" sounded so innocent; lust was ugly and ungodly.

One night the whole group of ministry students sat under the teaching of a special speaker. All of the speakers had been good, but this one was great. I suppose I especially remember him because God chose his message to get to me. It's amazing how God can do that: take a speaker's subject, which has nothing whatever to do with what God needs to tell you, and then tailor it, line by line, principle by principle, to apply it to a precise, specific, individual need.

And it wasn't just what he said: it was where his text was located. He'd had us turn to the first chapter of Ephesians. But it wasn't the first chapter of Ephesians that got to me; it was what lay on the opposite page: the last chapter and a half of the book of Galatians. A verse from the fifth chapter leapt off the page and nailed me right between the eyes: "And they that are Christ's have crucified the flesh with [its] affections and lusts."[1]

How could He? How could He put affection and lust in the same sentence? Not only had He thus painted them with the same brush, He was clearly telling me, "Call it affection or call it lust, but it's all coming from your flesh, and your flesh is supposed to be dead, crucified with Me."

By the end of the service I was a wreck. I sought out one of our Canadian executive staff whom I respected a tremendous amount and tearfully asked him to pray for me. (He was a young man, not much older than I, but very safely married.) I was an incoherent mess, babbling over and over, "How could God use affections and lusts in the same sentence?"

I don't think the poor fellow ever did have a clue what I was talking about, but it didn't matter. *I* knew what *God* was talking about, and I was finally ready to listen.

At the recognition and acknowledgement of this persistent, besetting sin, I felt so much shame at the dark condition of my heart. In response, God simply showed me how much He loved me, exactly the way I was. I holed up in my room with my guitar to get it all out in a song—a song that I call "Revelation at Rockford."

Lord, You love me when I'm up
And You love me when I'm down
You love me when I'm still
And when I'm spinning 'round and 'round
You love me when I'm bad
Just as much as when I'm good
You love me in a way
I thought nobody could

Lord, I want to love You
Please make me Your own
If it was left to me, Lord
I'd be left alone
I couldn't even come to You
You had to bring me to that place
And everything I am now
Is only by Your grace

But sometimes, Lord, I get rebellious
And then my life gets in a whirl
I want to get things right again
But Lord, I'm a stubborn girl
So if I ask You what Your will is
Remind me I've known it all along
And if there's any doubt that something's right
There ain't no doubt it's wrong

Lord, I want to serve You
But I can't do it on my own
If it was not for You, Lord
I'd still be alone, alone
I cannot even come to You
Except You bring me to that place
Only by Your mercy
Only by Your grace

Because You love me when I'm up, Lord
And You love me when I'm down

You love me when I'm on my knees
And when I'm busily rushing 'round and 'round
And Lord, if I am bad
Well, even then You love me too
I don't know why You love me
I'm just glad You do

I don't know why You love me, Lord
I'm just glad You do

So the Lord had pulled me back into line once again. How wonderful that we can come to Him over and over with the same sin, the same weakness. No rebuke; no put-down. Simply His Word: "If we say that we have no sin, we deceive ourselves, and the truth is not in us. [But] if we confess our sins, he is faithful and just to forgive us our sins, and to cleanse us from all unrighteousness."[2]

Over and over again we can come to Him, as many times as it takes for His work in us in a particular area to be completed.

I continued to hang out with Lucas, but I backed off a bit. We did things as a group with some other singles from the School of Ministry, and I got to know some more people. I realized that there was no special future in this "relationship" with Lucas, and I behaved accordingly.

Let's face it, ladies: we can usually answer that question pretty easily, even when we've just met the guy: "Is this the special one God has for me?" If the answer is no, then we should keep our distance and act in this man's presence as if we were already married to someone else. God can already see you married to that special person, be it a short way or a long way into the future; He lives outside of time. If we would just desire to see through His eyes, we might catch a glimpse too, and it might change the way we act in the present moment.

Yes, we can know, in most cases, if there is a future in a given relationship—*if* we will look squarely at God and ask Him. But most of us don't come right out and ask the Lord, because we really don't want to know. We'd rather stay in a half-squint so we can't see too clearly, put our fingers in our ears so we can't hear too well, and go blithely on with the "fun" of the moment. The only trouble is, there'll be hell to pay later. And no, I'm not cursing: I'm speaking literally. Hell is separation from God. When we choose to "enjoy the pleasures of sin for a season"[3] rather than embrace the will of God, we will reap all manner of things that are the fruit of separation from Him. There will be weeping and gnashing of teeth, right here on Planet Earth.

One night in Rockford a bunch of us had planned to go to a movie, and lo and behold, Lucas had a visitor: his older brother, who now lived in Indiana and was taking the rare opportunity to see Lucas while he was in a nearby state.

I sat next to Lucas at the theatre; his brother was on the other side of him. Man, oh, man, what I would've given for a good excuse to change seats. He was an absolutely awesome guy. He looked so much like the now-infamous Dr. Duncan Collins, ERP, but he loved God with all of his heart, and it was evident that his life was centred there and not on himself. Sense of humour—oh yeah! Tall. Good-looking. Sigh.

He was around only for the evening and the next day, just long enough for me to get to know him a tiny bit—and to be convinced that here was something God and I could really work with. And then he was gone, never to be seen again. And I'll tell you something, it is not tactful to ask Person A for Person B's address when Person A seems to really like you. Especially when they're brothers. So for once, I was tactful. I restrained myself.

Instead, as I returned from Rockford, I committed this hopeless fantasy to music, confiding only in my piano, a song telling this veritable stranger how much he reminded me of the most serious love of my life—the only man I'd ever really wanted to marry.

> How would you feel if I told you
> You reminded me of someone?
> How would you feel if I told you
> That's why I liked you at the start?
> How would you feel if I told you
> You were very much like someone,
> Very much like the only one
> Who ever really stole my heart?

And so began a song that went on to compare the two men: how similar they seemed, yet how fundamentally different they were in the end; how in the final analysis what was really important was how each of them—the old flame and the new one—responded to the Lord. Because after all, ladies, in the end, that's all that really matters.

It wasn't the kind of song I could ever sing anywhere. Most of what I write has various applications in many different venues. But this song—it was just a fantasy that never went anywhere. It was a beautiful song, and I played it over and over until I knew I would never forget it, and then I put it aside. The Lord just kind of tucked it away in my repertoire. He knew that there was a time coming, even though it was still a year and a half away, when He would want me to sing that song, and when the time came, there wasn't going to be any chance for a rehearsal.

Delightful Delinquent

My job with Youth for Christ took me to some interesting places. One evening I went to visit at a drug-and-alcohol-rehab halfway house. I had helped a teenager to get into the program, and I had promised him that I would join him for one of their evening sessions.

Running along the lines of AA's twelve-step program, they gave opportunity for several residents to get up and share. Then a well-heeled woman in her forties got up and took the floor. She introduced herself as Virginia Carmichael. She explained that the Lord had told her to come there and share about her son, Philip. He had had drug and alcohol problems since his early teens, she said, and was now incarcerated over on the mainland. She shared only briefly, then left the room, climbing the basement stairs toward the kitchen and the exit. On impulse I jumped up and hurried up the stairs after her. When I reached the top of the stairs, she still had not turned around, so I spoke her name.

"Virginia."

She spun around and clasped a hand to her bosom, then rolled her eyes and sighed with relief. "Oh!" She spoke in a hushed tone. "I thought you were one of those creepy guys following me up the stairs."

"I think I should see your son," I told her, handing her my YFC card.

She explained that it would still be a couple of months before he got out of jail. I took her phone number, and we promised each other that we would stay in touch. Then I bade her good-night and returned to the meeting.

Two months later I was on the ferry coming back from Vancouver to Victoria. It was late in the evening. I walked into the cafeteria to get a cup of tea. In the line-up, I found myself once again behind this poised and striking woman.

I spoke her name: "Virginia."

She whirled around, eyes big, hand to her heart in that same startled gesture. "Jesus Christ—!" and as I, now just as startled, wondered briefly if she were cursing, she finished her broken sentence: "...is so good!"

She told me that she was just returning from seeing Philip at the jail; she and her daughter had gone over to visit him because today was his twentieth birthday. She introduced me to seventeen-year-old Ginny. The three of us drank our tea together, and I told them about YFC's upcoming trip at Easter break: California Breakaway. Maybe Ginny would be interested?

Shortly thereafter Virginia phoned to tell me that the Lord had given her a message: it had appeared as an inner image, she said, printed out, reeling past her mind's eye like ticker-tape: "Philip is to go on this trip."

It turned out that he would be released from jail two weeks before our departure date. She would arrange, once he was home, for him to meet me at a restaurant for coffee. I could fill him in on all of the details, and he could make his own decision from there.

When the day came, I dressed in jeans and jean jacket, softening the denim with a silky pink blouse. I zipped on my black, high-heeled leather boots and brushed my hair out loose.

Philip and I met in the parking lot outside the restaurant, recognizing each other from the descriptions given.

"You goin' on this trip?" he asked, laconic, right to the point.

"Uh-huh."

He looked me up and down appraisingly, his gaze piquing my feminine vanity.

"I wouldn't mind goin'," he said.

A short time later, I was sharing this scene with a church group that I was speaking to. I concluded the story by saying, "God can use anything He wants," and everybody laughed. But there's something about this picture that I no longer find funny. Definitely some duplicitous motivation. I'll try to sort it out:

It must be obvious to the reader that, if more than twenty years later, I still remember exactly what I was wearing, I was extremely conscious of myself and how I came across in certain situations. It was very important to me how I looked that day. Clearly, I was looking to impress this fellow.

First reason, for my sake as a person: Here I was meeting, for the first time, this young tough who was newly out of prison. I had no idea what he would be like, but I wanted to impact him as a woman. As always, I wanted to be perceived as desirable—yes, on a sexual level—because that was still the way I received affirmation as a person.

Second, for the image of Christian women in general: Philip would already know, from his mother, that I was "religious." I felt a need to demonstrate to this stranger, in defence of Christian women everywhere, that "religious" girls were not necessarily dowdy and prudish.

Third, for God's sake: As an ambassador of God's kingdom, I really wanted this unknown youth to choose to go on this trip to California and, ultimately, get saved. So I was using myself as bait (as I see it now) to lure this young man into the kingdom of heaven.

Yes, God can use anything He wants, but He doesn't need our worldly devices. The Apostle Paul chose not to trust even in his oratory skill to influence the unsaved: he relied on the power of the Cross: "I determined to know nothing among you except Jesus Christ, and Him crucified."[1] I still had a lot to learn. Yet it seemed that God winked in good humour and let the chips fall where they might.

California Breakaway was a trip designed primarily for the mainstream high-school kids involved in YFC's Campus Life program. As the Youth Guidance counsellor, I had only two charges, and they would keep my hands full. One was Philip. The other was Valentine, a fourteen-year-old prostitute.

The two of them got along famously, a fact that made me quite nervous. (It was only much after the fact that Philip told me he had got Valentine to carry his drugs the day we went into Tijuana to shop. He didn't want to risk carrying them over the border himself. Drugs, on our squeaky-clean Youth for Christ trip? And over the Mexican border? I nearly croaked when I found out, but it was long into the past by then.)

In the opportunities I had to talk with Philip on that trip, I found him to be very open to spiritual things. Our trip was due to terminate back in Victoria very early Easter Sunday morning, and Philip actually accepted my invitation to go to church with me upon our return. But when the bus was at last crossing the ferry back to the Island, he told me he had changed his mind. Said he didn't want to go.

Now, usually in that kind of situation, I would respect the person's freedom of choice—just as God does with me, but in this case I felt to badger and manipulate him until he agreed once more to come with me.

At the service he was quiet and withdrawn. "Sullen" would probably describe it best. Afterwards, as people milled around visiting, we were accosted by my friend Allen, who, in spite of his philandering, had a solid knowledge of the Word of God and an unquenchable zeal for souls. The only thing he was lacking (as many of us are when we are newly in love with the Lord) was tact.

"Hi, I'm Allen." He had a wee hint of a southern drawl, an affectation from the type of preachers he listened to. The second thing out of his mouth was this: "Do you know the Lord?"

I cringed inwardly.

Philip answered, "Nope."

Allen barrelled on: "Do you want to know Him?"

"Yeah," came the answer. As simple as that. My jaw nearly hit the floor.

Allen grabbed Philip's hand and began to lead him in a prayer. The rest was history.

Later that evening, after all the wonderful events of that Sunday, seeing the miracle of a young man being born again, witnessing the reality of a "new creation,"[2] I found out the reason that Philip had tried to renege on my invitation to church: the young hooker on our California trip had invited him to come back to her apartment and share a little *ménage à trois* with her and her lesbian girlfriend. My shattered nerves! Talk about wrestling somebody out of the very jaws of perdition!

Philip and I became great friends. He was keenly intelligent, deeply sensitive, and fond of laughing. He was in love with God. The cigarettes, the drugs, and the alcohol simply disappeared from his life. He loved church and church people, and he had a great hunger for the Word of God. We spent hours over coffee in restaurants, sometimes with our Bibles, sometimes just talking about the Faith. He was a terrific disciple, and it never occurred to me that it should not be me doing the discipling. "Bid the older women," says the Word, "… to be reverent and devout in their deportment, as becomes those engaged in sacred service.… They are to give good counsel and be teachers of what is right and noble."[3]

I was an "older woman" as pertaining to Philip: he was twenty and I was twenty-eight. And I was older in the Lord too, having now known the Lord four years.

I wanted to "give good counsel" and be a "teacher of what is right and noble," just like the Scripture said. I wanted to be "reverent and devout" in my conduct, as becomes one "engaged in sacred service," as all ministry is.

But as we continued to spend a lot of time together, it gradually became more difficult to keep my deportment reverent and devout. When you're both seeking God and He is revealing continually more of Himself, there is much love and joy floating around, and it can happen that the emotions get caught up and confused. My old nature and its understanding of sexuality had been reigned in firmly as I'd grown in the knowledge of God, but it had not been tamed or disciplined. It was just held back, waiting and hoping, in spite of the best intentions of my new nature, to break free.

I'm sure that's one reason why the Word of God quoted above, in exhorting older women to be good counsellors, continues on in giving them their ministry directive as follows: "… So that they will wisely train the *young women*.…"[4]

But Philip and I saw no harm in our friendship. We were practically inseparable, talking together by the hour, sharing deep confidences. Our souls were being knit together, and although it seemed that there was an unspoken agreement to never admit it aloud, a deep yearning grew that hung between us like an ache.

Outwardly we were "self-controlled and chaste," as the Scripture above continues on to advise, but inwardly there was a warm fire of passion starting to burn. We both pretended it wasn't there, because we knew that it was wrong—knew that it could never go anywhere.

One day I called Philip to arrange to meet for coffee. I remember how upset I was when he told me, "I don't think God wants me to see you today." Not only was I disappointed not to see him, but I was ashamed that he, a new Christian, had obeyed God, when I, supposedly more mature in the Lord, had been turning a deaf ear to the same promptings of the Spirit in my own heart.

It was the first of many times that we would agree to remove ourselves from one another for a while. But we would always end up seeing each other eventually, either intentionally or by chance, and we would pick right up where we had left off.

Virginia seemed to think that I was the "cat's meow" and welcomed me without reservation into her home. She gushed over and over about how I had saved Philip's life. It made me feel proud, but it also made me uncomfortable. Sometimes I would implore her to remember to give glory where glory was due: namely, to God. Once I even said, "Yes, God has used me as an instrument of Philip's salvation, but I could just as easily be used by the enemy as an instrument of his complete and utter destruction."

Partly I spoke so strongly because I had become irritated with her praise, but also, a part of me was quietly concerned that if I could not bring myself to obey God in distancing myself from Philip, exactly that could happen.

It's never my intention to disobey
Just sometimes I don't hear so clear, Lord, what You say
So if I've been going my own way
Convict me now, Lord, as I pray

I need an answer that only You, Lord, can give me
Have I done my brother wrong?
If I've caused him to stumble, forgive me
Oh, Lord, hear my prayer, hear my song

I really do want to listen—I know You're right
Convict me if I'm in the wrong
Flood my wicked heart with Your pure light
Oh, Lord, hear my prayer, hear my song

Instead of Your peace, there's a storm within
Why is it so hard to call a sin a sin?[6]
I gave up my right to be where I have been
On the day I invited You in

And I'll receive now the word that You give me
I really do want to know where I'm wrong
If I've caused my brother to stumble, forgive me
Oh, Lord, hear my prayer, hear my song

When You said I was weak, You were sure right
But then, when I am weak, You are strong[7]
So flood this wicked heart with Your pure, pure light
Oh, Lord, hear my prayer, hear my song

Charming a Snake

Part of my job description for Youth for Christ was that I was acting-chaplain at Victoria's Juvenile Detention Centre. The director of the Centre was a Christian man, and once he had heard that Youth for Christ was doing a work in the city, he expressed his desire to establish a chaplaincy program. "Acting-chaplain" meant that although I was not an ordained minister, I was carrying on the effectual work of chaplain, under the direction and authority of YFC/Victoria's executive director, Doug Perkins, who was an ordained Baptist minister. Although I was not officially qualified, it had become clear that God's hand was on me for this type of work.

The kids at "Juvie" were kept busy with various programs most of the day, so the best time to meet with them casually as a group was lunchtime. Several times each week I would peer through the small, heavy window in the dining-room door and knock until I caught the attention of a staff member, who would then produce a key and let me in. I'd pick up a plate of food at the counter and seat myself at one table or another. Some of the kids saw these lunchtime visits as blatant opportunism on my part, and they gave me the derisive name "Free-Lunch." Others, those who were more in touch with their spiritual hunger, referred to me a little more respectfully as "The God Squad."

Every time I parked my little car in front of the building, I would pause and pray. I had to. My heart was racing and my legs felt weak. I was the Christian being thrown to the lions. The hardness of the kids I could manage—I knew it was mostly just an act of self-defence. And I loved those kids, even with all their put-downs and comebacks.

The staff was another matter entirely. Many of them were

openly hostile to a Christian presence behind those walls. It wasn't unusual to have a staff member talk a kid out of attending my occasional Bible studies right under my very nose.

There were some exceptions though. There was one fellow named Bradley, just a little older than I, who was always very kind and courteous. He was tall and nice-looking, with a dark, droopy moustache that I always thought made him look like a British rock idol. I found as time went by that I looked forward to seeing him there. I would peer through that little window and knock, hoping he might be on duty. When we were alone briefly, when he had to escort me through the building from one locked door to the next, he would chat a little—often about my faith, questioning me, sometimes challenging me, always pleasantly.

He became a little more familiar as months went by. He might touch my elbow and gently direct me through a doorway as he held the door open. Sometimes he would say, "You sure look nice today." And once he said that he liked my perfume. All of these little gestures were dynamite to a lonely heart. I enjoyed his company, however fleeting the moments, and my heart beat faster when he was in close proximity.

Then one day he made a mistake (or was it quite deliberate?): he told one of his teenage charges, a sharp, young Native boy, that he thought Nancy Fowler was really beautiful. It spread like wildfire among the residents, who were all delighted to be in on the secret. It was a secret no more.

Now when I knocked at the dining-room window, if Bradley was on duty, a corporate roar would go up among the kids: "Hey, Bradley, Nancy's here!" I would try not to blush as he let me in. He would just smile, seemingly not bothered a bit.

My sanctified womanly wiles were working overtime trying to figure out how to share my faith with Bradley in a fuller way. Happily, a great opportunity presented itself. The Billy Graham Association was promoting its new film on the life of Joni Eareckson Tada. All evangelical churches and parachurch organizations in the Victoria area received complimentary tickets to attend an advance showing. I was given two.

Great! I would invite Bradley: it would be an effective way of exposing him to the whole gospel, and in a relaxed and entertaining setting.

Just an aside, ladies: This activity is something that the late musician Keith Green termed "missionary dating" in a teaching tract of the same name. It's when a Christian dates a non-Christian, hoping to help effect a change in the non-Christian's life that will render him fit to marry. Not a good strategy, entangling your emotions in a situation that may or may not head the way you design. Get in too deep, and you may have trouble disentangling yourself when you have grown to love this person and you realize, too late, that he is not going to change.

Love, foolishly in this case, "hopes all things."[1]

Agape, God's great unconditional love, in us, is meant to "hope all things"—in situations into which *agape* has led us. *Eros* (romantic love), on the other hand, will blindly believe what it hopes to be true—or what it hopes will one day be true. There's a big difference between these two kinds of love. I would venture to say that the former is undergirded by God's will while the latter is driven, all too often, by our own will, which is frequently need-driven and wayward. Often in matters of *eros*, God keeps popping "error" messages up on our internal screen, and we just keep blithely deleting them.

My friend Allen was concerned about my interest in Bradley. "One of three things is going to happen," he said. "Right now, you're going to heaven and he's going to hell." (For Allen, in those early years, everything was reduced to heaven and hell.) "Number one, you still go to heaven, and he still goes to hell. Number two, you both go to heaven. Number three, you both go to hell."

The heaven-and-hell talk in this context is a little strong, and besides, in this book I'm more concerned with looking at the here and now of relationships and how they are fleshed out on earth. But Allen made a good point. When a Christian partners herself with a non-Christian, their respective spiritual states may stay basically the same, or she may influence him to draw closer to God, or he may influence her to pull away.

The Bible clearly cautions the Christian not to yoke herself with an unbeliever,² saying that ultimately both will find that they have little in common. "For what fellowship hath righteousness with unrighteousness?" asks the King James Version, "and what communion hath light with darkness?" Not only will the believer not be able to share with her spouse what ought to be the most important part—the very nucleus—of her life, but when life gets hard, as it surely will, they will find that the two of them are built on two very different foundations; consequently, they will not be able to draw comfort and strength from one another.

Too often, a young, immature Christian (or, God forbid, an older, shoulda-known-better Christian), torn with love for an unsaved companion, compromises and chooses to yoke herself with an unbeliever. Or the unbeliever, for love of the other, makes a superficial "commitment" to the Lord, which soon goes the way of the seed sown beside the path (Matthew 13): God's Word is quickly gobbled up by the enemy, leaving the ground barren and unfruitful. Not a pretty place to live out your life. No wonder so many pull up stakes and move on, looking for greener pastures.

Back to the story: I would invite Bradley to the *Joni* movie, and maybe sooner or later he would get saved and then we would see what might happen from there.

Bradley accepted my invitation. He picked me up at the Youth for Christ office early in the afternoon for the matinee showing. He would drop me off there later to get my car.

I don't remember much about the movie and how he responded: it's the afterward that sticks so vividly in my mind. It was a beautiful day in mid-October, and the sun was still very warm as we drove along Beacon Hill Road, winding beside the ocean.

Suddenly he swung the car into a parking space, coming to an abrupt stop. He turned to me and gestured with his hands and spoke rather angrily, which took me by surprise.

"What am I supposed to do with you now?"

I realized all at once that he was quite uncomfortable, that he had no idea how he was meant to entertain a young lady who was a Christian.

"If you were any other girl," he continued on, "I would head on over to The Snug"—this was the cozy little pub in the Oak Bay Beach Hotel, boasting an ocean view—"and have a couple of drinks. But I don't know what to do with you!" He was quite upset, definitely out of his comfort zone.

I tried to put him at ease, and we talked until the conversation grew more relaxed. Shortly he suggested that we drive to the breakwater and take a walk.

The breakwater is a long concrete wall, about twelve feet wide, that runs way out into the ocean at a gentle curve and does exactly what its name says it does, protecting the entrance to the Inner Harbour at Ogden Point.

I was wearing four-inch heels (which put me at six-foot-two, almost at Bradley's height) and a smashing mid-calf-length dress with a long slit up the side. As we walked, I thought we must look a well-matched couple. I had always liked the way he dressed. Casual blue jeans, with a good-looking pair of brown leather boots. He wore a light-blue dress shirt, comfortably unbuttoned at the neck, complemented with a tweed sports jacket. He knew how to dress, up or down, a fact that was a big plus in my books. Sometimes I'd had quite enough of tee shirts and dirty running shoes.

He was such a gentleman too, considerate and soft-spoken. He walked beside me, close, but not too close, not touching me, nor offering to take my hand. And it was a jolly good thing too, because I was a basket case. Outwardly I was walking along and talking normally, but inside I was a mess of desire. I could feel my bones desperately trying to do their job of holding me upright while my entire body felt like it was going to melt down into a puddle at his feet.

Out at the end of the breakwater we sat down, but not before he had slipped off his jacket and spread it out for me to sit on, saying that he didn't want me to get my dress dirty. The gesture undid me a little more.

We sat with our feet hanging over the edge of the wall, eight feet above the boisterous, sparkling blue waves, and we talked.

Sometimes he looked out across the water; sometimes I was aware of him looking at me intently. I just gazed into the distance. I didn't dare look at him. I knew what would happen if our eyes met.

Later we went for fish and chips at a great little place he knew, and then finally he drove me back to my car. I thanked him for the evening, said "Good night," and reached for the door-handle.

He spoke: "Could I have a kiss?"

I turned and wordlessly planted a single, soft kiss on his lips, then got out of the car. He didn't try to stop me.

I drove away. I got out of there. Vamoosed. I embraced the scriptural admonition: "Flee from sexual immorality."[3]

All the way home I cried out to God. I had kissed this guy; what now? As a Christian, I didn't have much of a repertoire to draw from in this genre. I didn't want to go any further than a kiss. Now I had used up the whole program on the first date. All the way home I kept banging on the steering wheel and crying out to God: "Lord, what will I do for an encore?"

Lord, I can't handle this guy, with all of his charms
What in the world am I thinking of *him* for?
The very first time, I fall right into his arms
Now what will I do for an encore?

He's such a nice guy, but someone else is speaking through him
He's so nice, he doesn't figure he needs You to renew him
I'm kidding myself thinking I can minister to him
And what would I do for an encore?

I can't handle this guy—he just does all the right things
And he knows that I love You, so what's he coming on for?
If I hum a tune that the worldly world sings
What will I do for an encore?

He's such a nice gentleman, he's hard to resist
But Your Spirit is telling me there's something amiss
And even *if* nothing's wrong with "just one little kiss"
What does a Christian do for an encore?

I can't handle this guy, with all of his charms
What in the world am I falling for *him* for?
The very first time, I fall right into his arms
Now what will I do for an encore?

What will I do for an encore?

I let myself into my basement suite, then climbed the stairs to look for Barb, my landlady as of these past few months. I was glad she was still up.

"Help, Barb!" I said. "I'm in trouble now!" I poured out the story of my wonderful afternoon and evening and the agony of my tumultuous feelings. "I can't handle this guy," I told her. "I don't know if I'm strong enough to behave myself."

She had been hearing about Bradley off and on over the last while and had been pleased when I told her he had agreed to come to the *Joni* movie with me.

Now she reassured me. "Don't worry," she said. "God will give you strength. You may be the only Christian he knows. God wants to minister to him through you."

I felt a little better. "Thanks, Barb." Then I laughed a bit ruefully and added, "But I don't think that's really what I needed to hear right now."

Downstairs again, I didn't feel so light-hearted. I got on my knees beside my bed. "Oh, God, help me," I prayed. "I feel so weak and vulnerable right now. I don't think I should go out with him again, but if he phones and asks me, I'm not going to be able to say no. Please help me. Don't let me be tested beyond what I'm able to bear."

It wasn't the first time that I clung to this word: "There hath no temptation [overtaken] you but such as is common to man: but God is faithful, who will not suffer you to be tempted above that ye are able; but will with the temptation also make a way to escape, that ye may be able to [endure] it."[4]

In the morning I climbed the stairs again to see if Barb had put on a pot of tea. She was sitting at the kitchen table with her lighted vanity mirror, doing her make-up. Barb was twenty years my senior, a beautiful and vivacious woman. She had a beautiful spirit too.

She smiled as she saw me, but there was a bit of grim tightness at the corners of her mouth and a hint of briskness in the tone of her voice, kind of like it was time to get down to business. "Oh, good," she said, "you're up." She pulled out a chair and poured some tea into the empty cup that she had set out.

I sat down and looked at her expectantly. It was obvious that she had something on her mind.

"I've been thinking about you all night," she said. "All I can see is this big snake. It's like you're playing a flute and charming this snake, and everything seems fine. But you make one false move and you're dead. Your ministry at Juvie would be destroyed."

"Thanks, Barb," I said. "*That's* what I needed to hear."

Just a point of clarification to the reader: Barb was not calling Bradley a snake. The snake here was the situation that the enemy of my soul was looking to use against me, for both my personal and public demise. I had seemed, on our date, to have things under control, but the situation was precarious. If the music of that flute were interrupted for a moment (and the music was symbolic of my obedience to God), that snake could strike in a flash and the spin-off could be disastrous.

The song above says, "He's such a nice guy, but someone else is speaking through him." Bradley's pleasant, gentlemanly words were having a seductive effect on my lonely soul, and the enemy was working overtime with those words, trying to break down my resistance, trying to get me to compromise, just a little.

Barb's words fortified me as I went off to work for the day, yet I still felt very weak. I continued to whisper to God all day in the vein of my prayer the night before: "I don't think I'm strong enough to say 'no' to this guy. Please don't let me be tested beyond what I'm able to bear."

That evening I wrote another song. This is the only time I have ever written two songs in two days—such was the intensity of the internal conflict. The second song was for my "First Love."

You are my first love, Lord
I want it to stay that way
You've taught me to love You, Lord
I never want to stray
Though I can't see You, Lord
Still I love You
It didn't come naturally
Lord, You taught me to

But sometimes it seems I'm so easily taken in
By the cares of this world and the deceitfulness of sin[5]
But our life here passes away
Like a vapour on a summer's day[6]
And only what's been taken to Your Cross, Lord, will remain

Your love is eternal, Lord
And so is our life in You
I want to love You more
Help me stay true
Though I can't see You, Lord
Still I love You
It didn't come naturally
Lord, You taught me to

The Lord is my first love
And I want it to stay that way
He's taught me to love Him
I never want to stray
No, I can't see my Lord
But still I love Him
It doesn't come naturally
But by trusting on Him

It doesn't come naturally
But by believing on Him

Three nights later I got a call from Bradley. He talked about how much he had enjoyed being with me. His voice was softer and kinder than ever. It made my heart feel so tender toward him. Then he said what a nice kiss it had been. His words made my heart pound in my chest so that I could hardly breathe. It hadn't been much of a kiss, but when that's all there is, it can leave you both pregnant with desire.

Listen to what the Apostle James said: "But every man is tempted, when he is drawn away of his own lust, and enticed. Then when lust hath conceived, it bringeth forth sin: and sin, when it is finished, bringeth forth death."[7] What a graphic metaphor in that Scripture!

Pregnant with desire—that's how I felt. The King James Version calls it lust. Once illegitimate desire has conceived, it's only a matter of time until it births sin. And sin ultimately ends in death. I thought about what Barb had said about the snake: "One false move and you're dead."

Barb knew what she was talking about. She had told me that that Scripture about lust conceiving and bringing forth sin was the story of her life. Years before, she had gone for counselling with her Anglican minister, looking for help for a very troubled marriage. But she found herself out of the frying pan and into the fire as the minister went "ga-ga" over her.

"The adultery began a long time before we ever hopped into bed with each other," she said. "It was in our eyes."

Finally, they ran away together, moving to Victoria. Eventually they married. He left the ministry and became an alcoholic. At length God restored him and began to use the two of them in a ministry to couples. But just two years into his sobriety, he suddenly passed away, leaving Barb a widow at only forty-four years of age. "Just like the Scripture says," she concluded, "it ended in death."

Barb's counsel was very much on my mind as Bradley and I talked on the phone that night. I was thinking, too, that before the end of the conversation he would surely ask me out, and I wondered what I would say. But he did not.

He never did call back after that night. Things went on as before at Juvie: he was pleasant as always, and I was always glad to see him. But he never did ask me out. Kind of strange, that. It wouldn't be until six months later that I would hear the explanation.

Progress of a Pilgrim

Over the past year and a half, I had continued, off and on, to see a lot of Philip, the young tough who had been so radically converted after the California Breakaway trip in the spring of 1981. He was delightful company—personable, sensitive, and intense. He did have trouble finding work and keeping it; what with growing up fatherless and then submerging himself in a hard-core party lifestyle from age fourteen to twenty, he was lacking in discipline and life skills in general. He had no vocational training, and he struggled with depression too.

But he studied the Scriptures by the hour and spent a lot of time in prayer, and this made him a richly spiritual companion. We enjoyed long conversations over coffee in restaurants, and I had, in a way, become addicted to his company. He met an emotional need in me, a God-given need to be loved and to enjoy true intimacy. Not that we had been physically intimate, at all, ever. But we had shared much, and our souls had been knit together at a very deep level.

I see in retrospect that God did not want me seeking fulfillment of these needs in anyone but Him. He knew that for me to become a whole person, I had to learn to come to Him with these needs, to let Him meet them. Only then would I be ready for a covenant relationship of the dimension that He truly desires for every marriage. But two people, neither of whom are whole, looking to each other to complete themselves—well, this is the working definition of co-dependency.

In my stronger, more honest moments, I would admit to myself that God had told me to stay away from Philip. He had the same conviction regarding me. But times of loneliness and weakness would creep upon us, and then we would begin to rationalize and justify, deceiving ourselves, picking the acquaintance back up. This was a recurring theme, this seesawing back and forth, "halting between two opinions," as the King James would say. "Doubleminded" and "unstable in all our ways."[1]

During the fall of '82, we were both earnestly trying to be obedient in this matter, and it had been a couple of months since I had seen Philip. But I thought about him almost constantly. Kind of like the syndrome where you go on a diet and then spend all of your spare time collecting recipes.

This very human propensity is reflected in Scripture: Romans tells us that when God forbids something, we end up wanting it all the more. "I would not have come to know sin except through the Law; for I would not have known about [lust][2] if the Law had not said, 'You shall not covet.' But sin, taking opportunity through the commandment, produced in me coveting of every kind."[3]

Another translation spells it out even more plainly: "But sin used this command to arouse all kinds of covetous desires within me!"[4]

The meaning of lust as used in this verse (evil desires, coveting) in the original Greek is "a longing, *especially for what is forbidden.*"[5] The fact that we know God has told us "No!" in a certain particular causes the spoiled child within to shout all the more loudly, "But I *want* to!" It is in this way that the "commandment" serves to further empower the desire.

I was yearning so much for any kind of contact with Philip; I thought that maybe a visit with his mother would soothe the ache a little. Some second-hand news would be better than none at all.

In the time that I had known Philip, I had had many long talks with his mother. Virginia had filled me in on her own story, how she had met the love of her life, and how he had left when Philip was only two and Ginny just a baby. She had never been interested in another man, hoping, I suppose, that somehow, someday, he would come back. She had never got over him; she referred to this obsession, in her dark humour, as "the Carmichael Curse." Now I felt like I was suffering from the same affliction.

So one morning, on my way to work, I dropped by to visit Virginia.

I knocked at the stately front door. It opened shortly, and there she stood, regal as always in her bearing.

Before she could greet me, I spoke: "Have you ever heard of the Carmichael Curse?"

Her expression remained grave. "Come right in, Nancy," she said, sweeping the door wide and leading the way to the kitchen and the teapot.

She knew exactly what I meant; she empathized with my emotional struggle. Yet she, too, had become convinced that Philip and I were not good for each other. She was gracious as always, and we had a nice enough visit, but there was a slight tension between us now that had not been present before.

I knew that Virginia had talked about me to various friends and prayer partners; it had come back to me via the evangelical grapevine. She had perceived what the Holy Spirit was saying to Philip and me, and each time she had seen us pick the relationship back up, she had become a little unhappier with the whole situation. I left her house that day a little sadder and a bit lonelier than when I had come. She had been a good friend, but it seemed that now I was losing her as such. I knew that when a person's ways please the Lord, He makes even her enemies to be at peace with her.[6] Surely the converse was true: by persisting in ways that were displeasing to God, I might suffer the loss of friendships.

It wasn't much after that visit that Philip and I ran into each other somewhere. We agreed to attend a church service together; surely there was no harm in that. We went to a Sunday evening service at the church he had been attending. I got nothing out of the service; I just sat there feeling like there was a black cloud of condemnation hanging over our heads. I didn't understand it. Granted, I felt a little guilty being with Philip, that dull, gnawing feeling you get when you're grieving the Holy Spirit and trying to ignore Him.

But this condemnation was more than that; it was huge. I felt that it was mostly coming from outside of me, not from my own heart. There was judgement zeroing in on me, like being trained in the sights of a spiritual submachine gun. When I whispered of my uncomfortable feeling to Philip, he nodded over his shoulder.

"That's one of my mom's friends behind us, a few rows back," he whispered in reply. She evidently was indignant at our disobedience. I was amazed how clearly I could feel it. It was a good lesson in how palpably people's attitudes can be projected in the realm of the spirit.

I thought it was so unfair of this woman, to sit in judgement of us like that. Didn't she know how hard it could be to struggle against the flesh? I wished she had the courage and the compassion to approach us and offer to pray for us. It might have helped us; we couldn't seem to help ourselves. Here we were, falling headlong into disobedience again.

Some nights later, Philip and I went for a long, moonlit hike around Thetis Lake. It was beautiful to walk and talk, finding our way along the trail by the soft light of the moon as it peeked here and there through the trees.

Then for a while I walked on ahead of him. When I turned around again and headed back to meet him, I could feel something in him pulling at me. Or was it something in me, pulling at him? I didn't care which—it was probably both. And I didn't care to resist it anymore. I came walking straight up to him, and with no warning at all, not to him, and hardly to myself, I planted a kiss on his lips.

Before Philip could reproach me, I went on the defensive: "Is there anything wrong with just one little kiss?" I asked him defiantly. I didn't expect an answer; the question was rhetorical. We both knew that I had stepped over the line—way over.

You might say that a simple kiss is pretty innocent. But it was not. Behind it was the pent-up power of a couple of years of unspoken yearnings on both sides. It was explosive. Nothing outward happened from there, and I never did it again. But it was like opening Pandora's box. Something got out, and I couldn't get it back in again.

Later that night—it was very late—we watched a movie at his place. I leaned against him, outwardly trying to follow the story line, but inwardly dizzy and distracted with the fragrance of shampoo that wafted from his hair. Virginia got up once and came to the living-room doorway, stood there a moment, then went back to bed. Her disapproval hung heavy in the air long after she was gone.

What was her problem? We weren't doing anything wrong.

Well, maybe there was nothing wrong with what the physical eye could see, but God does not look on the outward appearance: He looks on the heart. And our hearts were a mess.

I wrote to my friend Mary Kaye the next day. She had come from a rough past; now she was deeply committed to God. We had a great friendship, keeping each other accountable to our faith. She had been very open and transparent with me in talking about her own relationship struggles, and this gave me the freedom to speak frankly in my letter. As I poured out my heart, I summarized my feelings for Philip with a sentence that she had once spoken to me: "I don't want to marry him," I wrote. "I just want to sleep with him." There. I had said it. What an awful thing to say. But it was a pretty good definition of lust, and at least now it was out on the table where I could see it clearly.

God had been gracious to keep gently reproving us in our disobedience. But there was a proverb I had read that haunted me: "He, that being often reproved hardeneth his neck, shall suddenly be destroyed, and that without remedy."[7] If I was going to be stubborn and stiff-necked about submitting to God's counsel, specifically about letting go of this relationship once and for all, might there come a point of no return, where God would cease to draw me to repentance? Didn't I fear God? Couldn't I heed His warning?

> "Then they will call on me, but I will not answer; they will seek me diligently, but they will not find me. Because they hated knowledge and did not choose the fear of the Lord, they would have none of my counsel and despised my every rebuke. Therefore they shall eat the fruit of their own way, and be filled to the full with their own fancies.

For the turning away of the simple will slay them, and the complacency of fools will destroy them; but whoever listens to me will dwell safely, and will be secure, without fear of evil."

Proverbs 1:28–33 (NKJV)

I drew no consolation from the fact that this Scripture is from the Old Testament; I knew that even in the New Testament, the covenant of grace, there are stern warnings about our behaviour: "Be not deceived; God is not mocked: for whatsoever a man soweth, that shall he also reap. For he that soweth to his flesh (lower nature, sensuality)[8] shall of the flesh reap corruption; but he that soweth to the Spirit shall of the Spirit reap life everlasting."[9] I knew that I had been planting seeds into my lower nature, and although I kept repenting here and there along the way, I'd had cause to write an unhappy song, "Lord, It's Still Coming Up Weeds!" I didn't much like the look of this crop; I didn't want to "eat of the fruit of [my] own way, and be filled ... with [my] own fancies," as the Scripture above warned.

One of my pastors, Dr. Doug Roberts, preached a sermon one Sunday on the principle of sowing and reaping. He highlighted the grace that God has extended to us in Christ, saying, "God will always forgive you—" then he went on to complete his thought with a great big "but": "*but* He will not necessarily give you a crop failure." He went on to say that the bad seed we have planted will grow, but that the Lord will be gracious to help us mow it down, plough up the ground again, and plant good seed. However, this might well be a slow and arduous and painful process: fair warning to those who take God's grace as licence to live any way they choose.

I went down to the garden one morning
To check on some sprouting seeds
I discovered there to my horror
Everything was coming up weeds

'Cause what you plant is what you grow
What you sow is what you reap
And if you're not careful, before you know
You'll find everything is coming up weeds

It was a couple of things I shouldn't have said
A couple thoughts I shouldn't have thought
I pretended they were little insignificant things
But Lord, I knew they were not

'Cause what you sow is just a tiny little seed
But what you grow is a great big weed
You are deceived if you don't believe
That what you sow is what you reap

I'm filled with a godly sorrow
I've repented in deep regret
And I know I'm forgiven, but as sure as I'm livin'
There's a spiritual law in effect:

What you plant is what you grow
What you sow is what you reap
And if you're not careful, before you know
You'll find everything is coming up weeds

I've been pulling those things up by the roots
But the roots go down so deep
To my dismay I find that after all this time
It's still coming up weeds

What you sow may be a tiny little seed
But what you grow will be a great big weed
You'd better walk the walk 'cause God won't be mocked
What you sow is what you reap

Lord, lay Your axe right to the root
'Cause if there's one thing I don't need
In this earthly life with all its trouble and strife
It's a garden that's coming up weeds

I had been asked to sing for an evening service at the Mustard Seed, a little storefront church that reaches out to street kids. In prayer that afternoon, lying on my bed, I was having trouble seeking God about the event, as I was so concerned about my spiritual state with regard to Philip. I was realizing that a part of me had been trying to ensnare him.

A bit of Scripture came to my mind: "the snare of the fowler."[10] My maiden name is Fowler, so suddenly this Scripture held a very personal meaning. This was precisely Philip's dilemma: he was entrapped in my snare! I had been plotting, subconsciously, to see if I could cause him to stumble, because if I could get him to express desire for me, I would feel affirmed and loveable. It was the same spirit that had wound itself around almost every relationship in which I'd been involved, and as awful as I knew this subversive desire was, I couldn't seem to get a handle on it.

I rolled off the bed and onto my knees, and, beating my head on the mattress, I began to cry out: "Oh, Lord, deliver him! Deliver him from the snare of the Fowler!"

That evening at the Mustard Seed, following a time of worship, I got up with my guitar and sang a few of my songs. Then I hung around for the film they were going to show: *Pilgrim's Progress*. I'd always been curious about this story: I remembered many references to it in the book *Little Women*, but I'd never read it myself.

(*Pilgrim's Progress* is a brilliant allegory of the Christian walk, written by John Bunyan in the 1600s, while he languished in the Bedford jail in the UK, a prisoner of the Faith. The main character, Christian, meets many challenges and difficulties on his journey toward the Celestial City.)

Just as the film began, Philip showed up. He came and sat down in the empty chair beside me.

The movie started to minister to me immediately, and I could hardly stand the pressure. It seemed like every metaphor was speaking to my situation. I didn't know whether to stay or walk out. Half of me was resisting in royal rebellion; the other half was screaming inside, "Go for it, God—go for it!"

The climax for me was when Christian and Faithful, walking through the woods on the "narrow path," were suddenly caught in a large net. The one man cried out to the other, "It's the snare of the fowler!" It seemed that God was confirming in no uncertain terms the thoughts He had spawned in my mind earlier in the day.

Then, as if I needed the point driven home more clearly, two teenage girls seated behind us hadn't quite caught what had been said and started whispering back and forth: "The snare of the *what?* The snare of the *what?*"

Philip half-turned in his chair, intending to clarify the script to these girls. His mouth was just a couple of inches from my ear when he hissed in a stage whisper: "The snare of the *fowler.*"

I nearly fell off my chair.

In much more recent years, I have finally read this great classic, *Pilgrim's Progress.* Strangely, I found no reference to "the snare of the fowler." I reread it, just to be sure, and then found the complete work on the Internet and ran a chapter-by-chapter search through the text. Nothing. This re-emphasizes to me, so many years later, the sovereign design of God's speaking to me that night: The original book is chock-full of rich metaphors, yet for some reason, the producer of the film had seen cause to add one of his own. It was this diversion from the original, this bit of artistic licence, that providentially nailed me that night.

After the film was over and the service at the Mustard Seed had concluded, Philip and I found a little restaurant where we could order some pizza.

As we waited for our food, I told him how God had been speaking to me that afternoon and evening. I confessed that there was something in me that was trying to make him stumble. I hoped that "blowing my cover" like this—bringing my sin out into the light—would expose the enemy here and that he would have to slink away for a while.

We talked also about our on-again, off-again efforts to stay away from each other. For his part, Philip admitted that staying away from me had never helped his feelings for me to diminish.

"Same here," I told him.

It seemed like an honest enough conversation, but it was lacking in true wisdom. Sometimes in a situation like this, we reveal, in the name of transparency, things that really should be left unsaid. Telling someone that you are consumed with thoughts about him is not going to help him to cast down the same longing thoughts about you.

Letting Go

"Do not my words do good to him that walketh uprightly?" God asks.[1] Put another way, "If you would do what is right, you would find my words comforting."[2] I was not finding comfort in God's Word. It seemed that everywhere I read in my Bible, I found passages that made my heart feel heavy and uneasy.

Reading in Matthew one day, I was sobered by yet another passage. Jesus was talking about Himself: the stone that the builders rejected becoming the cornerstone. Then He said, "And whosoever shall fall on this stone shall be broken: but on whomsoever it shall fall, it will grind him to powder."[3]

God was telling me to cast myself upon Christ and allow Him to break me of the things that were keeping me from His will for my life. If I refused to fall on the Rock, eventually the Rock would fall on me and I would be crushed. Not because of petulant retribution on God's part: He is not like that. It would be the eventual outcome of refusing to align myself with God. I would simply, naturally, reap what I had sown; I would be stuck with the consequences of the choices I was making.

I didn't want that to happen. As much as it hurt to be broken, it was still preferable to the prospect of being crushed.

I needed to make up my mind to "Let Go."

Let go, let go
God's telling you to let go
I know it hurts, but it's worse
If you hang on—I know
It's never easy to fall on the Rock and be broken
But you must
Or the Rock'll fall on you
And you'll be crushed

You're so strong; you keep hanging on
Though many times you've heard God speak
Don't you know the same thing that you call strong
God calls stubborn and weak?
And every time you sin, the Lord Jesus
Under your stumbling feet is trod[4]
And it's a fearful thing to fall
Into the hands of the living God[5]

You've wondered what you might offer Him
As a fitting sacrifice
Have you forgotten you once made Him
A gift of your very life?
And now you wonder why He doesn't even seem
To hear you when you pray
He's not calling you to sacrifice
But to obey[6]

So let go, let go
God's telling you to let go
It hurts, but it's much worse
If you hang on—I know
It's never easy to fall on the Rock and be broken
But you must
Or the Rock'll fall on you
And you'll be crushed

You must
Be broken
Or be crushed

    I took a drive out to Sooke one day to have a visit with Lorna Smith. I wanted to talk to her about Philip. Deep down, I knew that he was not the right person for me—nor was he mature enough or stable enough at this point to become a husband to a woman eight years his senior, especially one who had "mothered" him in the Lord. But my continual disobedience had opened the door to great confusion in my life, and I had begun to think that perhaps the only thing lacking was a commitment on my part to the relationship.

I told her of the pain and the confusion, the on-again, off-again treadmill we had been on. Then I suggested that maybe the only reason for God's disapproval on our seeing each other was that I had not been willing to make a commitment to Philip. Perhaps that was all I needed to do: make up my mind to marry him.

Lorna had heard plenty abut Philip in the past, but even though I had asked her at other times what she thought about the relationship, she'd had no firm opinion. This time it was different. She prayed for me. She prayed, and she prophesied, and by the time she was done, it was very clear that God did not approve of this relationship, period. Lorna did not either. Mind you, she always tended to agree with God anyway.

Not long after, I went to one of my pastors, the Reverend Ted Follows, for some counselling. After a long talk, he prayed for me. And he prophesied over me as well. "My daughter," came the Word, "I am going to bless you soon. But it is necessary that you let go of what you are holding onto, so that you can receive what I want to give you."

That evening I headed up the Island. I had a speaking engagement with a ladies' group up in the northern part. I would spend the night with friends in Nanaimo and drive the rest of the way the following day.

Rod and Kathy were almost a generation ahead of me. I had met them through mutual friends in Victoria, and in the three years that I had known them, they had become like spiritual parents to me.

We talked a long time that night. I shared with them what Ted Follows had said; then I quipped: "The Lord says He's going to bless me soon. But He said He was coming soon too, and that was two thousand years ago. And I just don't have that kind of time."

I was turning God's special word to me into a joke, a cynical play on Scripture. I thought I was pretty clever, but Rod and Kathy were not amused. They sensed that God had an agenda with me that night, and they probed with their conversation, gently but persistently ferreting out the things they saw deep inside: the rebellion, the anger, the lust, the unbelief. Slowly I opened up, and as I did, I saw, too, the things that had taken root in me. One at a time they helped me to identify the things that bound me. They led me in prayer to renounce them, and then they prayed for my deliverance.

It was very late when we all finally retired. I was exhausted—I felt like I'd gone through surgery. I was in a kind of pain that was almost physical. My heart felt as though it had had roots all twisted and ingrown around it and now someone had ripped all the roots out. It felt like it was torn and bleeding, where those roots had been pulled free. But it felt clean, and it felt really, really good.

As I climbed wearily in between fresh sheets, Kathy appeared in the doorway with a steaming cup of tea. She had switched roles, from scalpel-wielding surgeon to Florence Nightingale. Her bedside manner was so soothing and comforting, and she sat there as I drank my tea.

"Now," she said, and then she gave me some advice that I have never forgotten: "God has delivered you, but you must walk every step of that deliverance."

I recall very little of the rest of that trip and the speaking engagement, but I do remember that I felt like a different person. I could tell that my entire countenance had changed.

It was January of 1983. My thirtieth birthday was just over two months away. It seemed that I was never going to get married. Why did I go on living as though I were on hold, waiting to do this and that "until I get married"? I had no decent furniture. It's one of those things that you unconsciously put off as long as your life seems to have "Status: Temporary" stamped across it. Well, if I was going to embrace the life God had given me, I'd better get on with it. I ordered a nice-looking couch and chair for my living room. It was, in part, a symbolic act of accepting my single state.

One Sunday toward the end of January, I saw Philip at church and I had a weak moment: I asked him if he'd like to get together later that afternoon. (I had been feeling terribly lonely—it would be so nice just to talk to him for a while.) He told me to give him a call after lunch.

After fixing myself a light meal in my suite, I called, asking him where he would like to meet. But he had evidently had a change of heart. "I don't think God wants me to see you," he said quietly.

I was furious. "Thanks a lot, *friend*," I said sarcastically. I slammed the receiver back on its hook, so hard that it was surprising the whole thing didn't break right off the wall. I stormed into my bedroom and threw myself down onto my knees, torrents of frustration and loneliness pouring from my eyes, words raging from my mouth.

"I'm so lonely, God! I'm so tired of being alone. Don't You care?"

I raged on in this vein for quite some time, gathering momentum with the power of the anger.

Then I cried out harshly, "Jesus, aren't You touched by the feeling of my infirmity?"

Immediately my own words arrested me. I had parroted something directly out of Scripture, but I had twisted it from a firm reassurance into an accusing question. I was pricked to the heart, and a spirit of repentance broke over me.

I was still weeping, but no longer in self-pity: now I was crying tears of pure contrition.

"Oh, Jesus, yes, you are touched by my infirmity," and I quoted back to Him His precious Word: "For we have not an high priest which cannot be touched with the feeling of our infirmities; but was in all points tempted like as we are, yet without sin."[7]

The presence of God came over me, soft and peaceful like a warm blanket, and I knew somehow that this battle was won, once and for all. Still on my knees, I pledged to serve Him single, if that was His will, one day at a time for the rest of my life.

His companionship was what I really needed in my loneliness, not Mr. Wrong. I was amazed by His faithfulness: no matter how many times I might blow it, as I had today and so many, many times before, He would still call me "friend." And if I would just remember to go to Him when I felt lonely, and if I would patiently wait, He would always, *always* meet me there.

When I've blown it once again
And no one seems to understand
When I've failed so miserably
And there's no one to even hold my hand
When I've fallen so far short
That I could never make amends
Oh, it amazes me, Lord
You still call me "friend"[8]

When I feel so all alone
And everyone has let me down
When I need a friend so bad
And there's no one around
Then in utter desperation
I fall down on my knees in prayer
And it amazes me, Lord
You always meet me there

But why must I wait till I'm so desperate
Before I let You meet me there?
Why let myself become so separate
Before You draw me back to prayer?

I know my righteousness is rags[9]
Lord Jesus, let your grace prevail[10]
It's of Your mercies that I'm not consumed[11]
Lord, Your compassions never fail[12]
Your mercies are new every morning[13]
Your faithfulness is great[14]
Oh, it amazes me
As I quietly wait

Oh, I need You, Lord!
I come to You and wait

    I wrote this song on January 25, 1983. Just six days later, Mr. Right walked into my life.

A Prophecy

The following is a prophetic word that was given to me while I was still chasing Mr. Wrong. I don't remember who gave it to me; whether it was a man or a woman, I don't even know—someone just handed it to me, I think at church one morning, saying that he (or she) thought God wanted me to have it. I don't believe that it was a word given for me in particular; rather this person had got it from somewhere and felt "led" to pass it along.

As is the case whenever and wherever God speaks, the message is for those who have ears to hear. If the shoe fits, wear it. If it ministers to you, claim it as your own. It certainly spoke to me.

On His Plan for Your Life

Everyone longs to give himself completely to someone, to have a deep soul relationship with another, to be loved thoroughly and exclusively. But God, to a Christian, says: "No, not until you are satisfied, fulfilled, and content with being loved by Me alone—with giving yourself totally and unreservedly to Me, to have an intensely personal and unique relationship with Me alone, discovering that only in Me is your satisfaction to be found—will you be capable of the perfect human relationship I have planned for you. You will never be united with another until you are united with Me, exclusive of anyone or anything else, any other desires or longings.

I want you to stop planning, stop wishing, and allow Me to give you the most thrilling plan existing—one that you cannot imagine. I want you to have the best. Please allow Me to bring it to you. You just keep watching Me, expecting the satisfaction that I AM. Keep listening and learning the things I tell you. You just wait, that's all. Don't be anxious. Don't look at the things you want. You just keep looking off and away up to Me, or you'll miss what I want to show you. And then, when you're ready, I'll surprise you with a love far more wonderful than any you would dream of. You see, until you are ready (and I am working even this moment to have you both ready at the same time), until you are both satisfied exclusively with Me and the life I have prepared for you, you will not be able to experience the love that exemplifies your relationship with Me, and thus perfect love.

And dear one, I want you to have this wonderful love. I want you to see, in the flesh, a picture of your relationship with Me and to enjoy materially and concretely the everlasting union of beauty, perfection, and love that I offer you with Myself. Know that I love you utterly. I AM the Almighty God. Believe it and be satisfied.

The Father

Part 2
Finding Mr. Right

A Date with Destiny

It had started back in November when Barb hollered down into my suite one evening. When I stuck my head around the corner of the stairwell, she was waving an envelope at me. "Are you interested in this conference?" she asked. "I went last year and it was very good, but I won't be going this year. You might enjoy it."

Later I perused the forms. Hmm. The Spiritual Leadership Conference. It was being put on by a Calgary church, at the Banff Springs Hotel. Banff was gorgeous in February, I knew, and the hotel was a beautiful landmark, one of the old Canadian Pacific Railway hotels, nestled in the majestic Rockies. It was more like a castle than anything else, with its lofty ceilings and ancient stonework. But to use up a week of precious holiday time to sit through long days in a conference somewhere, no matter how ambient the setting—well, I would rather go skiing.

No, I didn't think I was interested. But I thought that I should at least get down on my knees and ask God about it. And do you know—it was the strangest thing: once I had done that, I started to feel like I wanted to go.

First things first: I talked to Doug Perkins, my boss, about whether I could get the time off work. He said he'd put it on the agenda for the upcoming board meeting.

The verdict came back: Yes, I could go. Furthermore, last summer when the rest of the staff had gone to a weeklong national Youth for Christ staff conference, I'd been asked to stay behind and keep the office open. Consequently the board didn't think that this week I'd requested should come off my holiday time. Considering the subject of the conference, it would be a good refresher for me, they felt, as well as "continuing education" for my ministry.

Wow! That had been easy, and I wouldn't even have to "waste" any holidays. I had knocked gently and the door had opened wide. Suddenly my prayers had a bit more unction. "Lord, if You want me to go to this thing, what about travel arrangements? It's a long trip; really, it would be too much to drive it alone." I asked the Lord about it on several occasions, and each time, the name of a friend came to mind: Mick.

I had gone out with Mick a couple of times in the past, but it really had never been more than a friendship thing on my side, and fortunately, for once I had behaved myself irreproachably. I hadn't even held the guy's hand.

When I ran into him one night at a youth group meeting, I brought up the subject: "Have you ever heard of the Banff Spiritual Leadership Conference?"

"Yeah, I'm going," he said. Just like that.

"*How* are you going?" I asked.

"I'm travelling up by train. You should travel with me. It's only $108 return, and that includes a sleeping berth."

Wow. For that price, I could hardly even cover the cost of my gas. And the train ride would be a blast, almost a twenty-four-hour trip from downtown Vancouver.

I discovered something else in that conversation: Mick was engaged to be married. That was convenient.

Every door that I cautiously touched regarding arrangements seemed to fly open. The gentle urging in my spirit grew to a conviction: *Surely God really wants me to be at this thing. There's something I'm going to learn,* I thought, *or someone I'm going to meet.* As I finally boarded the train on January 30, I had a deep sense of rightness, an assurance of being dead-centre in God's will.

The conference began Monday afternoon. Mick and I walked into the first meeting, looking for a seat. I was aware of a fellow who half-turned in our direction as we walked across the back of the room. His awareness of me was split-second yet definite, or so I thought. There were some empty seats directly in front of this guy, so I led the way over there, plunking myself down in the chair directly in front of him. Not too subtle, I suppose, but my curiosity was piqued.

Praise and worship was in progress already, and I was very aware of this deep, rich, melodic voice behind me. The sound seemed to reverberate right through me. In between songs, I could hear him quietly praising God amongst the voices of the others around him. Such a heartfelt sound: I heard deep devotion in his voice. His praises sounded so strong yet so humble.

We were asked by the song-leader to gather in groups of four or five, with people we didn't know, to share our reasons for coming to the conference and our expectations now that we were here. As Mick turned aside to some others, I turned to face four people behind me. We all joined hands: I was next to this fellow, who introduced himself as Greg. I was kneeling on my chair, leaning against the back of it, and I felt dwarfed by his huge frame. It was such a nice feeling for one like me whose height had often made her feel like an amazon among pygmies.

Greg shared that he had come to the conference last year as a new Christian and had enjoyed it so much that he'd wanted to come again. He also mentioned being a counsellor at the Circle Square Ranch near Halkirk the previous summer. That was curious—I'd been to the same ranch just a year ago for a national YFC training seminar.

When it came my turn to share, I said that I hadn't been interested in coming but that the Lord had made it clear He wanted me to be there. "It's either for something I'm going to learn or someone I'm going to meet." (I said the former to take the intensity out of the latter.) "By the time I leave," I concluded confidently, "I'll know the specific reason why God wanted me here."

After everyone had shared, our little group broke up and I faced the front again as the praise and worship continued. My mind was already buzzing with excitement, and I got angry at myself: *Nance, for heaven's sake, he's the first dude you've even met here, and your thoughts are right out of control. Would you just shut up and put your mind back on the Lord and let Him do what He wants with you through this week!* I stomped my foot at myself mentally, pushed this fellow out of my mind, and centred back on the Lord. I really didn't think I'd talk to him again in the duration of the conference.

The next morning I was up in my room after breakfast, preparing to head down for the first session. Corinne, my roommate, was sitting in the armchair, holding very still. We had been put together at random, two single women, both twenty-nine years old. Both poised on the brink of official spinsterhood.

She was staring straight ahead. I didn't notice anything wrong—I didn't know anything about her yet, except for her age. Busy with myself, I was not being particularly sensitive.

"Are you going down now?" she asked.

"In a minute." I still wasn't tuning in.

"Uh ... " she hesitated. Then: "Could I ask a favour of you?"

I mentally scolded myself for being so insensitive and sat down in the other chair.

"Sure. What's the favour?"

She said that she needed me to pray for her, going on to explain that a fellow she had met previously had unexpectedly shown up at the conference. "I met him about a year ago," she said, "and I really like him. I don't know if he really likes me too or if he's just that friendly to everybody." Given her feelings toward him, she was feeling really uptight and distracted about the whole situation.

A mental image of Greg parked itself in the middle of my brain. I resolutely drove it out again and continued talking to Corinne. Then she mentioned that this fellow had counselled at Circle Square Ranch.

"Is his name Greg?" I asked.

Needless to say, that blew her away. "How did you know?" she asked.

"I met him yesterday," I said simply, "and yes, he *is* really nice."

My words were innocuous, but inside my thoughts were racing. *Three or four hundred people at this conference and I get paired with this particular girl? This is no coincidence: I know the Lord's hand when I see it.*

"Dear Lord," I prayed aloud, "I ask You to release Corinne from the awkwardness she feels in this situation. I ask You to help her keep her mind off this fellow so that she can seek You single-mindedly. I pray that You would work Your will and not Corinne's will in this situation."

"Amen. Amen," she kept agreeing heartily all through the prayer.

She probably wondered how I could pray so intelligently and so appropriately for her. She didn't know that I had a parallel prayer for myself going on in my heart: *Help me, Lord, to keep my mind off*

Greg. Help me to seek you single-mindedly. Let Your will be done and not mine.

I resolved before the Lord to respect this fellow as Corinne's "territory" and to wilfully refuse to draw attention toward myself. My flesh whined another dying breath, and my spirit settled in the peace of the Lord.

During the mid-morning break, I saw Corinne. "How's it going with Greg?" I asked.

Her face lit up in a big smile. "Just great!" she enthused. "I'm meeting him for lunch. But I didn't want to make it look like I was trying to get alone with him, so I told him to save a seat for my roommate too!"

It ended up that Mick, Greg, Corinne, and I ate all the rest of our meals together. She remarked to me once that it was so good to have Mick and me there because it kept things casual and friendly. I did my best to give Greg no more attention than the other two yet not ignore him completely. Either behaviour would have aroused suspicion.

It was very difficult, sitting across the table from him like that. The sound of his voice was so thrilling to me that I couldn't bear it, so I closed my ears to him. Consequently, in the course of the conference I hardly learned anything about him. All I knew was his name—and that he came from a farming family.

Every time he talked at the table, I'd stare fixedly down at my teacup, rotating it slowly with my hand, in place on its saucer. Not wanting to look at his face, trying to block out even the sound of his voice, I spent those times mentally crying out to the Lord: *Oh, God, God, God, help me. Keep my mind on You. Keep this thing in Your hands. Keep me in Your will.*

One evening I was coming down in the crowded elevator for dinner. The fellow who was squashed next to me looked at my name tag. All it said on it was "Nancy Fowler."

"You're from Victoria?" asked this fellow, a complete stranger.

"Yes, I am, but how did you know?"

"I've been writing to you," he said.

A couple of years earlier, I had been visiting my dear friend Margie Graham, from back in my Douglas Lake ranch days. Over the years since I had become a Christian, Margie had become increasingly concerned that nothing seemed to be happening for me in the marriage department. During this visit, she told me all about a certain young man, and she had, she said, told him all about me. She assured me that he was a fine Christian—a missionary actually—and that he and I would make a great couple. Partly to get her off my back and partly because there was just enough curiosity to leave me wondering if perhaps this might be the *one*, I took his address and, a short while later, wrote him a letter.

Since that time he and I had corresponded occasionally. He was stationed in Jamaica, and his letters were always very proper and very spiritual, each beginning something like a New Testament epistle: "Greetings in the name of our Lord and Saviour Jesus Christ."

Now this fellow in the elevator was telling me his name, and I immediately recognized it as this acquaintance of Margie's. We agreed to get together later that evening for a visit.

I went and sought out Mick. I was completely blown away by this amazing "coincidence," and I needed to tell someone about it.

"Do you think this is the reason that God wanted you to be here?" he asked.

"No," I said with sudden conviction, "this is not the reason I was to come, but it is the confirmation that I am exactly where God wants me, right now."

On our last evening there, some of us singles were sitting up late in the hotel's ice-cream parlour. Greg was talking about taking a walk downtown, as he had no inclination, he said, to turn in yet. I sensed that he was hinting for company, so as the party dwindled, I excused myself, thinking Greg could then ask Corinne if he so wished. "Good night, all," I said. "I'm going to go look for a piano."

I went up to the room to get a jacket (I was a little chilly), then I returned to the mezzanine to see if the conference room was deserted and the piano free. I really felt a need to draw close to the Lord, and singing and playing was the best way.

Greg and Corinne, along with another fellow, were now sitting and chatting in a lounge area just outside the conference room. I breezed by, giving them a smile and putting a finger over my lips, which meant, "Don't tell anybody I'm in here—I want to be alone." Greg made a piano-playing motion to let me know he understood what I was up to.

For maybe twenty minutes I was alone in there, in the quiet semi-dark, and I sang my heart out. Then Greg and Corinne slipped in, taking seats in two different sections. I continued to sing, sensing that I was ministering to them. They seemed to take part in my worship as they sat quietly.

I moved from one song to another almost without a break, not wanting to give them an opportunity (or an obligation) to say anything. The songs were "unto the Lord," and I wanted my attention and theirs focussed upward.

After some heavy worship songs, I thought to lighten it up with a love song. Just as I began the introduction, Corinne walked out.

Oh no, I thought, *now Greg's here alone with me and I'm playing a love song.*

Then she walked back in, and I thought, *Oh no—now she thinks I'm singing this because I thought she was gone.*

She came to the piano and quietly set a glass of ice water down at the side of the keys. Bless her heart. My throat had been bothering me all week and she knew that: I'd been coughing a lot at night. She whispered that she was exhausted and was heading up to bed. I said "Good night" and settled back to the song.

How would you feel if I told you, you reminded me of someone?
How would you feel if I told you, that's why I liked you at the start?
How would you feel if I told you, you were very much like someone—
Very much like the only one who ever really stole my heart?

How would you feel if I told you, you reminded me of someone?
And just how much you're like him, I'd really like to see
Oh, how would you feel if I told you, you were very much like someone—
So very much like someone who meant so very much to me

But I love the Lord, and this man despised Him
I told him the Truth; he just walked away
I began to dream of the day that God would change him
And since then I've been just dreaming time away

This was my "fantasy love song," inspired by a fleeting acquaintance in Rockford, Illinois. I had never before sung it for an audience. Singing it for *two* people (Greg and Corinne) had seemed like a good idea, but...

As I sang, my mind raced ahead to the verses that were still to come. *Oh no!* I thought, *I can't finish this with Greg sitting here alone in the dark. He'll think I'm singing it for him.* I had a sense of the Lord sitting next to me on the piano bench. He was laughing.

I didn't plan this, Lord; I didn't!

I know," He seemed to say. *I did. Keep singing.*

Oh, he was tall... you are taller
He was good-looking, but not quite like you
And in my mind, the old fantasy grew smaller
As I looked at the reality of you

I couldn't look at Greg, though out of the corner of my eye I could see him sitting motionless with his feet up on the chair-back in front of him. I closed my eyes and kept singing. Too late to stop now.

But he lived so far away, and you live much farther
Heaven only knows when I might see you
Sometimes I wonder why I even bother
But I loved that man—and now I think I love you

Oh, how would you feel if I told you, you reminded me of someone?
How would you feel if I told you that's why I liked you at the start?
Now how would you feel if I told you, you've made me forget all about him?
How would you feel if I came to you and offered you my heart?

Oh, how can I sit here saying you remind me of this person?
How can I even compare you when you're really worlds apart?
He despised the name of Jesus, and he's living still in darkness
But you walked out of darkness
Oh, the light shone in your darkness
You walked out of darkness—
You've got Jesus living in your heart

Instead of finishing the song there, I played a quickly improvised instrumental solo. No way could I just stop. Then with a couple of chord progressions, I made a sharp detour away from the love-song theme and broke into a boogie-woogie. At the end of that song, he interrupted.

"Are you really lonely?" he asked.

"Sometimes I am; sometimes I'm not."

"Well, your songs really sound that way."

I explained that because my songs were written at extreme times, they were inclined to portray intense highs and lows.

"You've never been married, eh?" and so began what seemed a highly personal conversation for two such veritable strangers.

He shared with me that he'd married a seventeen-year-old girl when he was only nineteen—because he'd got her pregnant. Then she'd miscarried after the wedding.

What an irony—what a tragedy. I found myself inordinately relieved to hear that there were no children from that union, which had finally been severed four years ago.

"You must have felt really ripped off when you had to marry her," I said.

"No," he said, "I knew that it was my responsibility to commit my life to her and to learn to love her."

My goodness, this is a different kind of guy, I thought to myself.

"But," he went on, "she never really made that commitment, and after three years, she just suddenly left one day."

As the conversation progressed, I was now crawling around on the low stage on my hands and knees in the dim light, looking for a power switch for the sound system. The monitors on top of the piano had been left on, and their hiss was really starting to bug me.

He sat in silence for a bit; then he concluded ruefully, "Yeah—it's really easy to get married."

"Oh, really," I replied, peering up from behind a speaker. "I hadn't noticed!"

"Oh, but it is," was his answer. "All you have to do is get pregnant."

"What?!" I demanded.

"Oh—not you—you're too old for that."

"*What?!*" I shrieked, pretending outrage.

"No, no," he replied, a bit flustered. "I just mean you're too old to be that stupid."

I returned to the piano bench. He was now sitting in the front row, just a few feet away.

"I used to think I would never marry again, but now I know I will," he said.

I felt a sudden tightness in my throat, but I managed to say with studied casualness, "What makes you say that?"

"I mean, I know I need to be, for the ministry God's put me in."

He talked about how effective he'd seemed to be in counselling the teenage girls at Circle Square Ranch.

"Of all the girls that I led to the Lord, though, after they left, they all fell away again, except for two. I finally realized they never did see Jesus: they only saw me."

"Yeah—I know what you mean. I find myself ministering mostly to young guys—I seem to get along with them better than with the girls. Can't imagine why." I allowed myself a smile, and he laughed.

"Yeah, right!"

He went on to tell me how careful he had to be in talking to girls, how quick they were to misinterpret his friendliness. As he explained this, he was lounged out across about six chairs, his feet crossed, his hands folded across his stomach, a picture of comfortableness in spite of the stern, straight-backed chairs. The way he was sprawled, his shoulders looked about six feet wide. I wondered if he thought that I was too "together," too spiritual, too mature, to misinterpret his friendliness. I was feeling less together by the minute.

I also thought of Corinne. I imagined her lying awake, wondering how long Greg and I might be down here alone, together. So I made a move to head up to bed. Astounding to me, that I should care so much about someone else's feelings as to lay down my own desire and do the right thing by her. It's what I call amazing grace.

We walked to the elevator. I felt small beside him, even though I had high-heeled boots on and he was only in stocking feet. What a nice feeling, to feel so dainty beside a man. But I had to block that very feeling; I could not afford to indulge it. So I frowned suddenly down at his socks and scolded in a motherly voice, "Where are your *shoes?!*"

"In my room," he said simply. If I was trying to embarrass him, it certainly hadn't worked. Water off a duck's back.

In the elevator I punched the "8" for me and the "3" for him. Such a short trip to the third floor! He hesitated, talking, and the door closed again before he could get his hand in it. I couldn't be sure, but it didn't seem that he had tried very hard.

The eighth floor: I stood against the doorjamb, one foot up against the edge of the door, holding it open for a moment.

"I'm still going for that walk downtown," he said. "Would you come with me?"

I pictured downtown Banff, store windows lit up in the cold and the snow. Clear, starry sky. Walking and talking.

"No," I said. "I'd have to go to my room to get some warmer clothes on." (*And Corinne would know,* I thought.) "If I get that far, I should jolly well be sensible and go to bed." And off I went, amazed again at the grace with which God was empowering me.

It was 2:30 A.M. I lay in bed, pushing away thoughts of Greg. *If I can just get through tomorrow morning without letting go of my feelings,* I thought, *everything will be all right. We'll be on the train shortly after noon.*

God Has Some Fun

I slept a short five hours. Corinne, Mick, and I had breakfast together. Greg did not join us. When Mick left the table, he said he would hold seats in the conference room for the four of us. After the meal and back in the room, there was a quick flurry of packing for us girls. I headed down to the front desk to check out. Mick and I might have to leave before the morning session was quite over, so I had best take care of this now.

I was surprised and pleased to see that Greg was at the front desk ahead of me. *Thank You, Lord!* I had taken care to put a business card in the breast pocket of my jacket, where it would be handy for just such an opportunity. With one smooth motion, I retrieved it and extended it to Greg. "If you're ever in Victoria," I said as casually as I could, "look us up." Mental emphasis on the "us": *Us. You know, Mick and me. We'll all get together. Old times' sake. Buddy-buddies.*

Greg slipped the card into his shirt pocket.

I finished checking out and came into the morning session a bit late. There was an empty seat waiting for me between Mick and Greg. It was such a treat, especially sweet since I had not manipulated it. A gift from the Lord, it seemed. Corinne was on the other side of Greg.

All through the conference, I had worked at staying out of the way as far as Greg was concerned—in deference to Corinne. I was allowing God to do as He chose. But now there came a little breach in my pledge. For one small moment I stooped to a little feminine ploy. It might seem silly and insignificant to others, but to me it spoke volumes about the deceitfulness of my heart.

It happened so quickly that I didn't have time to catch myself. Sitting there with Greg on my left, I was finding the room a little chilly, so I pulled my jacket from the back of my chair. I was going to slip my left arm into the sleeve first, but lightning-fast the thought went through my mind: *If you put it on that way, Mick will naturally help you with the other arm, but if you...* and as quickly as the thought came, I changed my course and instead slipped my right sleeve on first. Of course, Greg helped me get the jacket the rest of the way on. I smiled and whispered "Thank you" to him, but inwardly I cringed at my subtle connivance. It exhibited a lack of trust in God's ability to put me together with this man, or at least an unwillingness to be still and let Him do it His way. I sat before the Lord, inwardly apologizing.

Some people might mock me, those devoid of spiritual understanding, at my concern over such a thing. But I know that this is the very arena where spiritual skirmishes are won and lost: on the battleground of the mind.

Praise and worship had begun again. Full circle from the first meeting, there I was, hearing that rich, melodic voice again. Only this time, it was beside me, not behind me.

As I sat there trying to concentrate on the speaker, I couldn't help but notice that, in spite of my high-heeled boots, his knee, right beside mine, was higher. And I was acutely aware, as we were sitting so close together, that his shoulder loomed above mine. Just sitting beside his big, strong frame made me feel perfectly feminine.

I made a distinct point of directing any whispered comments at Mick instead of Greg, still trying not to give Greg any inordinate attention.

The speaker was finished. We stood again to sing. The room was charged with the anointing, full of the presence of God. I was having trouble holding back my tears. The worship leader had us all join hands during one long prayer. Greg's huge farmer hand engulfed mine. I hung onto it as hard as he was holding onto mine—the emotion of the moment, I rationalized for his part. I wondered what would happen if I moved my fingers—if I caressed his hand in some small way. I had to hold myself firmly back; hold my fingers still.

As the leadership began to serve communion, passing out the

wafers, they asked us to go to one person and "break bread" with them, as an indication of love and servitude. I sat down, leaning forward, elbows on my knees, eyes shut, seeking the Lord. *I can't make a move, Lord.* It would be most fitting for me to share with Mick, especially since he was on the outside of the aisle. But I wanted awfully to share with Greg.

I waited on the Lord, seemingly interminably. As I finally sat up and opened my eyes, I found that Mick, Greg, and Corinne were all holding a part of their wafers out to me. Gratitude to the Lord surged through me as the four of us shared together, an appropriate end to the fellowship we'd had throughout the conference. The "wine" was circulated; then we rose to sing again.

Great singing—the Holy Ghost was sweeping through the place. We worshipped, most of the congregation with their hands lifted up. My eyes were closed. Suddenly I had the most uncanny sensation. I opened my eyes. Greg's arms were stretched up high, out to either side of him, palms turned out. His right arm was over my head, overshadowing me. I felt the Lord speak to my heart: *That arm is your protection, your covering. That's where you're going to be standing for the rest of your life, underneath that arm.* I began to cry.

Mick looked at his watch, then at me. Train to catch. I had to say good-bye. Greg and Corinne both had their eyes shut, lost in worship. I reached behind Greg to get Corinne's attention. She gave me a big hug and a kiss. Mick and Greg were shaking hands but ended up in a bear hug. As I pulled away from Corinne, I thought, *I've got to shake Greg's hand and get out of here.*

It was no use. As I tried to reach for his hand, I found myself folded up in his arms. For one brief instant, ecstasy. As I broke away again, I heard myself say, "I love you, brother." Immediately I thought, *I can't believe I said that.* Then, *Oh well, I say that to all my brothers.*

Then Mick and I were out of there, hustling down to the lobby. But as we waited for our cab, Greg showed up, seeming to be taking care of some other business at the front desk. I wasn't sure what: I was too dazed to think straight at this point.

"Hey, Greg," Mick addressed him, "you'll have to come to Victoria sometime. I'll give you my phone number."

"He has my business card, Mick. If he wants to get in touch, he can."

"Well, anytime you're in town," Mick continued, "remember, you've always got a place to stay."

"Oh, I'll be out there," Greg said. He turned to walk away, then paused and looked back, hesitating. Seemed he was going to say something. The strangest look passed over his face, as though he might cry. Then he was gone.

We had a few minutes to kill at the train station. Mick spotted an old-fashioned scale, the kind where you put in a penny to find out your weight and your fortune. He urged me to climb on, then I turned the knob to find the question I wanted answered. I made a crack at him about having just left the Spiritual Leadership Conference and now, only moments later, turning to divination and fortune-telling.

"Stop at that one," he interjected. The question read: "Am I lucky in love?" I put in my penny and the response popped up: "No—better take up cards!" We hooted with laughter, causing others in the quiet station to eye us suspiciously.

On the train I took my seat while Mick went off to find the observation car. Grateful for the pillow that was there, I curled up against the window. My body was exhausted; it felt like it was disappearing down into the upholstery. My mind, on the other hand, was running at triple speed. I had kept a tight mental control clamped on myself all week, "casting down imaginations, and every high thing that exalteth itself against the knowledge of God, and bringing into captivity every thought to the obedience of Christ."[1] Now I could safely let go, and I felt myself spiralling down, down into pleasant thoughts of Greg... *Greg.*

The porter, an old East Indian fellow, came and stationed himself in the seat opposite me.

"That your boyfriend?" he asked, nodding his head at Mick's empty seat.

"No—he's just a friend. He's engaged to someone else."

"Oh... you gotta boyfriend?"

"No."

"Oh... haven't found him yet, eh?"

"No."

"*How* old are you now?" (This was getting bizarre.)

"Nearly thirty."

He shook his head and wagged his finger at me. "I tell you," he said, "you go out and find that boy, you get married and settle down and have a couple of kids. Then you be happy."

I patiently but somewhat wearily explained that the Lord had everything under control and that I only wanted His will for my life.

We talked awhile about our respective faiths. Then, sensing my fatigue, he kindly reclined the double seat into a bed and got me a blanket and two extra pillows. He tucked me in, for all the world like a concerned father. Then he went on his way.

I lay there for fully two hours, my body again appearing (and trying) to sleep but my mind still racing and cavorting. I wondered if I should say anything to Mick.

When Mick returned to our car, I gave up the pretence of resting and visited with him awhile. The porter came by again and began once more to express, to both of us this time, his concern at my single state.

"Oh, you don't need to worry about Nancy," Mick assured him glibly. "She's got more lines out than a troller in season. She's bound to snag something."

Our dinner reservations were not until the 8:00 P.M. sitting, so in the early evening Mick and I went down to the lounge car for a cup of tea. In the course of the conversation, he happened to mention Greg and Corinne.

As nonchalantly as I could, yet nearly choking on the words, I said, "So...do you think Greg and Corinne would make a good couple?"

He looked surprised. "No, as a matter of fact, I thought you and Greg would make a way better couple, and besides that, I thought he was really interested in you. But you sure were acting weird!"

He looked even more surprised as, at the end of this short blast, I grabbed him by the arms and shrieked, "Did you really—did you really think he was interested?!"

"Well, what's the *matter* with you? Why didn't you *do* something about it?"

So I told him about Corinne's confiding in me and about my resolution concerning the situation, to respect Greg as her territory. He sighed in exasperation. "Women!" he said.

At dinner we joined a pastor whom Mick had met in the observation car. He seemed to assume that Mick and I were a couple. Once we straightened him out, he began to question me about my marital status. The day's focus on me and marriage was beginning to get ridiculous.

He shared with us about Ann Kiemel's story, as told in her book *I Gave God Time*, how, at the age of thirty-five, going about her business of serving the Lord, she had suddenly met an Idaho potato farmer—a big, strong fellow, fallen in love, and got married really quickly.

"A farmer, eh?" I commented, to Mick's obvious amusement.

The pastor went on to speak of a gal who had travelled in ministry with him and his wife. Although she was twenty-nine or thirty, whenever she was questioned about marriage, her response was that she only wanted to serve the Lord. The three of them were put up one evening by an old farm couple. The girl met the farmer's son, a big, strapping fellow. Love at first sight: they were married very shortly thereafter.

"A big, strong farmer—how nice." I smiled blandly across the table at the pastor, all the while whispering laughing threats and reprimands out of the side of my mouth at Mick. He was poking me under the table and nearly gagging on his food in his delight at the Lord's irony. The pastor must have thought us strange—or at least very easily amused.

After the late supper, I was ready (I hoped) for an early bed. I climbed to the upper berth in the quiet, dark car and sat there with my legs dangling through the curtain as I organized my things.

I felt someone take hold of one of my boots. Peering out, I saw the porter. He whispered that he wanted to talk to me and gestured for me to follow him. Strange.

He led me to an empty stateroom, allowed me in ahead of him, then closed and locked the door behind us. I was not afraid, but I was certainly on my guard. I sat down in the chair that he indicated; he settled himself in a chair opposite and then whispered intensely, secretively:

"You wanna get married? Then I set it up for you."

As I began to protest, he assured me that I could meet with this fellow and see him "two, three times, and if you don't like him, we call it off."

I was aghast, but I tried to answer in a level manner. My response surprised me as much as it surprised him:

"Look, I told you that the Lord is going to take care of me, and as a matter of fact, I just met a guy in Banff, and I think I'm going to marry him. Thanks anyway for your kind concern."

I calmly unlocked the door and stepped out with a polite "Good night."

Finding Mick in the observation car, I sat down in the seat beside him. "Mick, I think our porter's a weirdo."

When I related my story, he disagreed with my conclusion. "Probably just a cultural thing," he said.

Still, I was not keen to turn in until Mick was ready to settle himself in the lower bunk. So we sat in the dark, watching the snowy mountainsides rattle past the train. He talked about his fiancée; I talked about Greg. We were a couple of basket cases, putting up with each other's one-track conversation.

"What are we going to talk about *now*?" I would inquire of him brightly every time there came a lull.

"Oh, Greg probably," he would reply resignedly, rolling his eyes.

By midnight I was so exhausted and so hyper I thought I'd never be able to relax. When I finally settled in for the night, sleep did not come easily. As I lay in the small berth, it seemed large and empty. I couldn't remember ever feeling so alone. Not so much lonely, but separated—as though part of me were missing.

My mind mused over all the amazing coincidences of this trip:

Being roomed with a girl who knew Greg and very much liked him—a situation which gave me a clear choice of putting things totally in God's hands or of taking them into my own.

Running into that fellow, the friend of Margie Graham's: God's assurance that He had me in exactly the right place at the right time.

Having that feeling as I'd stood next to Greg in the last meeting—the sense that he was to be my covering.

Having all these references made to me about marriage—and big, strong farmers, ever since getting on the train.

The thoughts went on and on. *Greg.* I wasn't even sure of his last name. At first I'd thought it was "Christianson," and I'd thought, *Good name! Son of a Christian.* But I wasn't sure if that was right after all. He'd said it more like "Christenson." I didn't know—I had consciously refused to look at his name tag all week. I hardly knew a thing about him.

The rhythm of the train rocked on, the wheels clacking monotonously, farther and farther away from Banff. As I finally drifted off to sleep, I was confident of one thing: I was completely relinquished to God's will in the situation. I knew that I only wanted of it what He desired. And I knew that whatever He chose to do, it would be good.

A Valentine's Letter

The following Wednesday, five days after returning to Victoria, I walked into my office at Youth for Christ and found a pink phone-message slip on my desk. A co-worker had taken a call for me the day before at 5:10 P.M.

She had got his name wrong. "Craig Christenson," the note indicated, had phoned while I was out, and "is going to write to you."

I couldn't breathe. I looked out the window. It was a beautiful day. My life was changing; I could feel it. I made myself breathe, slowly and evenly.

My co-worker had added a postscript: "You are very fortunate to be getting mail from this fellow, as he sounds quite nice on the phone."

No kidding.

The rest of the day was going to be a dead loss as far as work was concerned.

Unbeknownst to me, Greg had faced a bit of a challenge in tracking me down. When I'd given him my card in Banff, he'd slipped it into his shirt pocket. But he never saw it again, even though he searched through all of his stuff several times. It was as if God chose to foil my one attempt to take matters into my own hands. So Greg went home to Wetaskiwin knowing only two things about me: my name, and the fact that I worked for a Christian organization in Victoria. Youth for Christ was the second place he phoned.

I received that message on the ninth of February, exactly one month before I would turn thirty. Time crept by over the next few days as I waited for a letter. The highlight of the day was picking up the Youth for Christ mail on the way to work. The rest of the day seemed nothing more than an interminable wait until the next day and the next trip to the post office.

As I waited, I prayed. "Lord, if this is really going to happen, then give him the guts to lay it out in the first letter."

The letter finally arrived, on Valentine's Day, of all days. This is how it happened, as recorded in the reply I quickly penned:

February 14
My dear Greg:

I had a feeling I'd get a letter from you on Valentine's Day. I was heading into town in time to get to the Detention Centre by noon to have lunch with the kids. With me was Kitty, a twenty-year-old girl who's staying with me right now: I was going to drop her at Manpower on my way to work. Stopped by the Post Office to check YFC's mail 'cause I have a key. Found your letter there—ran out to the car waving it at Kitty like a crazy woman. She knew I was waiting for such a letter, as I had probably mentioned your name to her three or four (uh) hundred times.

"Well, open it!" she shrieked.

"No way—I'm dropping you off first, then I'm going somewhere alone to read it."

She wailed that it wasn't fair—why didn't I skip lunch at "Juvie" and go for tea with her? We compromised: I dropped her at one of our favourite restaurants and promised to be back in fifteen or twenty minutes. Then (being a romantic) I drove down to the ocean to find a suitable setting in which to crack open this letter.

Sliding down a muddy path in a new pair of heels, I climbed to a rock at the water's edge where the waves were smashing in against logs and boulders while the sky above threatened to storm.

With the wind whipping my hair around and tearing at my dress, I must've looked like I was filming a schmaltzy commercial—maybe for perfume or something.

Before I was halfway through the second page, I was chilled to the bone, and, practical romantic that I am, I headed back to my car to finish the letter.

The truth was, this letter—five wonderful, long pages—seemed to be full of nothing but chatty news. This was nice, but was this all? I was standing on a rock scant feet from the foaming water, in a full gale, getting soaked in the sea spray, freezing, and afraid that at any moment the wind might tear this precious epistle from my hands. All this, for friendly conversation? I gave up my posturing and went back to my warm little car. I could finish this letter in more comfortable—if less romantic—surroundings.

Halfway through the third page, I came to a paragraph that was different. "Well, Nancy," it began, and my breath caught in my throat, because I knew the tone was changing after all.

Well, Nancy, I've been debating with myself, whether to say some things or not. These "some things" concern you. I don't even know where to begin. I'm getting shaky just thinking about it.

The night I listened to you play and spent that time with you, I experienced some things that I haven't experienced for three years. All of a sudden, I was tongue-tied, shaky, totally lacking in control and cool. I guess you might call it similar to "first-date fears." It was nice. It was great. Praise God I can still feel that way. I had forgotten what it was like.

You were the first person in three years that I had let myself respond to. Sure, I have been with others, but never emotionally in that way. And, I might add, the first Christian, which is something that adds new dimension. I have abstained from any intimacy (emotionally or otherwise) on my part since becoming a Christian, because I wasn't sure I could handle myself. I've never had to say "No" to myself since I got married, if I didn't want to. The next step has always been the bedroom.

I believe God is teaching me greatly in this area. How to control myself, and what to look for in a relationship. Also none have really "turned my crank."

So, taking this time to share some of me has left me vulnerable because I have "shared some of me." It also could end what might have been even a friendship. I hope not. You stir me as few do, and when I get rid of all of my "need to impress" (which I hate), I believe we could share deeper things. I was disappointed when we parted, not getting to know you as well as I would have liked. Also, I wasn't sure about you and Mick and didn't want to overstep.

This is incredible. Oh, the fears of falling in love. Anyway. If I haven't scared you off...? Time will tell.

Love,
Greg

God had answered my prayer: Greg had "laid it out" in the very first letter. I would not appreciate, though, for years to come, what a big step this was for Greg, how hard it was for him to make himself so vulnerable, to be the initiator, to risk rejection in this way. In every relationship he had entered into, the girl had always made her intent clear before he had ever made a move. He had never before had to put himself out on a limb like this. Already, at the very beginning of our courtship, God was laying a new foundation, His way: letting the man take the initiative. And although I didn't understand the full significance then, I sensed that it was a fearful thing for Greg, and I appreciated his transparency.

I responded in kind, in the remainder of that first letter of mine.

> *Thank you for taking the risk of sharing your feelings. You didn't catch me by surprise at all—I had prayed much that God would let you share what you did. After the first couple of pages I was beginning to think you would finish it in the same tone—just very general—however friendly. Then when the tone changed, part of me (my spirit) was casually saying, "Of course," while the rest of me was freaking out and saying, "I just don't believe it!"*
>
> *I could write volumes to you, but I think I'll try to keep it short and to the point—so I can get it right in the mail.*
>
> *There's one question and one request that occur to me right off:*
>
> <u>*When*</u> *are you coming to visit?*
>
> *Please will you phone me <u>soon</u> so I can talk to you!*
>
> *If I seemed cool and non-committal at the conference, it was fully intended. Because of another situation—personal dynamic—I felt obliged before the Lord to do nothing to encourage you. When I write more later, I'll explain if necessary. But in response to something you said in your letter, no, there's nothing with Mick and me. He's really seriously engaged. I did go out with him a few times a year ago, but I was never comfortable with him... I knew I wasn't interested in him but could sense he had serious expectations (which he denied), so I cut it off as gently as I could.*
>
> *That's why it was ironic that when I prayed about whether I should go to Banff, then prayed about travel arrangements, Mick's name kept coming up. I spoke to Mick about it finally and sure enough, he was going.*

So we proceeded to arrange to travel together. Still, I wasn't that sure if God knew what He was doing—I thought it could be difficult. Then Mick told me he was engaged. So, not only did that afford me a good and irreproachable travel companion; not only did it give me company for meals, etc., and a "covering" to protect me from sudden involvement (sounds like it held you back a bit!), but it also gave us (Mick and me) a chance to get to know each other as friends without the possibility (for him) or threat (for me) of a relationship. Finally I am completely at ease with him.

But not to digress too much—I believe the Lord contrived the situation mentioned above (not Mick but the other) to constrain me from you—so that I would have a clear-cut choice of either putting you (and any possibility of a relationship with you) into His wise and capable hands—or of mucking ahead impulsively in the flesh as I certainly would have if not for His precious grace.

The first few days after leaving Banff, I felt like part of me was missing—I felt lonelier than I can ever remember feeling. But that feeling lessened as I got back into my routine. I'm used to my single life, and I do like it in a lot of ways.

Most of the time I have to block you out of my mind, because I can't bear to think of how long it might be before I see you again. And I'm scared too—like you said in your letter, "Oh, the fears of falling in love."

Time to turn in for the night. I am so over-tired lately: I'm way behind on sleep. Even when I do get to bed at a decent time I find myself lying awake, thoughts just a-buzzin'. Mostly your fault.

Please phone me soon—you can call me after midnight because you're more likely to catch me then. And if you don't get me (but get Barb or Kitty) make <u>sure</u> you call back the same night or I won't go to sleep at all.

I have committed this matter many times to the Lord—I trust you're doing the same.

This is crazy, Greg. I don't even know you.

Fond and formal regards,
Nancy

I folded the letter inside a Valentine's card that had a lovestruck prairie dog on the front. The message inside the card was

"I gopher you." I posted it the same day, then went home to once again begin the agony of waiting.

That evening I wrote a "Love Song." This would be the song, I decided right then, that I would sing at the wedding. It sounds like I was way ahead of myself perhaps, but in my heart of hearts, it all seemed like a foregone conclusion. I knew it was happening.

I wrote a letter to my sister Polly in Toronto. "I've met a guy," I said, "and it looks like it could be serious." That was all I said about Greg, but she wrote back and said, "Nance, in all these years, you have *never* used the word 'serious' in connection with a guy. I know this is presumptuous, but if you might be getting married, would you consider the last weekend in July? I'm going to be home then anyway for a class reunion."

I also wasted no time tracking down a copy of Ann Kiemel's book *I Gave God Time*. My curiosity piqued by the pastor on the train, I wanted to read the story of how God had brought a husband into her life. I had enjoyed her free-flowing poetic style in the past, and now this new book touched me deeply. So many of the things she said rang a familiar, almost prophetic note in my heart. I wrote down many of the phrases that spoke to me, substituting names and details of my circumstances into her writing:

> i suddenly realized that going to [Banff] was an adventure unlike any other in my life. outwardly i denied any real meaning or purpose behind this trip ... but subconsciously i must have known there was a plan-in-the-making
>
> i had [travelled] to [Banff] that day out of sheer obedience, knowing this was ordered by God. the timing perfect
>
> it all seemed so amazing and overwhelming that this man next to me was going to be my husband ... that i was going to leave everything i had ever known ... to put my entire life under [his] authority and love and care
>
> i looked over at ... this big, strong, sober, determined man sitting next to me. for the first time it was so clear ... so obvious. This was God's man for me ... His

perfect choice in all the world. He was the one I had waited for, these [thirty] years[4]

i have decided that a man of the earth can make it through anything... if some day, we are stranded on the other side of the world with no one... and no money... [he] will be able to take care of me[5]

the secret throughout was that we were both obedient. we were listening to God's voice... not our own. we were giving Him time, and putting no confidence in what we personally thought or felt[6]

the peace transcended every barrier[7]

remember that LOVE never fails because it is primarily a commitment, not a feeling[8]

The First Date

I had no way of knowing that Greg had gone out of town to work and would not receive my letter for ten long days. Every night I made sure that I was home before midnight, after chasing juvenile delinquents around on the streets of Victoria; but night after night there was no call. Sleep was difficult.

I had a week's holiday coming up right away. I was planning to head up to the Kamloops area to visit some friends and do some skiing. If there was any chance of getting together with Greg, that would be the time, since I would have already covered a significant portion of the distance between us.

I was planning to leave on Friday, right after work.

Wednesday evening, Barb opened the door at the top of my stairs and called down into my suite: "Nancy?"

"Hello!"

"You're not to leave on your holiday until Saturday morning."

I came to the bottom of the stairs and looked up at her pleasant face. "Why not, Barb?"

"I don't know why," she replied with a strange smile. "I just know you're not supposed to leave on Friday night."

Friday night at 11:00, I invited Barb down for tea. It helped to have company while I waited to see if this was the night the call would come. As it got later, I became less and less able to keep my mind on the conversation, more and more caught up in my waiting and wondering. Finally I could not keep up the charade any longer. I slid off the couch onto my knees and cried out, "Pray with me, Barb!"

"Oh, God," I wailed, "please, I submit this situation into Your hands. I only want Your will here, Lord. Please have Your way."

Barb's prayer was not quite so pious. "Heavenly Father, I believe

You've put these two young people together, and I don't believe You're going to keep them waiting around. So Holy Spirit, right now, in the Name of Jesus, I ask You to speak to Greg and tell him to pick up the phone and call."

I was still on my knees when the phone rang. I screamed softly and ran to pick up the receiver. I couldn't bear it if it wasn't him. "Hello?"

"Hello," said a wonderful voice.

"Hi," I said quietly, suddenly a little shy. "Greg? Just a minute, please." I tossed the phone over my shoulder, and Barb and I exchanged a triumphant hug while the receiver bounced off the floor, suspended by its curly cord.

"I'll be waiting up," she whispered as she headed up the stairs. She knew that I was going to want to talk to her once I got off the phone. What a great friend.

I recall that our conversation lasted about forty-five minutes, that is, if you could call it a conversation. There was a whole lot more sighing going on than talking. We did get down to business on one subject, though, and that was a plan to meet the following week during my holiday. I would drive from Kamloops; he would drive from Wetaskiwin; and we would meet, once again, at the Banff Springs Hotel.

It was a 330-mile drive to Banff from Kamloops. I would have to make an early start to be there for lunch. I spent the night with friends and set my alarm for 3:30 A.M. By 4:00 A.M., I was motoring east in the early dark in my little navy blue four-door Fiat.

After I'd driven for about an hour, the engine started to sound a little rough. Sounded like it was running on only three cylinders. It got worse as time went by. I stopped at the side of the road, got out, and opened the hood, groping in the dark for the distributor cables. Somehow I just felt led to wiggle all the attachments, in case one was loose.

It ran well for quite a while after that, but just as the sky was starting to get light, the engine began to lose power again. I had to shift into third; I just couldn't keep the revs high enough for fourth. Then I had to shift down to second, and finally I found myself droning along on the shoulder at a crawl in first gear, praying nervously. Then the engine quit completely.

I was still over two hundred miles from the date of my dreams. I was sitting there wondering what to do when faith suddenly rose up in me. I laid my right hand on the ignition, closed my eyes, and prayed the prayer of faith. "Lord God, I have submitted this thing to You all along, and I believe it is Your will that I go to Banff. I take authority over the devil in Your name and command him to take his hands off this vehicle *now*." I prayed then for a while in tongues and then sat quietly, waiting on the Lord, hand still on the ignition.

After a bit, I had a sense in my heart that I should pull out the little manual choke knob. Now anybody who knows anything at all about engines knows that you mostly need the choke while the engine is cold. It had been running now for several hours. But this was not a time for common sense; it was a time for trusting God and obeying whatever foolish thing He might ask of me. I pulled out the choke and turned on the key. It fired right up and away we went. After a few miles, I shoved the choke back in. The car ran like a top the rest of the way.

As the miles slipped by, I became more and more confident that God was going to get me there just fine. Now my mind was free to become more and more nervous about my date. Every once in a while on that long drive, I pulled a little bottle of spray perfume from my purse—a delicate fragrance I had just bought—and applied a few more shots. Alternately, out came a small aerosol breath-freshener for a couple more squirts. There was one other thing I kept doing over and over: yielding the upcoming events of the day to the Lord.

At long last I parked outside that beautiful old Canadian Pacific Railway hotel. I don't recall where Greg and I actually found each other, but I have a vivid memory of walking beside him through the long halls of the Banff Springs Hotel to one of the restaurants. It was warm inside after the refreshing March weather outside. He pulled his ski-jacket up over his head (it was a pullover style), and as he did so, his black velour shirt rode up to his shoulder blades. I reached out to pull it down for him. His back was warm and sweaty. *He must be as nervous and excited as I am*, I thought.

Once we were seated in the eatery, I asked him, "Do you pray in public?"

"I'll pray anywhere, anytime," he assured me.

My kind of guy. "Then would you mind praying and committing this day to the Lord?"

He gave a nervous laugh. "I've already done that, about four different times on the way here."

"Would you do it again, with me?" and I reached out and took his hand. I hardly let go of it for the rest of the day.

The other notable thing about our lunch date was that we had no lunch. We both found that we had no appetite. He ordered coffee, and I ordered tea, and we talked and talked and talked. As I was drinking my tea, I looked down into my cup and was reminded of a recurring theme in this same hotel a month earlier.

"Do you know," I said, "that all those meals we ate together with Mick and Corinne, I didn't hear a thing you ever said? I had to block out the sound of your voice, because it was blowing me away so badly. I would just stare down into my teacup, turn it slowly on the saucer, and pray over and over for God to help me."

He laughed. "I wondered what you were doing with your teacup all that time."

It was a spring day in Banff, sunny and mild, and we spent the afternoon walking around the town, enjoying the sights and one another, still holding hands. We found ourselves touring the Banff School of Fine Arts. By this time, we were holding *both* hands, which sometimes made walking difficult. We were in an unreal, euphoric state, and we had a great deal of trouble making sense of some of the exhibits. I remember an odd heap of headless female bodies, made of flesh-coloured cloth, stuffed to give them dimension, sprawled in a corner, and I remember that we both tried to suppress our giddy laughter—and that we both failed completely. We must have appeared to be very unsophisticated, a couple of hicks who did not appreciate "fine" art.

Greg had told me in our phone call that he loved the hot springs in Banff and that he wanted to take me there, so we had both packed our bathing suits. At Sulphur Mountain I changed in the chilly locker room and padded out in bare feet on the cold concrete looking for Greg, wading into water so hot that it took my breath away.

What a strange thing, to be on my first date with this man with whom I was head-over-heels in love; to be so determined to keep this relationship absolutely right in God's eyes; and now to be together in this hot pool, almost completely naked. I'd never thought of bathing suits in quite this way before, how it's quite permissible in our society to disrobe like that and think nothing of it. Suddenly it seemed so extremely immodest, even in my demure one-piece.

His body was massively muscular. I couldn't take it all in so soon. I wasn't ready yet; no—I had no right to yet. I didn't dare let my eyes wander too far from his face; I allowed myself only to take in his right shoulder and arm. He had his right elbow resting up behind him on the side of the pool. I carefully refrained from looking anywhere else: facing him, concentrating just on his face as we talked. I just wouldn't look at the rest of his body. I was sure that the greatest blessing would come to our marriage (for even now I was sure that this was where we were headed) if we did not indulge in anything before its time. "Don't excite love, don't stir it up, until the time is ripe," say the Scriptures. At length I came closer and gingerly rested my head in the crook of his shoulder, my heart pounding with the newness, and yet comfortable in a kind of foreknowing familiarity. We talked on.

Toward the end of our time at the pool, I prayed a strange prayer. "Oh, Lord," I said aloud, "any fool can fall in love. But teach me how to be a friend to this man."

As I rinsed off in the warm shower in the locker room a short time later, I suddenly had the sensation that all of my emotion, all of my passion, had been doused with cold water. All of the feelings were simply *gone*, and in their place was just this very plain—not unpleasant, but very plain—sense that Greg was ... a nice guy. Just a great guy, and that was all.

I had always wondered what happens in marriage when you wake up one morning and find that the passion is gone. I was finding out, and it was only our first date.

As we walked side by side to the parking lot to find his van, I kept glancing up at him, almost expecting to see someone else there. The feeling I had, walking beside him, was so much like the-boy-next-door kind of thing that I really didn't think it could be the same man beside me that I had arrived with.

Greg broke the silence in the van. "Do you kind of feel like you've had a cold shower?"

I looked at him in surprise and answered shakily, "I sure do."

"Don't you remember what you prayed in the pool?" he asked. "You should be careful what you pray for; you just might get it."

I talked to him then about that fear, of what happens when the passion fades in a relationship.

"Passion will come and go," he said, "but God is the Author of those feelings. Just trust Him with them. The feelings may go, but He will bring them back again."

What was it that I just read recently, and where? Yes, it was in Ann Kiemel's book: "Remember that LOVE never fails because it is primarily a commitment, not a feeling." And I know that God has promised in His Word that He is able to keep that which is committed unto Him. I will commit this love to Him, and He will preserve it.

I had also read—somewhere—that God never designed the heights of passion to stay at their original level throughout the marriage, because He knew we wouldn't be able to function properly, or to even survive that sustained, fevered pitch.

Surely God wanted to be Lord over my emotions—He would know best what to do with them. The thought gave me reassurance, here in the parking lot of Sulphur Mountain Hot Springs. I yielded my feelings—or this strange lack thereof—and let go of my fear of the future, and sure enough, the feelings came back. Not in a big whoosh, the way they had left, but gradually, gently, kind of like standing in front of a fireplace when you're chilled to the bone, slowly thawing, warming in front of the flames, until suddenly once again you can barely stand the heat.

"Let's go up the Sulphur Mountain gondola," Greg suggested spontaneously. I was quickly learning that this was his nature, very unlike mine.

We barely caught the last ride of the day, and as it was late in the ski season, we were the only ones aboard. The little restaurant at the top was shut down, and the place was deserted except for a security guard, who discreetly pretended not to notice us.

The view was magnificent and we watched the sun go down, and while I was busy watching the sun go down, Greg sneaked a kiss, his lips on mine.

I protested: this was way too soon to get into this if we were going to keep ourselves pure. Greg was oblivious to my concerns. He was just flat-out excited at what God was doing. He hadn't so much as held a girl's hand since he'd got saved a year and a half earlier, and now God was giving him freedom. He must have given me a hundred little kisses from the time we got back in the gondola till we arrived at the bottom.

It was getting dark quickly, and we suddenly realized we were absolutely starving. We found a trendy little steakhouse and enjoyed a great meal together. As we ate, Greg told me about a girl, Eva, a mature believer of about my age, back home in Wetaskiwin. They had been helping to lead the youth group together. A third party, a young married woman with a penchant for prophesy, had had a dream that Eva and Greg were getting married. Eva had already felt that God was telling her—in spite of her inclinations to the contrary—that Greg was the man for her.

When the time for the Banff Spiritual Leadership Conference was approaching, Greg told Eva that he wouldn't be going this year as he was very short on cash. (Ever since coming to the Lord, Greg had found that a process of financial stripping had begun in his life.) Later Eva came back and told Greg she felt so strongly that God wanted him to go to this event that she wanted to pay his way.

In retrospect, after meeting me and feeling that God was going to bring us together, Greg felt so guilty about it all happening on Eva's nickel that he borrowed money from a businessman in his new church home and paid her back.

My goodness, God certainly did move in mysterious ways, His wonders to perform.[3] And I'd thought that the story of how God got *me* to Banff was unusual! Well, I didn't much care at this point *how* Greg had got there; I was just so glad that he had. But as I thought about it more, I realized that I owed quite a debt of gratitude to this young woman who had obeyed God in this way.

As we finished our meal, Greg changed the subject and made a confession:

"I was praying this morning that God would send a terrible snowstorm and that we would be stranded here for several days."

I laughed and thought nothing more of it.

It was getting late. He had a long drive ahead of him; I had a *really* long drive ahead of me. We said our good-byes and headed our separate ways.

I hadn't even quite got out of Banff yet when the snow started, and within a few minutes, I found myself in the worst snowstorm I have ever driven in. Obviously Greg had forgotten to cancel his prayer! And he had been admonishing me, just several hours earlier, that I should be careful what *I* pray for!

The flakes were so thick and heavy that I couldn't see anything but dizziness—even at thirty miles per hour with the low beams on. It was barely below the freezing point, that certain temperature where the wiper blades clog up and freeze every five minutes. I couldn't see a thing through the wet, snowy, streaky glass. Every time I tried to stop so I could clean off the wipers, the car slipped and slid all over the place. Then each time I tried to get up to speed again—if you could call it speed—the tires spun and caused the car to fishtail from side to side all over the road.

The highway was just an expanse of white with more white swirling in the blackness above it. I had no sense of whether I was in my lane or the other one. The road was deserted except for the occasional mammoth truck, and as the headlights bore down on me, I would steer the little Fiat just to the right of the glare, hoping to give those big wheels a wide enough berth without slipping into the ditch on the right.

It wasn't long before I was exhausted, and my eyes felt like they were bugging out of my head from the strain. I prayed continuously, and at length the snow thinned to sleet and then to rain. I made my weary, winding way through the mountains as far as Golden, and there I stopped and found a room for the night. Even though it was one o'clock in the morning, I phoned my mom and asked her if she thought her wedding dress would fit me.

The next morning I drove on to Revelstoke, where I stopped for gas. My little car had run fine since that scary difficulty on the way up. I checked the oil. It was down a bit, so I topped that up too. And so, because I had just put in a pint, it hit me with a shock when, about fifteen miles shy of Kamloops, I glanced down and saw the oil light flash. I knew immediately that this was serious. Acting instantaneously, I flipped the key, killing the ignition, then coasted to a stop beside the highway.

I lifted the hood and found the entire engine splattered with smoking black oil. *It's probably terminal,* I thought. *Probably the head gasket.*

This was back before the time when everyone and his dog had a cell phone. But I had passed this way before; I knew what to do. I grabbed my purse, locked the doors, and stuck out my thumb.

In Kamloops, I tracked down an old mechanic who had worked on other wrecks of mine years back. He was busy all day, he said, but tomorrow, Saturday, his day off, he could help me. My lonely little Fiat was left out on the side of the road all night, and I stayed with my friends again.

In the morning, as the mechanic drove me back out there in a little red Fiat that looked like a first cousin to mine, he said, "If I can't fix your car, I'll sell you this one."

Well, one look under the hood confirmed to him what I'd guessed: "Looks like you've blown your head gasket."

He poured a whole lot of oil into the crankcase and told me to drive into town, to his shop, very slowly, keeping the revs low. He thought the car was worth rebuilding, but it sure wouldn't happen soon enough to be of any use to me.

So we did some paperwork, exchanging ownership of the two Fiats, and I got ready to leave.

"Just one more thing," he said. "Before you leave with my car, I need a ride home."

I dropped him at his house and was introduced to his wife, who threw up her hands and exclaimed, "He always sells the car we're driving!"

And then I was on my way, looking forward to this "holiday" being over so that I could go home and get some rest.

Facing My Fears

Back at work, I took the first opportunity to sit down with our Executive Director, alone in his office, to let him know that I had met someone special. In the past there had been a lot of good-natured teasing from him and the other staff members about the various young men traipsing in and out of my life. "This time it's different," I told him. "I can't bear it if you joke around about this." And I punctuated my announcement by bursting into tears, much to his surprise. I was taken by surprise as well.

Within a few days, I received a letter from Greg. His trip home had been a little less eventful than mine:

I arrived home from Banff Friday morning at 5:15 A.M. I got north of Calgary and pulled over for three hours. (I slept from Banff to Calgary quite a bit, but it wasn't restful. I had to keep waking up to stay on the road. God is truly watching over me.)

Friday I was in a daze and quite tired. After a little nap in the afternoon, Friday night was better. It was then that I started to come alive. God by His Spirit was coming alive in me, in areas particularly concerning sex and women. After one and a half years as a Christian, I can finally begin to understand God's idea. It was our meeting Thursday that brought it all together. I'm free. I'm finally free. I'm not driven by my body. I can truly see God's hand.

Saturday was another tremendous day. God just keeps growing in me.

Sunday was even better. I am almost speechless. God grew so big in me, I almost couldn't contain Him. I found myself praying most of the time. Communicating with my Lord. Oh, God.

Something big is just around the corner. I sensed something Sunday afternoon that I couldn't explain. It was as if God was saying to me that something was about to happen to me. I have never sensed God that big.

Well, I know you have been going through a lot too. I trust that you got home safe and sound. I will pray that you get rest.

Nancy, I wish I were there to help you relax.

When I read that line, I got down on the floor and started to cry. Only God could have known how much that last sentence would impact me. I was (and still am) a very intense person, easily becoming driven and even oppressed by the very desires and talents with which God has gifted me. At that point in my life, it was caring for the wayward youth of Victoria that drove me physically and burdened me emotionally and spiritually, often to the point of exhaustion. It was a work that I loved, yet sometimes it threatened to undo me.

To have this man recognize this tendency in me so early in the game, and for him to express an earnest desire to help me relax, made me weep for the relief, the sanctuary, the covering, that promised to be mine in the very near future. It was a preview of the wonderful provision that God was making in this relationship to give me a refuge from my own personal storms, a respite from my tensions.

Greg could see the burden that I already carried, and he knew that added to that now was the overwhelming excitement of what God was doing in our relationship. He gave me some simple but wise counsel:

Please take time to stop and reflect and rest deeply in the Lord. I know your head is racing. God will work it out.

Then he finished the letter:

I prayed Thursday that any feelings I had for you would be inspired of God. It's too soon to tell... but I do miss you very much. I want to satisfy myself right now by saying terribly romantic things. The urge is almost overwhelming. I never dreamed that spending a day as we did could have such an incredible effect in so many areas of my life.

Meanwhile, Doug Perkins had announced to his Youth for Christ staff members that we would all be attending a Bill Gothard conference, called "Basic Youth Conflicts," in late April. It was, he said, excellent foundational teaching. The conference would be in Vancouver. I began to think that it would be a good time for Greg to come for a visit. We would have a whole week together; we would be well occupied; it would be Christ-centred. I mentioned it to Greg over the phone and followed up shortly thereafter with a letter.

Hi Greg:

I'm sending you the info on Basic Youth Conflicts, just in case you decide you can come for it. We had to send in our group registration today, but I got the address so you can write in separately if you like.

I don't really mind when you come, so long as you come soon! But the seminar would give us something to do—a good focus. If you come, then you could spend the weekend (first) with me in Victoria. I'll just leave it up to you and the Lord.

Hey—do you know why I think you should come out for that seminar? You're right-handed and I'm left-handed, so if I sat on your left we could hold hands all day and still take notes. Make sense?

I had a lot to think about on my drive home. That experience at the pool really shook me up—when it suddenly seemed that all the overwhelming feeling I had for you was gone. I was so grateful that you pointed out what you did—about how you would've felt bad if you were still "in the world" and that happened, but that knowing God, it didn't rattle you at all. You also reminded me of the prayer that I prayed in the pool.

But still it was a strange experience: it was like I suddenly saw you in a naked light, not suffused with the glow of all those rosy feelings. But you know what? I found out that, "feelings" aside, I really do <u>like</u> you! And what a relief that is.

Although the feelings did slowly warm up again while we sat in the ice-cream parlour later, I felt much more mellow and relaxed (not so intense)—also much more accepting and at peace about having to leave you again.

That night (at the Spiritual Leadership Conference) that we talked after I played the piano, you asked me if I was afraid of getting married. I *said no, but I think I lied. The experience of losing that feeling showed me one (and <u>only</u> one) area of my fears: what do you do when you wake up and the romance has worn off?*

On the way home, the Lord had much quiet time in which to speak to me. He reminded me, reassured me, of what He has slowly been getting through my thick head these past five years or so: LOVE IS PRIMARILY NOT A FEELING BUT A COMMITMENT.

And He assured me again that when I come to the place where I'm willing to <u>make a commitment</u> to someone and to then <u>build that commitment on the Rock</u>, He will sustain it. Feelings will come and go—and I thank Him that He created those feelings. But they are not what I can build on or be guided by. I have to keep building on Him and being guided by Him.

Gotta go now. Sure do miss you.

I folded the letter and stuck it inside a card that said, "I never knew what I was missing... until I met you! And now I'm missing you!"

The opening phrase from that card somehow lodged itself in my brain and stayed there until it became the theme of a new song: "I Never Knew."

I never knew what it meant to be really loved
To be really loved
Till I found you
And aside from what I have in my sweet Lord above
There's no other love
Like what I've found in you

And for once the time has come
That I don't want to turn and run
I want to learn how to love you the way you love me
And by the grace of God
And through faith in His Son
I want to make you as happy as a man can be

I never knew what it felt like to be cherished
Really cherished
The way you cherish me

I never knew what it felt like to be honoured
And I feel so honoured
The way you honour me

I never thought the time would come
I'd really trust someone
But I'll trust you and honour you as long as I live
And by the grace of God
And through faith in His Son
I want to give to you everything a woman can give

I never knew what it could mean to really know someone
For two to be as one
One in Jesus
And as we grow to know each other I just want to pray
That we'll grow every day
In Jesus

We can learn how to love
In the love of the Son
Because His love is much greater than the love in you and me
So by the grace of God
We can grow to be one
As together we discover all God meant it to be

Yes, by the grace of God
And through Jesus His Son
Together we'll discover all God meant it to be

It was very difficult to be so far apart and to have our means of getting to know one another limited most of the time to phone calls and letters. But looking back, I see the marvellous forethought of God: I believe He ordained our courtship to be long-distance partly so that it would be documented in writing. If we did not have such a wonderful relationship now, I would not be interested in sharing these letters—I would not even be interested in reading them myself. But as it is, and with my dear husband's blessing, I am happy to share our epistles.

There is one challenge in reading these letters, and that is the time line: our letters were always crossing one another in the mail, so a letter might be addressing something that the other had written up to a week earlier. Interspersed with the letters were almost nightly phone calls. The letters are, for the most part, recorded chronologically, so the reader should not expect that they flow perfectly in subject matter from one to the next.

March 14
Dear Nancy,

Good morning. I wanted to write last night but was too tired. I was feeling rather romantic and missing you. Nothing a good night's sleep can't fix. Now I feel good as new. Ha!

Actually, it's still quite early, and once I get it together, I will miss you as much as ever. I think I'll go talk to the Lord for a bit. That always helps bring things into perspective.

Well, this is somewhat frustrating. I'm speaking of this distance between us. Actually it stinks. God, give me grace and understanding. This is probably the best thing though, I think (speaking as the rational person I sometimes wish I wasn't). It definitely helps to keep things under control (physically) and allows time to sort things out. It still stinks though. I want to see you, to talk to you, to know you, now or whenever I want. I'm selfish and I don't care if I am. I want, I want, I want. I bet you didn't think I threw temper tantrums.

It's been a good week, like most. Yesterday was probably the most interesting. Eva called and arranged a meeting. She had found out about you. I hadn't told her personally, not knowing how she would receive it and being afraid of the worst. Believing that she had been told "of God" that she and I were to be together and not having it happen could be devastating to her—at least this is what I have been afraid of.

She is still quite sure about her and me. Regarding you, she believes that I'm starting to let myself come out of my shell and that I'm being healed of my past. Although she expected that this would happen (i.e., another woman), she now has to deal with it.

She doesn't believe God would put a man and a woman together in our (yours and my) circumstances. And what she says does make a lot of sense. There are probably a hundred reasons why she and I ought to get *together. So anyway, we prayed, and I agreed to give it all to God, which I did in a way that I've never done before.*

I trust my God. I must continue to rest it all in Him. It comes down to whether Eva can continue working with me. I say yes; she says she doesn't think so. Let the chips fall. She is not a spin-head, and she truly, truly does love the Lord. I respect her and her convictions.

I went out to share with my pastor, as it concerns him (because of the youth group), and besides, he is a friend. He told me of a circumstance in his past, almost identical. He, appointed youth leader, worked with a gal who played piano: she had dreams and visions; he had nothing. She <u>knew</u>; God never said the same to him.

Anyway, he ended up not marrying her, and they continued working together. His telling me this helped me tremendously. At least I'm sure now that I'm not being rebellious against God.

God will continue to deal with me, directly and not through someone else. I rest in You, Lord.

Regarding the "prophetic word" that Eva's friend had given her: This is potentially a dangerous practice, to presume to speak "the Word of the Lord" into someone else's life. I am a hearty supporter of the prophetic ministry, but the prophet should never presume to direct the course of another person's life.

The safest thing for the recipient to do is to hold that word in his or her heart (not trying to bring it to pass) and allow God to direct further in other ways (through His Word, His peace, and the working out of circumstances). Later, that prophetic word may become a confirmation, after the fact, as other things continue to line up (if they do), and this in turn will be the assurance that this word truly was from God. The prophetic word should never be considered the primary leading.

New in the Lord though Greg was, thankfully he had the wisdom to trust that God would lead him personally.

Sometime in March, Doug Perkins called me into his office. "Your support level has started to drop off. You'd better mention it in your next prayer letter."

I had never yet asked my "prayer partners" for money. In the beginning, as YFC's secretary, I had received a salary from the general fund. Then when Doug asked me to officially become Youth Guidance staff, he had laughed and said, "The *bad* news is that now you get to raise your own support." He asked me to get together an address list of possible prayer partners, and he sent them a letter explaining how he had come to recognize that I should be working with these troubled teens. He explained also in the letter that I would be receiving my salary "by faith."

Believing that this change in my job description (from secretary to youth worker) was God's will for me, I asked Him to confirm His leading by providing finances. His answer was immediate and gracious: although I myself never mentioned money in a newsletter, from the outset there was not a single month when my entire salary did not come in. Sometimes it came in dribbles; sometimes in gushes: either way, I went home with a full paycheque every month.

Now with Doug's request, I agonized over the wording of a letter. I just couldn't bring myself to tell these friends that I needed money. Then I remembered something I had prayed at the beginning of my Youth Guidance ministry: "I will never ask for money, Lord. If my support ever drops off, I will simply question whether You still want me here."

And so I tore up my wretched efforts at a rough draft and wrote the usual fare: an exciting story about something God was doing in a kid's life. I closed the letter with this paragraph:

> I would covet your prayers for the whole direction of my work with Youth for Christ. It's a time when God is shaking everything that can be shaken. He is teaching me to loosen my grasp on everything in my life that is comfortable and predictable, and to cleave only to Him, that I might hear His voice saying, "This is the way, walk ye in it." I feel a need to reassess, to confirm, that I am still doing the things, and only the things, that *He* has called me to do—because I am
>
> His servant,
> Nancy

At the end of March, my paycheque was short of the full amount for the first time. It made me nervous. I got on my knees beside my bed that evening and told God all about it. While I was still praying, the phone rang. It was the head of the finance committee of my church. For over two and a half years, they had maintained their pledge to provide fifty percent of my salary. My heart leapt. God was answering already!

"Nancy," this man said, "we are in a difficult financial time at the church. I'm sorry, but we have decided that we have to cut your support back by two hundred dollars a month."

"Praise the Lord," I said, with a confidence I didn't feel. "I was just praying about my salary. This must be God's answer."

Once I hung up the phone, I thought, *This can't be a coincidence. This must be God's answer. It's just not the answer I was expecting.* And then another thought came to me: *If I'm getting married, then I would be leaving my job and moving away. I wouldn't need my support anymore. Wow!*

March 12
Dear Greg,

It's hard to know what's going on. It's frustrating having you so far away—I want to be getting to know you in a steady, normal way.

I was so bugged at the Terry Talbot concert last night, being out with other people. Seemed like you should've been there with me. Went for coffee with friends later, but I was irritated with everyone (not outwardly) and couldn't get home soon enough. If I can't be with you, I'd rather not be with anyone—socially. I miss you less when I'm alone. I don't think that makes sense, but it's true.

Last night I spoke for the Women's Aglow banquet. Afterward I was flying high, but then the enemy laid a bum trip on me. I guess I knew it was him, but I was so drained from the ministry that I couldn't fight back. It had to do with you and it really upset me. Barb prayed for me when I got home but it didn't really lift till sometime later. Such joy and relief and clarity when it lifted. I'll tell you all about it sometime if you'll <u>just come and see me.</u>

I had flippantly said to Greg on the phone one night that I was nervous about our relationship. I suppose that if I had taken the time to articulate my feelings, I would have said that I was afraid of it moving forward into marriage—and even more afraid of it not. The night of Women's Aglow, all those fears precipitated.

Lorna Smith had driven in from Sooke for the Aglow banquet. I only had a brief moment to speak with her at the beginning of the evening. She asked me how it was going with Greg. (Of course, she had heard all about him.) I said that it was going fine, but that I was really scared: I could sense that the time was rapidly approaching, I said, when I would have to make a commitment to Greg, and I was afraid of that commitment, even though it was what I wanted.

She furrowed her brow and said, "You shouldn't be scared."

I had no time to think about it then, but once the meeting was over and I was packing up and heading home, her words and her facial expression came back to me. Why had she said that? She must mean that if this relationship were really ordained of God, there would be no fear. I deeply respected her discernment. If this was what she thought, if this was not God's will... I couldn't bear the thought. My mind was suddenly running away with panic now, fearful that I was mistaken about Greg and that I would have to give him up. I was in an awful state by the time I got home, and even though Barb prayed for me, I found no relief.

At length, even though it was very late and I was sure that Lorna would have retired, I phoned her. As soon as I heard her voice, I began to weep, blurting out my tortured thoughts between sobs. She was quick to reassure me.

"I only meant," she said, "that God doesn't want you to be afraid."

Then she prayed for me, and the sweet peace of God enveloped me again. Of course! How silly of me to be tricked like that. It was a time for joy, and the enemy was just trying to rob me.

My letter continues:

Greg, remember last week on the phone when I said I had a real peace and patience about waiting to see you again? Well, that is definitely no longer the case. That's the main reason I'm lying awake again tonight—I'm totally agitated. Well, I've finished my warm milk and cookies—going to try to sleep again. Please make it soon, Greg. I want to talk to you face to face again.

I sure am missing you. It almost makes me angry to sit here and write you another letter when I know you won't even get it till the middle of next week. Just got your last letter today. Thank you. I read them over and over.

There's been a lot happening in my heart and in my mind. You won't hear me saying anymore that I'm scared of this relationship. It was just a cute (though true) thing to say, but it seems that it wedged me open to a whole pile of fears that were certainly not from God. It's been good in the long run, because I've had to face some hard issues, but I want faith and trust—not fear—to be my motivation.

You're talking about being set free from some things in your past. I've been going through some healing too. Last night I sat up late talking to Barb. I wanted to talk about some of these fears. I found myself relating details out of a painful time, issues I thought were long buried. (I have so much I want to talk to you about.) I shed some tears over some things I thought I no longer had any feeling for. Barb prayed for me—she's very gifted in the area of inner healing. Neat lady to have around at a time like this.

When I came home from that Women's Aglow meeting all bent out of shape with fears about my relationship with Greg, there was more troubling me than what I thought Lorna was implying. As I talked to Barb about my fear of committing myself to marriage, I found myself suddenly blurting out, "What if I give my whole heart to this guy and then he goes and dies on me? What then? What will happen to me then?" And I began to cry.

It was suddenly obvious to me what this was about. Seven years before, when I was still living a heathen, hedonistic life, I was involved in a relationship that was cut short by an accident. I had the traumatic experience of seeing my boyfriend, Derrick, crash his hang glider and then die a day and a half later in hospital.

Although this was a very difficult time for me, the pain did not go as deep as it might have. Because there was no sense of God in my life, I was without solid principles to live by. Commitment and marriage were not even considerations back then. Life was for the moment. Living with a partner was one thing; to ever burden one another with notions of future expectations was quite another. I believe that because of my lack of serious intent in that relationship, I was shielded from the full impact of bereavement. If I had already come to the point of making a lifetime commitment to this young man, my loss would have been much greater. As it was, there was a deeper part of my heart that had never before made itself vulnerable.

Now I could sense very clearly that God intended for me to give over to Greg every last part of my heart. To refuse to make myself completely vulnerable in this way would be to cut myself off from some of the potential joy. We can only know joy to the degree that we are willing to risk sorrow. We can only know love to the degree that we are prepared to risk bereavement or betrayal.

I was terrified of this risk. The loss of this boyfriend seven years earlier had proven to me that things like this don't just happen to other people; they can happen to me. So, long before I would finally call Lorna that night to find reassurance about what her words had meant, I had to deal with this fear of commitment, which was really a fear of losing the person that I might commit to.

It was wonderful that God had ordained for me to live under the same roof as a woman who carried on a quiet, unofficial, and unpretentious little ministry in inner healing. Barb helped me that night to pull out the stops and trust God with whatever He, in His unfathomable wisdom and purpose, might choose to bring my way. She prayed with me for the healing of those old wounds, and I willingly opened up my heart and got ready to give it all away.

Lots of Letters

March 15
Dear Nancy:

God bless you! Oh, how I have been finding out that the blessing is in the giving and not the receiving. The old cliché "It is better to give than to receive" has taken on an entirely different meaning. No longer is love just an emotional high or a warm feeling. The Spirit of God within me wells up in unspeakable joy. Totally different from anything I've experienced in the past. Maybe one day I will be able to understand and express the love that I feel in my heart.

Well, where are you these days? I've had a little time in thought. What I feel for you, I could feel for many others. Why you? Of course there are several admirable things about you and some that I am specifically, romantically attracted to. But why you? Whatever my silly, analytical mind comes up with, so what! It's you and you only that matters. My heart misses you. I have a sense of part of me "missing." Is this too romantic or revealing at this stage of the game?

Greg and I talked on the phone almost every night. He confided in me something that he had told the Lord back in Banff at the conference where we'd met. A bunch of us had gone for a swim and a Jacuzzi on the second evening of the conference. He said he'd watched me climb out of the hot tub. "I was looking up at those long legs, and I said, 'Lord, I want one like that.'"

I was pleased.

During another phone call, he said to me affectionately, "I was thinking about you today."

"Were you?" I answered happily.

"Yes, I was taking off your bathing suit."

This time the response was anger, and it came fast and hard, surprising even me. "Don't you dare lust after me!"

I can in no way recall how Greg responded to my outburst. But I do remember the feelings that fuelled my anger. I wanted this relationship to be different—it *was* different, from anything I had ever experienced before. This relationship was a gift from God, and to have Greg express what to me seemed a lusty thought threatened to sully the beauty and holiness of what God was giving to us.

Make no mistake about it: If Greg had not been sexually attracted to me, I would have been disappointed. That's putting it mildly—I would have been devastated. But...but I...I didn't want him to express it. Or at least not so blatantly. Oh, I don't know *how* I wanted him to respond.

This was the first hint of the difficulty that I was going to experience in reconciling the earthiness of sex with the holiness of God. God, however, has no problem with this juxtaposition. It was a holy God Who created sex. I now believe that He takes great delight in this act, enjoyed within the boundaries He has set; and I think it is one of the most amazing and complex things that He has come up with.

But back then, it was confusing. Years earlier, as an unbeliever, I had partaken freely of anything I'd wanted in the area of sex. Then as a new Christian, sex had become a paramount temptation that continually threatened to pull me away from God's perfect will. Now finding myself smack in the middle of courtship, I had no positive frame of reference in which to set my sexuality or Greg's. Holy sex was, at best, an ethereal ideal at this point. At worst, it was an oxymoron.

March 16
Dear Nancy,

A most fond "hello." Oh, for a better and more meaningful way to greet you. Try to imagine me speaking to you in person, with no one around, and about twenty minutes to say hello. Only twenty minutes now. Now, let's go for coffee and catch up... "Yes, miss, espresso, please. Two? Yes, two... Take my hand. Ah! That's better. "

No matter what my imagination does, there is no substitute. Sometimes it only aggravates the sense of separation that I feel. That, though, can be good. Some of my lows are my highest highs.

"Missing you so intensely," says Greg now, "meant that I had something worth missing—and that was wonderful."

It's grand to know that I can feel and that it doesn't matter how I feel. Feelings are a blessing of God. I can only praise God that I am not controlled by them. They come and go. I asked the Lord to be in my feelings concerning you. He knows exactly where I am.

I am going to share something with you that I would only share with you. Not that I could share it with anyone else. But here is a part of me that no one else sees:

What I feel intensely at any one time does not mean that I love you. <u>Sharing</u> that feeling—or rather, feeling free to share it—does. As I share my highs and lows, I want to believe that they don't scare you off or necessarily draw you closer. I am not keeping—and I refuse to keep—anything from you. I pray God: I want always to show you all of the inner me. This is not "baring all," but I don't want to hide anything from you. I want honesty. If some things do scare you off, praise God; if not, praise God. I want to be free to feel when I'm with you or corresponding. Not necessarily to react to those feelings—just free to feel. I guess that's the part that I want to be separated to you.

Writing this is helping me to bring together what has been a somewhat confused mass in my head. Psychoanalytical maybe, but it helps me to understand why part of me seeks a companion. To share this with you does not put me in a place that makes me feel too vulnerable. I count it joy to be able to share. Anyway, thanks for listening. More on this as it develops.

"I wanted to be free to be myself when I was with you," he says now, "with no fear of being judged or condemned. I was comfortable in God, secure in His love, and now I was finding that I was comfortable and secure in the same way with you."

If I were to write every time I think of you, I would have nothing to say. Although I want to share my thoughts with you, you're just an image in the semi-conscious part of my mind, constantly there, but neither directing my life nor affecting it. I want to tell people about you, and often do, but I don't think they really care. At least not as much as I would like them to. I want them to feel what I feel. They can't. These are _my_ feelings. I guess I'm frustrated, huh?

March 20
My dear Greg:

I've had two dreams about you coming to visit in the last couple of nights, and both times you forgot to hug me when you arrived. It was so anticlimactic; I felt very let down. Perhaps the Lord is revealing another deep-seated fear! Would you be so good as to make a note of this? Maybe just a little memo to yourself that you could pack around with my pictures: "*N.B.—DON'T FORGET TO HUG NANCY WHEN YOU SEE HER AGAIN." Thanks very much—you are so considerate.

I meant to ask you on the phone last night how your cold is doing. You sounded fine. But I woke up all stuffy this morning. That's your fault—for trying to kiss me over the phone. Next time I'll just keep talking.

It was great to talk to you again last night. Do you know—I just love the sound of your voice. I could listen to you for hours. And although it is frustrating (as we were saying) to get to know each other over the phone, I _am_ getting to know you. Even last night I felt more comfortable and "at home" with you than before. Not that I ever felt _uncomfortable_ with you. I want to know you more and more. It seems like I could go on forever getting to know you and never get tired of it.

Another beautiful day. I've come home from church and have had lunch. Now I've got the "après dejeuner" groggies: I'm trying to get a couple of pages off to you before giving in to an afternoon nap. I nearly always nap Sunday afternoon. It's a time I'm very jealous of—I often will go for lunch with friends after church, but then I like to hog the rest of the afternoon just to me and my Lord. Whether asleep or awake, it's a pleasant time to rest in Him.

God really spoke to me through the sermon this morning. Part of it was Mark 4:26–29. In this relationship I go through phases of being like an impatient farmer who wants to dig up the seed and see if it's sprouting yet. I know it's good seed and good ground—and I know the Lord is sending both rain and sun. I need to just go quietly about my business and let my Lord take care of the increase. When the harvest is ripe, it will be obvious. Meanwhile, there are other chores to be done.

When I'm at peace and in close communion with the Lord is when I feel the most peace about you. (That's a good sign!) Right now the peace is so full and warm, it's like basking in the sun: the love of the Lord together with my feelings for you.

Wish I could have a hug right now.

Love,
Nancy

March 21
Dear Nancy,

God bless you. I praise the Lord that we know Him. He always helps us to keep things in perspective, and He knows just how we are feeling. It certainly makes the distance between us easier to bear.

Today I'm lonely. I haven't felt this way since I don't know when. I seem to be in a world of my own. I know that all that's happening to me right now is building me. My life in the past two or three years has been one of many new and exciting experiences. I have been very much single, to come and go as I please. Although I don't know the future, I get excited knowing that my God is leading. He is looking after my highest good. All this fancy-free living seems to be coming to a stop. Nothing in particular gives indication; everything, in every particular, does.

You know, you make a good diary.

I seem to be lost, somewhat. Maybe this describes my day better than loneliness. The circumstances I find myself in are somewhat alien to me. I know that I have to start setting specific direction. God, guide me. I must set goals and work toward them. God, help me set big goals. Put the stretch on me. I have confidence knowing that He is my strength.

Nancy, I want to tell you "I love you." I mentioned this earlier (in the phone call). In past experience, I've found that I've said this too easily, however sincerely. I don't know what girls think when this is said to them. Since coming to the Lord, I've become afraid to say this to anyone, for fear of misinterpretation.

When I have said this, I have not meant, "I will be yours forevermore." That is a decision, a commitment. What I *was* saying (back then), and what I want to say to you now, is, "I'm in love with you," "I long to be with you," "Thoughts of you thrill my heart."

Because I say this or want to say this to you, am I being selfish? Am I going beyond my limits? Is this an area where I have to practise self-control? I know that this aspect of love is "blind" to rationale, but so what? I think it is a necessary part of what God intends in a relationship.

I'm sitting across from the airport right now. I feel like jumping on a plane—to anywhere. Not that I want to escape, even though I'm feeling somewhat out of control. I'm just going through a phase-change—unfamiliar territory. I feel excited and impulsive. Praise the Lord. Do I ever love this experience!

I pray God that He starts to bring some things together concerning you and me. That doesn't mean things will change, or at least not to my satisfaction. As a matter of fact, I don't know specifically what I want it to change to. There is so much involved: distance, work, commitments, emotions, direction. I do know what I would like right now, and that is to have you near, and to know you and have you know me in every way possible. You can't always get what you want—just what God says is good for you.

Don't you just love to grow and learn? Maybe one day I will write a letter you can understand without having to decipher words and thoughts. When I get one, I'll send it to you.

Thanks for listening.

Love you much (may I?) and miss you dearly.

Greg

March 21
Dear Greg,

Another letter was waiting for me when I got home from work today. I had run upstairs to check the mail slot, holding my breath and pretending I could stand it if there was nothing there. Praying for strength in case there wasn't.

Went down to my room and made myself pray for fifteen minutes before I opened it. (Such a legalist!) Actually, I was a bit tired and speedy from the day, and I wanted to unwind before the Lord—let Him rest me so that I could enjoy your letter more. I don't know if that's why it blew me away so much—but, oh, Greg—it sure did. After a couple of lines, I had to grab my head and pray some more—it was so powerful. Cried a bit, then read on.

Seems every letter I write, I'm talking about crying again. It's something I do easily—maybe I could teach you something in that department.

Obviously this is the letter about "feelings" you were referring to Saturday night on the phone.

Sometimes in my more insane moments, I thank the Lord that you're so far away. There's something unspeakably precious about getting to know you this way... or is that just a cheap rationalization, translated "beggars can't be choosers"?!

I was so delighted with your letter that I roared around, cleaned up my whole suite, did some laundry, and decided to take myself out for dinner. I'm my favourite date in your absence.

That's where I am now, having a coffee while deciding what I want to eat. It's already 8:30 P.M.

It was either last night or this morning in chatting with the Lord that I was impressed with something about time—as it pertains to our relationship. In the Lord there is no time—He created it and is Lord of it. Now how did it go...? It started with the scripture coming to mind, "Be anxious for nothing...."[1] He showed me that I've been dealing with two opposite kinds of anxiety: one, fear (of things with you moving ahead too quickly); the other, impatience (about things moving too slowly). Both portray a lack of faith and trust in God's timing. Both are mutually incompatible with faith.

Hey, I'm getting blessed just writing this down! Either that or buzzed from the caffeine.

Anyhow, this is not the first I've mentioned this subject to you. But the understanding (and spiritual implication) is getting fuller.

Hey, Greg—while I think of it—please don't throw away any of my letters. I think I'm going to write a book sometime, and they could be valuable as an outline or catalyst of thought. I'm at least three-quarters serious. In fact, I've already written the first chapter.

Here I lapsed into a long digression about what had happened at Juvie that day. Then:

Well, I should finish this off and head home. This caffeine stuff makes me as verbose on paper as in person. This has been almost as much fun as really having dinner with you. Except—I guess I have to pick up the tab. Hey, it's okay—this one's on me!

Much love,
Nancy

On the return train trip from Banff after first meeting Greg, I had begun writing the story of how I met him. I finished it within a week of getting home. It was this epistle that I was referring to in the letter above as "the first chapter." It has become the first and second chapters of Part 2 of this book.

Now, given all that he had said about sharing freely, in his letter of March 16, I decided to send him my version of how we met, explaining that I hadn't had him in mind as the audience when I wrote it. "If I had," I clarified in the cover letter, "I probably would have omitted some things, fearing I would be saying too much."

The cover letter goes on:

You talked about this kind of thing in that last letter on "feelings," about how you want to believe that regardless of what you share of your inner self, I would neither be scared off nor drawn closer simply by what was shared. (What is drawing me closer to you is not so much what you have shared but the fact that you have shared it: that you've been willing to open yourself to me.)

So in wanting to send you this story, I found I was facing the same thing, not wanting to say "too much." But this was not written with any manipulative intent—I never even thought about you reading it. I just wanted to record what happened from my point of view—as well as some of my thoughts that were going on at the time—just because it seemed important to remember.

A note about the love song in the story—the one I sang you that last night in Banff—hey, Greg—it's your song—even though it was written a year and a half before I met you. It was a fantasy song, written after briefly meeting a fellow whom I never got to know. In appearance he was very much like the heathen doctor that I "fell in love with" five years ago. My mind spun itself a tale about getting to know this second guy—and so the song was written. For some reason, it was at that point that the hold the first guy had on my emotions was broken. It was as though I recognized that if I could now fall into such an infatuation just because some-

one <u>looked</u> like someone else, it probably indicated that there was about as much substance in the one "relationship" as in the other—which was no substance at all.

So my mind was freed from both of them. But I still liked the song and was sorry there was no reality behind it, therefore no reason to sing it—except to myself. Singing it that night in Banff for you was the first time I sang it <u>to</u> somebody—not that I intended to sing it to <u>you</u>. It was just a song that I thought of singing—then Corinne left—then I had that brief conversation with the Lord on the piano bench—and so it went.

So by the end of the song, I <u>was</u> singing it to you, and pretending (both to you and to myself) that I wasn't. Oh, "the heart is desperately wicked and deceitful above all things, and who can know it?"![2]

But how obnoxious! to sit there and sing to you: "I loved that man, and now I think I love you," and "How would you feel if I came to you and offered you my heart?" (Hey, Greg, how <u>would</u> you feel?)

A little later, mid-afternoon now: Having a coffee on the way home from work. Tonight is floor-hockey night at Juvie, but I won't be playing: my back is still sore from last week's game. Must've pulled a muscle. I think it's turning thirty that's done it to me. So I'll just ref tonight.

I dreamt about you all night again last night. Kept waking up and going back to sleep—hard to tell what was real and what was dream. It seemed like you were really there.

Of all the dreams I've had of you, there's never been anything lusty. This is a great blessing, because many times Satan has tried to work at my mind through off-colour dreams. Lust hasn't been an easy area since coming to know the Lord (I guess 'cause it was too <u>easy</u> an area before—pun intended). I've learned many hard lessons and been deceived too much. One hard thing was arguing with the Lord about my feelings: "But Lord, it's not lust—it's real, genuine affection." Then one time He showed me a verse in Galatians 6: "They that are Christ's have crucified the flesh with its affections and lusts." "Oh, God," I screamed inside, "how could You possibly put <u>both</u> those words in the same sentence!" And I went on to learn—the hard way—that a seemingly pure, sweet affection can very much be of the flesh ("inordinate affection" is spoken of many times in the Word) and that as such it reeks as much of death as does lust.

An aside to the reader: Contrary to what I wrote in that last parenthetical statement, I realize now that there is actually only one reference in the Word to "inordinate affection."[3] Evidently I had *noticed* it *many* times!

Just to clarify myself to you—I don't believe that what I feel for you is of the flesh. Yes, it's physical (praise God!), but I believe it's inspired of God, because I went to the Cross with it immediately at the beginning: i.e., offered it up to death. And I believe He is raising it up now. Hey: resurrection love!

Back to the dream: Aside from just a memory of you being there, a feeling that permeated the whole dream, there's one part that I remember clearly. You were lounged in a big chair. I was standing in front of you in my dressing gown—I'd been lying down because I wasn't feeling well. (That part was real—I actually woke up half an hour later quite sick.) So I was telling you that I was feeling ill, and I said, "Do I look really pale and sick?"

You gave me a big grin and said, "No, as a matter of fact you look beautiful."

I laughed and said, "Actually, I was just cruisin' for a compliment."

It was so real—sounded just like something I'd really say!

Whereas often these all-night dreams make me more frustrated at your absence, not so this time. I seem to be returning to a state of peace and patience again. Maybe I really can wait till the end of April to see you again.

Love,
Nancy

A letter dated March 22 talks at length about Greg's new job opportunity, managing a mini-mall. Then it continues in the usual spiritual and personal vein:

God is growing me again today. I look forward with great anticipation to the coming months. All heaven is going to break loose, praise the Lord.

But you've got your life and I've got mine. It seems as though we are worlds apart. Here I go again. Please, Lord, do something divine and supernatural. Get us together somehow. (That's the first time I've prayed that.)

I've never been able to set up something with you in my head, nor have I tried. And now that this job is coming up, things look less bright concerning my "hop-a-plane" lifestyle. I'm not too concerned yet though. Too many other things happening that keep me from dwelling upon a rendezvous with the love of my life. Although I dearly want to be with you, I can't even conceive a definite "coming together." I trust that God's got perfect timing and that He will reveal it to me. In the meantime, my heart aches with uncertainty. This is a period to learn. Lord, help me keep my emotions in line so that I can hear You.

It's time to quit. I can't even build a sentence. Getting late.

To my love, good night.
gc xo

March 24
Dear Greg:

I'm tired. Sitting up in bed—don't know how long I'll last. This is getting too unreal again. I need to talk to you in person. Sometimes I think I understand what you say; sometimes I don't think I understand at all. I want to talk to you; I want to be able to bounce things off you, to say, "Is this what you mean?" or "What are you saying here?"

No, I'm not going to say "I love you" in a letter—if I tell you that, I want to tell you to your face.

I told God (and it was only three weeks before I met you) that I never, ever, ever want to be in a dead-end relationship again. I've had enough of the kind of relationships that had a whole bunch of emotions and nothing else: relationships where a lot of warm feelings blotted out the Truth, conveniently muting God's voice so that one could enjoy the pleasures of sin for a season. In doing so, one is drawn into a deception which by its own nature is so deceptive that the deceived doesn't even know she's being deceived until God in His mercy shines His light into the darkness and in His grace gives her the guts to embrace the light and go back to the Cross.

Those kinds of "gardens" come up weeds for a long, long time, and digging out the roots is a painful thing. God can bring glory out of anything—granted: only He could have thought of using manure to grow beautiful flowers.

But there's the hard way where you get broken and nearly crushed in your pig-headedness and then God does a miracle as you repent...

Or you can do it God's way from the beginning: obedience—the <u>easy</u> way.

God can do anything He wants with me—He can break me again and again if He sees fit and I'll still praise Him. He can destroy me if He wants and I'll still love Him and trust Him.

I was thinking here of Job, how he said of God, "Though He slay me, yet shall I trust Him."[4] I wanted to be spiritual and to respond like Job no matter what God might require of me. Really though, don't we have to come to this level of trust, in every area of our lives, eventually?

The letter continues:

But for my own part, I never want to find again that I've gone my own way and caused untold pain for myself and someone else.

Oh, Greg—I care so very much about you. This is different from anything I've heard myself talk about before. (I am remembering what I have said to others in the past…)

I suddenly have no confidence in my ability to love God's way. I want Him to teach me how to love you—really love you. I want all or nothing—I don't want to play any games. I've played games all my life, especially before I knew the Lord. Sometimes I hold back on saying things to you because they've been said before and have lost their power. Same with little gestures of affection—they've all been done before (to others) and have lost their specialness. I want to refrain from expressing what I feel for you until somehow it's real and old things are blotted out.

Already my ungodly past was rearing its ugly head and leering with a malicious eye on my hopes for wedded bliss. I now realized that what I had known of relationship and love and sex "in the world" was a far cry from the way God designed things to be. There was a line being drawn between two perspectives, a tension between two powers in my life: on the one side, guilt and despair—that I had perhaps unwittingly and permanently ruined something unspeakably precious, and on the other, faith and hope—that God, in His great love and power, could restore anything.

I began to pray that God would wipe out all of the old notions and teach me everything that He ever intended love and romance to be.

It would be a long time before God could completely let the old things pass away in this area of my life and allow all things to become new.[5] Yes, by faith, at salvation, old things pass away, but when we then continue in the old carnal ways (or just stumble into them now and then) after receiving the knowledge of the Truth, we deeply wound ourselves. We also further empower the old nature, which is supposed to be dead, and thus we keep binding ourselves to our old sins, even though God is wanting to remove them from us, "as far as the east is from the west."[6]

The letter continues:

My dear Greg—I hope you can understand what I'm trying to say better than I can—because I haven't got a clue what I'm feeling or why.

If you were here right now, I'd probably say some angry things (though I'm not angry at you) then I'd put my arms around you and hang on to you till I felt better.

I feel a lot of pain right now, and I feel like crying. Oh, God—what are you doing in me now?

Yes, Greg, I love you, and I'm so happy that you love me.

Greg's response to my little meltdown came after the usual postal delay.

Well, doll, how was your day? I received two of your letters today. Now, don't do anything rash. By the sounds of it, you feel pretty much the way I do. If you must express yourself (frustration), scream. It's not ladylike to swear. Let me do that.

I don't know how you are feeling or thinking today. This writing is for the birds. The girl I relate to is hardly more than a figment of my imagination.

I might as well not dwell on my frustration.

March 24
Dear Nancy,

Hello!!! I just can't say it well enough with pen and paper, but I trust that you get my drift. I know: XOXOXOXOXOXOXOXO...! Ah, that's better.

Well, Eva seems to be happier than ever, thank God. The Lord is doing tremendous things for her. I sometimes think that the inner healing was needed by her and not me. I don't know though if she's coming or going with regards to me. I pray that she is set free. We are working together better now than ever. Lord, show me where she's at. I pray that she is not building up for a fall.

Nancy. Do I dare ask? Or is it too early? Oh, go for it.

Lord, what is the next step? I'm trying not to make plans, but my feelings toward Nancy are not dwindling, so can I assume that we will be seeing more of each other on a regular basis? I know this is what I want. How much of my desire is Your desire, Lord? I hope it's all You and that things are happening to bring us together somehow. I pray my wants are Your wants, 'cause I know what I want.

I somehow get the idea that all this good feeling is sinful (old concept—like, if it feels this good, it must be wrong). I'm speaking of my own desire to have you near. I guess that idea is just a defence mechanism—I want to protect myself from being hurt. Am I confusing you?

Winter keeps dragging on here—more so now than in January and February. When spring comes though, it will happen in a hurry. God is God.

Part of me is missing.

It seemed to me that Greg was speaking of the season both literally and metaphorically. There is a passage in the "Song of Songs" that very much speaks to this metaphor:

> My beloved responded and said to me,
> Arise, my darling, my beautiful one,
> And come along.
> For behold, the winter is past,
> The rain is over and gone.
> The flowers have already appeared in the land;
> The time has arrived for pruning the vines,

And the voice of the turtledove has been heard in our land.
The fig tree has ripened its figs,
And the vines in blossom have given forth their fragrance.
Arise, my darling, my beautiful one,
And come along!

Song of Solomon 2:11–13 (NAS)

"When spring comes, it will happen in a hurry," Greg had said. I have learned something about the seasons of our dreams and desires: If it is not God's time, then even though you try as hard as you like to make something happen, it will be about as productive as banging your head on a brick wall. But when God says, "It's time," you'd better get out of the way, because it's going to happen so fast it'll make your head spin.

I think we both had the sense that God was moving, and that He was moving swiftly.

Needs and Expectations

Sunday, March 27
Dear Greg,

    Good afternoon, sweetheart. Here is a song I wrote last night just before bed—I was going to write you and was too restless. Didn't have anything new to say anyway. This was a song that came quickly—probably completed within fifteen or twenty minutes with music and all. It's a really pretty tune.

As I lay me down to sleep
My thoughts drift toward my lover
I pray, Lord, in Your hands him You would keep
And with your soft love cover
And Lord, if You'd awake him for just one minute
(As I'm sure he's long since retired)
Put into his mind just one small hint
Of my thoughts—my desire

I've written him 'most every night
Till I can write no more
It's hard with him so far from sight
Him whom my soul longs for
And Lord, if he's lying awake right now
Let him think of me awhile
And Lord—if we might see each other soon somehow
So I could hear him—and see his smile

But Lord, I trust Your perfect time
In peace I rest in You

*I'll neither rush ahead nor lag behind
As I'm so prone to do
Lord, I believe that You've brought us together
And I trust whatever You do
And Lord, if You've designed this to be forever
Only let it be in You
Only let it be in You*

It's actually time for my Sunday afternoon nap right now, but I'm waiting for a cake to come out of the oven first. Had some milk go sour, and that's good for chocolate cake. I'll try to eat the whole thing before my nap. Hey—do you know that I overeat when I'm lonely?! You'd better come to visit soon or you may not recognize me!

The Lord continues to do many deep things. Today in church I was greeted by an intense friend-in-the-Lord: Kim. He shows up about every six months with no warning. Last I heard from him was sometime in December when he phoned me at 3:00 A.M. one morning (collect!) just to say he was in prayer for me and the Holy Spirit had told him to phone. Proceeded to tell me exactly where I was at in the Lord concerning several things (he was right on), gave me some fast counsel, assured me of his love and prayers, and said good-bye. It was at a time of crisis both in my job and with Philip.

(Excuse me—care for some hot chocolate cake with ice cream?—GOOD!)

Anyway—today it seemed he greeted me with a warmer hug than usual. I was thinking, "Okay, Lord, what have You got on the agenda today?"

Kim asked, "What's new?" and I said, "I'm in love," and told him a bit about you. He was pleased—liked the sound of it. Then he said, "Hey, I'm in love too—God's put me together with a beautiful woman in Prince Rupert." I was delighted for him and also for the greater freedom it gave me to fellowship with him.

And fellowship we did. Went for lunch after church and God spoke to me through him so much. Talked about the feelings that had come out of his new relationship (on both sides): quite unexpected anger, hurt, withdrawal, and rejection, as God began to heal many things in both parties.

We talked about how these old (unrecognized) hurts come up as a bar-

rier between our heart and the other person's love, causing us to seem to turn away from the very thing we want the most.

I thought I was going to break and completely shatter in the middle of the restaurant. Kept having to ask him to slow down and let up; I only had one small piece of Kleenex in my purse, so I didn't want to let go. So every time he saw my eyes fill up with tears, he'd back off a bit, but the Word went forth and will prosper as I get alone with the Lord now.

Talking to Kim, I could finally understand where my last letter to you came from—the one that was so angry. I was really reacting to some things you had said...

Yeah, this growing is good.

During that lunch with Kim, he shared with me that he could not marry his new love yet, because she had been married before and was not yet legally divorced. But, he said, they had made the mistake of already sleeping together, and now they couldn't undo that step. He urged me not to make the same mistake. "Be obedient," he implored me. "Do it God's way."

Spending some time with the Lord on March 28, I jotted some disjointed thoughts and prayers on a yellow legal pad:

God, I pray that whatever is happening in Greg through the different things I am writing, whatever things are being stirred up: joys, hurts, fears, hopes—that he can and will receive them as from Your hand, not as isolated and hard-to-understand emotions, but as evidence, in part, of the deeper work You are doing in him. I only pray this because I've begun to see the deeper implication of what is happening in me—and I want to receive it as from Your hand, Lord, that I might always grow through this...

Lord—help me to keep Your vision in mind, not to let it be obscured by the push of my own selfish needs and expectations.

Lord—help me to distinguish between <u>faith</u> imparted by Your Spirit (regarding this relationship) and <u>presumption</u> that tries to grow out of my needs and expectations.

Lord—there is something here that is born of the Spirit. Don't let it be trampled by what is born of the flesh: i.e., my needs and expectations.
Oh, GOD: crucify my NEEDS and EXPECTATIONS!
"God is the Lord, which hath shewed us light: BIND THE SACRIFICE WITH CORDS, EVEN UNTO THE HORNS OF THE ALTAR" (Psalm 118:27, KJV).

I sent the notes off to Greg. A couple of days later, I wrote a letter that explained the notes more fully:

March 30
Dear Greg,

Came home from work just now and found another letter waiting. This time I prayed again for God to speak through the letter—to use it to stir up anything He wants—and to make me grow. Seems when I do that the letters are great and don't cause painful or mixed feelings... In the last letter, I mentioned a scripture: Psalm 118. God gave it to me when I was spending some time with Him before you called Monday. Here is why it ministered to me...

I was seeing how these "needs and expectations" were taking hold of my heart and moving me away from the peace of God's perfect love. I had ended up on the floor feeling like I was on the altar—on my back—asking God to cut these things out quickly before they got firmer hold. Moments later, reading the Word, this scripture (Psalm 118) hit.

It ties in with a part in a book I finished reading a few days ago: <u>Hinds' Feet on High Places</u> (Hannah Hurnard). Today I looked up this passage again. What a ringer!

It's in the chapter called "Grave on the Mountains": "She put out her hand and with one final effort of failing strength, grasped the natural human love and desire growing in her heart and struggled to tear them out. At the first touch it was as though anguish pierced through her..., and she knew... that the roots had wound and twined and thrust themselves into every part of her being."

The priest comes from behind the altar—offers to take it out for her. Then she says this:

"'I am afraid that the pain may cause me to try to resist you. Will you <u>bind me to the altar</u> in some way so that I cannot move? I would not like to be found struggling while the will of my Lord is done.'

> *"The priest put forth a hand of steel, right into her heart. There was a sound of rending and tearing, and the human love, with all its myriad rootlets and fibres, came forth.... He cast it down on the altar....*
>
> *"Nothing but ashes remained, either of the love itself, which had been so deeply planted in her heart, or of the suffering and sorrow which had been her companions.... A sense of overwhelming rest and peace engulfed Much-Afraid."*[1]
>
> *This is one of the final incidents in the story of how Much-Afraid, with her companions, Sorrow and Suffering, journeys from the Valley of Humiliation to the High Places—where the Great Shepherd replaces the plant of Longing-to-be-Loved (which has been rooted in her heart) with the Flower of Love. Her name becomes Grace-and-Glory; those of her companions become Joy and Peace.*
>
> *I feel like I should read it again!*

Romans 12:1–2 exhorts us to present ourselves as "living sacrifices." I once heard a preacher make this humorous observation: "The trouble with living sacrifices is that they keep getting off the altar." This was Much-Afraid's concern, that after dedicating herself to the Lord, she would grow faint of heart and would pull back from the consecrated life.

I could relate. I had committed and recommitted myself to the Lord and to His will, first in my single life as a new and growing believer, and now in this most important of all relationships. I asked God to bind me also to the altar, to hold me to the promises that I had made to Him. "Take me at my word, Lord—the words I say to You in my stronger moments. Require of me the vows that I have made."[2]

Greg and I spoke frequently during this time about "needs and expectations." I sensed that these things could cause real trouble in a marriage, and that coming to terms with them before we began our life together would prevent a lot of misunderstanding and heartache.

I once heard someone say that "expectations," in the context of relationships, is defined as "pre-meditated resentments." Funny, but painfully true.

Dear Greg,

I was looking around the house for an envelope when I found this card—I bought it five years ago and have been waiting ever since for someone to send it to!

*Love,
Nancy*

The card went like this: "Boy, do I feel bad... I'm shaky... my nerves are shot, my legs buckle. I'm short of breath, my heart palpitates, my mouth gets dry!!..." and inside it said, "Wow! Being in love with you ain't easy!!"

*April 8
Dear Nancy,*

I've thought of you often today. Trying to picture you here in my apartment. I've been longing to be pampered these last few days, but not even getting any satisfaction from my imagination.

He describes his new job managing the mini-mall, how it has him on the run day and night, how burned out he is getting. Then:

With things so hectic, I've wanted to retreat to you. I can't imagine you here, not easily at least. I've often wanted to crawl into bed and have you hold me while I rest. I've tried to imagine it. It doesn't work. Maybe if we had shared this intimacy, I could relate, but thus far I have nothing to grasp onto.

You know, I don't even know who I am. It's like I'm zooed. I've even had a hard time relating to Christ in the way I'm used to. He is showing me another side of Him, taking me to another experience.

I, also, recently finished reading <u>Hinds' Feet on High Places</u>. Very good. I, too, can relate to Much-Afraid and some of her experiences. I wonder where I am in the journey. Am I going up a mountain, down into a valley, or through the forest? One thing I know: God, I want you to cleanse me. Place in me that fear of You—the fear that will cause me to love you so much that I don't want to hurt You.

Well, these days I don't know how I feel about us, meaning, I don't understand. My heart (gut feeling?) feels no "check." But my head does not understand. The fact that my heart does not "check me" gives joy. I pray for understanding. I think that there are still some wrong motives in my desiring to be with you—these motives being "expectations and needs," inspired by my "self." (This is probably why I don't understand.)

Isn't the Lord wonderful—purging and making us pure! Lord, bring me along, that I may soon spend time with Nancy.

As he writes this letter, he has been moving stuff from his old residence to a suite at the little mall. In the process, he has stumbled onto some correspondence from some old girlfriends.

As I was packing some of my belongings, I ran across some old letters. Praise the Lord that we now are motivated by faith and not feelings. Feelings come up dry, with no fulfilment and always more questions, with no inner hope of an answer. Those letters were written by people responding only to "feelings." Very impulsive and flippant people. Actually, I found the letters to be very shallow and boring. I find this somewhat surprising. (Why?)

I've been alone too long; it is hard to imagine someone in my life. That person would almost be as close to me as my Lord, in that I would always be semi-conscious of her, always considering her desires and point of view, in everything I do. That's hard to relate to. This thought takes considerable meditation, which I'm not up to right now. Oh well, I will cross that bridge when I come to it.

I can't really say I'm "in love" right now. Thoughts of you do not cause me to "drift off." I'm feeling very matter-of-fact.

I want to be with you. I love your letters, and I'm happy to have someone to love.

Good night and God's love,
gc

The Breakaway Letters

Youth for Christ was making its annual Easter pilgrimage, California Breakaway, with two buses full of fun-seeking teenagers. I climbed onto the charter coach, exhausted from late nights and last-minute preparations. What a luxury, to flop down into my seat, close my eyes, and daydream of nothing but Greg until I dozed gratefully off to sleep.

It wasn't long before a staff member from Vancouver (we had teamed up with them this year) plopped herself down in the seat beside me, disturbing my stolen rest.

"You'd better get back there and build some bridges," she advised me a little sharply. "Building bridges" was the going vernacular in "Christianese" for establishing relationships—in this case, with kids. She indicated to me that some of "my" kids were out of order.

I reluctantly roused myself and made my way to the back. Sure enough, a delinquent kid named Ryan and his none-too-virtuous-looking girlfriend, Sheri, were lying sideways in their seat, locked in a passionate embrace with legs entwined. Not a pretty sight in a public place, surrounded by teenagers most of whom were "good" kids.

I slid into the seat behind them, leaned over the seatback, dodging a wayward leg, gave them a big smile (which belied the awkwardness I felt in confronting them), and said, "Hi!"

I explained that their intimacy was causing embarrassment to some others; that it wasn't appropriate—could they please sit up a little straighter and try to control themselves? Fortunately, they were good about it, and I ended up staying there and chatting with them for quite a while. I was glad that that staff member had called me to task from my dreamy reverie.

Oh, God, help me get perspective. I've got no right to sit around starry-eyed while there are kids all around me lost, ignorant of Your ways, Your great love, Your abundant Life. Help me, Lord; give me that burden—the aggression that I usually have to reach out and get to know kids.

When after thirty hours we finally got off the bus and found our hotel for our first real sleep of the trip, I found that this young "lady" Sheri was assigned to my room, so I was especially glad that I had not inadvertently made an enemy of her at the outset.

This little incident with Ryan and Sheri highlighted to me the vast need in the teenage culture for some understanding about modesty and purity, and it reinforced my desire to conduct myself impeccably in my relationship with Greg. People would be watching.

I would not be able to receive any letters from Greg in the ten days I was to be away, but I phoned him when I could, and I wrote to him every spare moment I could find on that trip.

April 2

Sweetie—How can I be farther away than ever and feel even closer than before?! San Francisco, on a beautiful, warm, sunny, and windy day. Sitting down at Fisherman's Wharf, all kinds of funky things going on around me. Outdoors, writing on top of my purse, with a coffee and a big oatmeal cookie beside me. Separated from the rest of the group—praise the Lord!

Greg-honey: These late-night phone calls are quite devastating. Are they so intimate and dreamy just because we are sleepy at that time of night? You should call me sometime early in the morning to get a picture of the real me—well—another part of the real me. I'm a grump in the morning and have no sense of humour till I've been up for a couple of hours. More true confessions. Grumpy in the morning, cold feet at night... anything else you want to know?

(Actually, I realize that you did talk to me in the morning once—the day after my birthday. I guess I wasn't grumpy then, 'cause I was talking to YOU.)

After we hung up last night, it took me an hour and a half to get to bed; I was pretty buzzed. When I finally did get to sleep, for four short hours, it was all dreams. Too bad you don't dream—or don't remember them. Here's one for you from last night:

I was in Wetaskiwin—it was so good to see you again. We were "catching up," sitting at a table with most of the members of your family and my family. It was good (and safe!) with everyone there visiting, but I wanted to be alone with you. Slowly the party dwindled till only your sister was left. She was hesitant to leave but did finally, after admonishing us to behave ourselves.

Then we were alone. It was INTENSE. Eye contact. "Just think, Greg..." I said, "tomorrow night..." (whatever that meant). Then we leaned across the table and kissed. I mean—it wasn't just a kiss: it was a KISS. I got such a rush that I nearly passed out.

As we straightened up again we realized there were people everywhere. "Oh, well," I said, "there aren't that many people in the bleachers."

You turned and looked behind you—we were in a gymnasium and the bleachers were packed. You gave me a look that said, "Let's get out of here!" and you went striding off into the crowd as I scrambled to pick up my jacket and purse. As I hurried out, I thought I'd lost you in the crowd, but the way you moved was so familiar that my eyes riveted to you immediately, even though you were walking in a mass of bodies.

Just as I was about to catch up to you, my clock radio went off, and I stumbled out of bed and into the shower with the feeling of that KISS still very real inside.

Remember how we were talking about keeping our act together when we see each other again... and you kept saying, "The Lord will keep us"? Well, just as I was sitting here reading in Isaiah, the Lord showed me a beautiful scripture (42:6, KJV):

"I the Lord have called thee in righteousness, and will hold thine hand, and WILL KEEP THEE, and give thee for a covenant of the people, for a light of the Gentiles."

Phew! What a promise.

"For a covenant of the people, for a light of the Gentiles," God had said. He was reminding me again that people would be watching. To the people of God, we would be a reminder of the covenant

He keeps with those who trust Him; and to the unbelievers, we would be a light in the darkness.

In a little gift shop at Fisherman's Wharf, I bought a postcard with a sketch of a hippopotamus on the front. I wrote on the back:

> *How can I explain that this card made me think of you?*
> *Remember I told you about the dream where you had turned into a hippopotamus? Seriously, that was one of the times, one of the ways, that God quickened this scripture to me: "Look not on the countenance nor on the stature of the man, for God looks on the heart." I think it's 1 Samuel 15:13[1] He first gave me this scripture a couple of years ago. At the time I thought, "Oh no! God's going to put me together with a pygmy with acne." Yet many times lately, God has quickened this scripture to me—most recently in explanation of why He has allowed the long-distance factor in our relationship. Almost everything I know and love about you is what I've learned about you via letters and phone. I'm beginning to feel such a deep bonding in the heart, in the spirit. When I think of how foolish my pygmy theory seems now (because there is certainly nothing lacking in either your countenance or your stature) and I ask, "Lord, what did You mean: 'Look not on his stature nor on his countenance'?" the Lord answers, "That? Oh, I just meant that that's <u>not</u> what I build the relationship on: that's just a BONUS!"*

Because ours was a long-distance relationship, I didn't get much opportunity to look on Greg's countenance or his stature; I was getting to know his heart. Looking back, it was a blessing that we weren't allowed to get too distracted with externals.

Typically a relationship starts out with a strong physical and emotional attraction. Generally speaking, the needs of body and soul in this life are allowed to reign pre-eminent while the spirit remains largely underdeveloped[2] or even dead—in the case of those who have not yet been regenerated by Christ.[3] As we develop a relationship with a member of the opposite sex, whether we indulge all the passions of the flesh or even if we restrain them tightly, the physical and emotional elements are a tremendous distraction, at the expense of our spirits. However, just as "the spirit of a man will sustain his infirmity,"[4] so I believe that if the spiritual side of a couple is well-developed, it will carry them through many a rough spot later in their life together.

I'll say it again: Even though it was awfully difficult to be so far apart geographically, I now see that it helped us to develop spiritually as a couple. "This was the Lord's doing, and it is marvellous in our eyes."[5]

It's amazing to realize that up until this point we'd still only had *one* date. Excitement was building toward the second one, and it was coming up fast.

April 5
Greg, oh, Greg—

Exactly three weeks from now, you'll be in Victoria—you'll be with me. It'll be so different—so much has happened since we saw each other in Banff. I think we've grown together a lot even though we've been apart. Oh, Lord, prepare us for that time together. Don't let us take a single step outside of You.

Well, honey—this is it. The beach! The nicest day-at-the-beach I've seen in the three years I've been coming on Breakaway. The breakers are rolling in with a steady, undulating roar, blue-green fringed with frothy white. A cool wind, the sun baking down, the sand warm and dreamy...

Hey—I need somebody to put suntan lotion on my back for me. I guess I'll just have to wait. I find myself envious of couples around me. I wish you were here. I keep imagining you in every situation with me.

I even thought that way on the return train trip from the Banff Conference, when I had just met you. Thought a lot about me being with you, you being with me—in every imaginable situation. I couldn't think of a single place where I wouldn't be glad to have you with me; not a single person that I know (or might ever meet) that I wouldn't be proud to introduce you to. I've never known anyone before whom I could say that about. I want to know you more; I want to love you more. Twenty days from today and still counting.

April 6
Dear Greg,

You said in one of your letters, "If I wrote to you every time I thought of you, I'd have nothing to say." That seems to be the case with me right now. Nothing to say. I just want to talk to you. (Of course, having nothing to say has never stopped me from talking before—there's no reason it should now.)

Sitting here in the coffee shop at our hotel; the gal who was eating breakfast with me has left. Having a cup of coffee now because the tea failed to bring my energy and enthusiasm for the day to a suitable level. I'm going to have to seriously withdraw from coffee after this trip.

HOW CAN I SAY THAT I LOVE YOU? I DON'T EVEN KNOW YOU!

I fill him in on some of our activities—and some of the challenges of keeping warm-blooded teenagers behaving with a degree of propriety. I continue:

Oh, Greg, I'm bored with writing trivia to you. I want to be with you. I think about you all the time. I just want to be with you. It's not right that we not be together. Every night when I'm trying to go to sleep I think of you. I imagine your arms around me. I hesitate to write that down, but I <u>know</u> you must know that I think about that. I've never felt right thinking such things of anyone before (since coming to know the Lord) and I would determinedly "cast down imaginations." But it was wrong before because I was only ever dreaming of things inspired by a spirit of fornication: that is, the fantasy (when I gave in to the temptation) was inspired by selfish desire for immediate gratification, and it shied away from any notion of commitment and responsibility. My fantasies of lying in your arms—to the contrary—are born of a desire to be committed to you and only you—for always. And before God, I don't feel conviction for such thoughts. Mind you, I try to keep the thoughts very "clean," because it will help us to keep things in line when we're together again. I hope you understand and will do the same.

I well remembered one of my pastors, Dr. Doug Roberts, saying during a sermon, "Spiritual battles are won and lost on the threshold of the mind." I knew it was true: What I allowed myself in fantasy, I would have a tough time abstaining from when the opportunity presented itself.

April 7
My dear Greg:

I can't believe it's only six days since I talked to you on the phone. Again that funny, unreal feeling is settling in—where you don't seem real to me. One reason that feeling sets in is because you're too good to be true, Greg. When I remember you again (as there are times during the day when the flurry and distraction preoccupy me and I forget that you are there—somewhere, far away—but very much <u>there</u> in my life), the remembrance comes with such a sweet shock. I have been alone so, so long; independent for too long. So many times I have cried out to God for comfort and companionship in a man—and so many times He has asked me to wait and wait some more—it was sometimes hard to believe that He really intended to finally bless me. You talked in a letter about "old concepts" ("if it feels this good, it must be wrong"). Similarly, I think I've suspected, subconsciously, that if I <u>really</u> submitted my singleness and loneliness to God (as I finally did), He would keep me that way, single and lonely, all my life. In my heart of hearts I believed that scripture, "They that wait on him will not be disappointed,"[6] but still the fear and distrust would creep in when I was most tired and most lonely.

(I'm lying in bed now as I write, and I'm really leaning on these gals to shut it down and get into bed. We're all over-tired tonight. They're distracting me, but I'll try to pick up where I left off.)

Greg, when I say you're too good to be true, I'm not being unrealistic or giving you more credit than is your due. I'm not saying you're perfect—I'm just saying you're perfect for me. There's quite a difference between the two. And I simply thank God for you. I may be blind right now to any faults you have, but I don't doubt that they're there! Again, I just trust that God is going to use both good things and not-so-good things about you to continue His precious work in me. It's in His hands.

Sweetheart. I want to see you again. (Have I said that before?) Over and over I picture you in my mind's eye, lounged out on a couch or something, propped up on your right elbow. I always imagine just standing and looking at you, then coming over, sitting down, and leaning up against you.

Oh, Greg, I want to be with you. I have an ache inside me like a pain that won't go away. I know it wouldn't be all roses—but hard times with you would be so much better than no time with you at all. Oh, dear God—what more can I say? Greg—just put your arms around me and hold on to me.

Good night.

Home Again

Finally I was home from California. There was a letter waiting for me.

April 5
My dear sweet Nancy,

    God bless! Well, I wish you were here with me. I need someone to pamper me. You come to mind first. My back and shoulders and feet need a massage. My shoulder and neck muscles have been taut for almost a week. I've been running on very little sleep.

Here he goes on at length about his job at the mini-mall.

    Well, I think of you often, and your California tour. I find myself somewhat jealous of the people with you. They seem to be getting more of you than I do. I want those smiles and laughs and conversation that you share with them....
    I talked to Eva on Sunday. Once I knew for sure that I was going to Victoria to see you, I felt I had to tell her. I have sensed that she is growing "toward" me, and I know that every time I'm with her, she grows closer to me. That is why she had to know, as she may feel she has to quit working with me. I'm getting more comfortable all the time concerning my feelings toward you and my relationship with Eva. I don't want to see her hurt, but at the same time I cannot take responsibility for her feelings.
    My relationship with you has not changed my feelings toward her—a good indication that any feelings I have toward her are purely "family." Whether or not yours and my relationship develops fully will not change my relationship with her on my part.

There is so much more I would like to share, but must rest. Good night. I long for you.

gc

    I wrapped up a delicate ceramic figurine that I'd bought in the States for Greg. It was a dear little mouse in a long pink dress and matching bonnet. She had a couple of heart-stamped letters in her tiny paw that she was putting in a mailbox.

    With it I sent a card with a bunch of funny little mice all over the front of it. Inside it said, "Have a mice day." I signed it, "Quantitative and qualitative romantic endearments." I enclosed another letter:

April 12
Dear Greg,

I find myself often looking at myself through your eyes, as it were. Wondering, "What would he think of me now?" Like—when I was staying in Kamloops just before seeing you that day at Banff, our first (only—so far!) date: I bought myself a cute little nightie—knee-length instead of long, for a change. Got up the next morning, walked by a mirror, and took a look. Yeah, nice. Especially with the unmatched sweat-socks I was wearing—different coloured stripes. I've got a real flair with things like that.

Or, sitting up late, sewing, hair back in a greasy bun, white "beauty" mask on my face—and my glasses. "Would he still love me now?"

I went to our church office today to have lunch with Barb (she works there as secretary) and one of our pastors, Ted Follows. I wanted to talk to him about your coming to visit. Barb had said that you were welcome to use her spare room, and I thought that sounded great at first, but then I didn't feel at peace about it. I don't think I could go to sleep if you were in the same house. And besides that, I could picture myself getting up early to make you coffee and bringing it into your room... sitting and talking while you drank it. I just couldn't handle it—I know it would be taking liberties that don't belong to me yet. Finally the hard lessons God has taught me—about myself, the weakness of my flesh, and the perfection of His way—are sinking in.

Yeah, well—Ted exhorted me to "abstain from all appearance of evil"[1] and to give no "occasion to the flesh."[2] Neither do I want to be a stumbling block to those younger "sheep" who watch me and my example. I want to do it right.

I know where I'll try to arrange for you to stay—it will be perfect.

April 11
Dear Nancy,

♪ I just can't get you out of my head. ♪ Isn't that tremendous?! Maybe I just ought to become a songwriter. Isn't it wonderful how music can give more feeling and depth to our heart's cry! Praise the Lord for music. God is good.

Back to the song. I'm very romantic these days. I am more able to imagine you with me, doing various things together, sharing life. Some things are comfortable; others are not so comfortable. It has been so long since I've identified myself with another person. I'm almost afraid to come into situations where there has only been me to consider. I'm speaking of social situations. I know that the day you come to church with me, a lot of heads will turn. Many will be anxious to meet you. Others will be afraid to impose. Others will… anyway, there's going to be a lot of talk. Maybe I'm building this up. Who knows? Anyway, what will be will be. I will surely know your name by the time the day is out. Slow down, Greg.

God, give me understanding.

I mentioned before that my heart is clear but that I sense no direction. I can see an outcome but no track to run on. God will show me the truth. I believe that, given any situation, a person seeking to know the truth will eventually find Jesus.

God, show me the truth.

I've noticed that I have slipped back to old habits and sins, unawares and unintentionally. I've started back now with the daily routine that I initiated at conversion, to bring myself back on track. I've been praying that God would give me understanding in regard to the meaning of "the Cross." I've never had revelation on this. What means "return to the Cross," huh? God is giving me revelation, making me aware of little things that have crept back.

Nancy, please be patient with me. Sometimes I feel so immature and naïve, unworthy, egotistical, proud, know-it-all. Oh, God, humble me. Purge me, tear out those roots that go so deep. Restore unto me the joy of *my salvation, and renew a right spirit within me.*[3] *Lord, show me where I am at. Clear my thoughts. Don't let me sit in the comfortable pew. Show me the root of my feelings for Nancy. Give this relationship purpose, O God. Lord, the uncleanness that lurks in my mind is empty. The human side of my thoughts does not give purpose. Is this why I sense no direction? Am I standing in the way?*

Lord, Nancy is the desire of my heart. If in fact she is not <u>Your</u> desire in my heart, Lord, take her away. But Lord, do it gently.

Nance, let's pray, pray, pray. For God to work the fullest in us, we must die to self. I want to die, Lord. Your way is better. I know this, Lord. For Thou art God. God, I'm fed up with my <u>self</u>.

Dear Diary, er... Nancy, thanks for being my diary—a vessel that records and keeps intimate, personal thoughts. Thank you, God, for this gift.

April 18
Dear Nancy,

Just "Hello" seems inadequate. Any type of written greeting is inadequate. I'm tired of it. Or maybe I'm just too tired.

Things are happening so fast. So much, so new. There are some seemingly very important decisions to be made fast. Much is at stake.

He gives some details here about difficult circumstances at work, which may catapult him into a position of much greater responsibility.

Lord, what are You doing? By worldly standards, all is tumbling down. I can't fully see the other side. I'm tired. "In my weakness, You are strong."[4] *So many details. Oh, God, I can't keep track. Help me to rest. Lord, I can't do it myself. Help me to turn it over to You, constantly.*

Dear Nancy, where do you fit in to all this? My conceptions of you are extremely limited.

Because there is so much to do and timing is so important, I've even had reservations about coming out to Vancouver. I'll have to see what the week brings. I know that would hurt you, disappoint you. It would hurt me also.

I rest in You, Lord.

I need something right now. I can't put a finger on it though. Because I don't know where you fit in, I can't even look to you for support. (I don't know how this sounds; I don't know what I'm trying to say.) I guess I'm not sure of my role, maybe that's why. I'm not sure I even want you here right this instant. Too much to sort out, let alone trying to romance you and consider you and your place in my life. I want you here but don't want you here. I just bet that you would have the right words, right now, although I can't conceive them myself.

Nancy, I'm going to sleep for a couple of hours, as I have to work at midnight. I know, I know the Lord is shaking and replanting, getting things in order. I know my Lord. His will be done. Amen.

April 12
Dear Greg,

Sweetheart, gee I needed to hear your voice last night. What a delight to come straight out of a deep sleep and talk to you.

Only twelve more days till I see you. It's going fast now.

I'm even more excited at the prospect of flying up next month and joining you and the kids in your youth group for that weekend at the Circle Square Ranch. How amazing—just yesterday afternoon I was picturing being back at that ranch again where I did my YFC training, then on the phone you say we'll be going there when I come up in May!

I drove home for lunch today for a change. Was thanking the Lord for my food, paused to pray a blessing on you and remembered with a delighted shock: "Oh, yeah—that's why I wanted to drive home—to check the mail." Ran upstairs and found three letters all at once. What a pig-out! There was such a sweet tenderness when I read them. I love your letters so much, Greg.

I don't feel like writing a long letter: I'll probably talk to you on the phone soon, so any news I wrote now would be obsolete. But I did want to say that I was thrilled in my heart to have you say you don't feel "in love" right now. When you say it that frankly, there isn't room for hurt or misunderstanding.

The last couple of phone calls, I haven't felt very much "in love" with you. But more and more all the time I think I LOVE you. I know you know the difference. And besides that, I think I just plain _like_ you a lot.

P.S. Got a lot done at the office today. Really trying to start all over in this work—get my motivation back and do it with my whole heart.

Sunday, April 17
My dear Greg,

I sure haven't done much writing to you this week as compared to before. Don't know why. It seems like with it being so close to your visit now, I'm too impatient. I can't stand it now. Before, I was counting the days; now I just feel numb, like I should just hold my breath and not even think until you show up.

You know what it's like? When I used to drive home to Castlegar to visit my folks, either from Kamloops (300 miles) or Vancouver (400 miles), the first few hundred miles seemed relatively easy. The destination was so far away, I wouldn't even think about it; rather, I'd just settle down and enjoy the drive. But the last sixty miles (from Grand Forks) was interminable: it seemed longer than all the rest of the miles put together. By then I was so full of anticipation at being home, I would drive like a fiend, and still those last miles would drag. I grew to hate that stretch of the trip, though probably the scenery is as beautiful there as anywhere in God's creation.

Anyhow, I've begun the last "sixty miles" of this "trip." A week, just seven days from now, I'll be sitting with you, maybe having supper in a restaurant as I am now—maybe heading off for the evening service as I will be in a few minutes. Hey, it doesn't matter if we're standing in the rain eating Big Macs—I'll be with you!

I wonder what will happen to my emotions this week. Maybe I'll get really nervous and uptight about seeing you and spending all that time together. Especially this week, I must take unto myself the whole armour of God, and—after having done all—stand.[5] I am not ignorant of the enemy's devices:[6] I won't be surprised if he tries to assault me with fresh doubts and fears.

Sometimes the enemy really tips his hand. When he troubles himself to throw confusion, doubt, fear, etc., into a situation such as this, it really only serves to convince me of God's purpose in it. If it wasn't of God and didn't have such potential in the Kingdom of Heaven here on earth, I really don't think the enemy would bother.

God, give me discernment as to what is an attack of the deceiver and what is my own (quite natural) nervousness and anticipation.

I remember when I was driving to Banff for our first date, Greg—I was very calm and settled till about the last half hour. Then suddenly, such a rush of excitement and anticipation, I could hardly breathe. I just wanted to get the initial meeting over with so I could settle down and enjoy your company. When I went into the ice-cream parlour to ask the waitress if you had been there, I could hardly squeak the words out.

I keep imagining meeting you at the airport. It's going to be so neat. I'll continue this later. Must rush for church. Love you!

We talked on the phone later that night, and I finished up my letter in the morning.

After talking to you on the phone last night again, there's not much to say. It's so drab and lacklustre to try to put things on paper after having the reality of your voice to hang on to.

I'll just sign off now and not bother to write anymore this week—you wouldn't get it before I see you anyway.

Looking forward so very much to having you here. You are constantly in my thoughts and in my prayers. I feel more freedom with you all the time.

I send you my love, my Love.
Nancy

The Second Date

I scanned the faces of the people streaming into the baggage area, looking for Greg. I saw him before he saw me, and I considered his appearance in a detached manner for a few moments. Was he good-looking? You know, I really couldn't tell anymore. I couldn't tell if he was handsome or plain. I only knew that he looked like my husband, the face that I would be searching for in situations like this for the rest of my life. It was my husband's face, the face that I loved, and this was the beginning of our second date.

In my little red Fiat, bombing back toward Victoria from the airport, I sang him the chorus of a new song:

> I want to put my arms around you
> And never let you go
> I want to tell you all the things I know
> You already know
> And I'll tell you once more in a letter
> If you really want me to
> But I'd rather wait till you are here
> To say I love you

Back at the house, I introduced him triumphantly to Barb, then we descended to my basement suite. In the evening I would take him to the home of some friends, for propriety's sake. But for now we could enjoy some time together. I remember sitting down at the piano while he sank gratefully onto my new couch. He had pulled an all-night shift, after working the previous day, and had gone directly to the airport with no rest. The hour-and-a-half flight with its intense anticipation had tired him even more; now he was starting to unwind.

I began to sing a favourite chorus of mine from church: "Jesus, How Lovely You Are." Just as though it had been planned in a script, he arose from the couch, came and stood behind me with his huge hands on my shoulders, and joined in with a beautiful harmony. It was too perfect; I couldn't believe how perfect it all was.

Then I sang him my new song. It wouldn't be long before he had found his own part in this song too, and in years to come, it would become a favourite of ours to sing at weddings, anniversaries, and Valentine's banquets.

How many times have I written?
How many times have I said I love you?
How many times have I told you how badly by that love bug I've been bitten?
But still, I want to tell you: I love you!

How many times have you said in a letter
You long for me and wish that I were near?
I thought that I'd get used to this, but it's not getting any better
Babe, I miss you and wish you were here

I want to put my arms around you and never let you go
I want to tell you all the things I know you already know
And I'll tell you once more in a letter if you really want me to
But I'd rather wait till you are here to say I love you

How many days must I keep counting?
How many nights must I feel so all alone?
My heart keeps getting emptier; my loneliness keeps mounting
And this place I live no longer feels like home

I want to put my arms around you and never let you go
I want to tell you all the things I know you already know
And I'll tell you once more in a letter if you really want me to
But I'd rather wait till you are here to say I love you

How many times have I written?
How many times have I said I love you?
How many times have I told you how badly by that love bug I've been bitten?
But still, I want to tell you: I love you!

When I finished singing for Greg, I joined him on the couch. He was crashing fast. He reclined wearily, saying, "Come lie with me," and pulled me into his arms. I was very nervous about being horizontal with him, and I lay very still for the couple of minutes it took him to fall into a deep sleep. Then I gingerly extricated myself and fled the scene, up the stairs to where Barb and the teakettle were waiting. We lapsed into comfortable conversation, and everything seemed back to normal, the way it had always been. But suddenly I remembered that nothing was the same at all; things were fast changing, and I shrieked, "Akk! Barb! There's a man asleep downstairs on my couch!"

Monday we made our way across to the mainland on the ferry. The Bill Gothard conference was beginning at 7:00 in the evening. We arrived a few minutes late at the coliseum, which was filled with ten thousand eager registrants. Before we even found our seats, we could hear this man's teaching resonating through the building.

"So, young ladies," was the first thing I heard him say, "you think you've found the man you want to marry. You'd better take a good look at how he treats his mother, because how he treats her is how he's going to end up treating you."

I glanced up at Greg as we circled the huge seating area, looking for our section. His eyes met mine, and we exchanged an ironic smile. It looked like the teaching was going to be quite appropriate for us. As for how he treated his mother... well, that would be evident when I flew to Alberta in a month's time to meet his folks. But I was sure there wasn't going to be a problem there.

The conference would run Monday through Thursday, evenings only, then all day Friday and Saturday. I would spend several days early in the week visiting some of the youth-detention facilities in the area. I'd been able to secure clearance for Greg to accompany me into most of the places.

Tuesday night, the conference wound up at 10:00 p.m. Greg drove me to my brother's girlfriend's place, where I was staying. He would then drive to my brother's place for the night again. But first we sat in the car and talked a bit. It turned into a lengthy conversation. He was sharing his concern and confusion about the situation with Eva back home, about these prophecies that he would marry her.

"When you think about the situation, what do you feel?" I asked him.

"I feel confusion, and doubt, and guilt, and fear," he answered.

I was shifting into ministry mode: "Those feelings are not from God," I assured him. "Those things are all trademarks of the enemy."

I asked him if he would let me pray for him, and with his assent, I launched into an aggressive spiritual assault against the powers of darkness. I took authority in the name of Jesus over confusion, doubt, guilt, and fear, and commanded that the enemy shut his mouth regarding this matter; that Greg be able to hear God's voice only.

There was a stillness that came. We sat in silence for several long minutes. I could sense that a release had come, but I had no idea how effective and complete the release had been until he spoke.

"Nancy..." he said, and suddenly I couldn't breathe, because I knew things had drastically shifted back out of ministry mode. I knew what was coming, and yet it was coming upon me unexpected:

"Nancy, I want you to be my wife."

He hadn't asked me; he had simply made a statement. But obviously, it required an answer. And surprisingly, I found that I wasn't ready to give him an answer. I struggled in silence. This was so big. Finally I responded, hesitantly:

"I know that's what I want too," I said, "but I don't feel I can give you a straight answer right away. Could you give me a few days?"

How crazy was this! I'd been telling friends, even before the first date, that I knew I was going to marry this guy, but now that the time had come, I didn't feel ready. I knew the relationship was ordained by God, but I was overwhelmed with the magnitude of the commitment.

Greg was not fazed by my hesitance. He knew that I loved him and wanted to spend my life with him. He was also coming to understand, very quickly, my fearful and cautious nature. But he was enjoying the excitement that his pronouncement had given him, and he was ready to celebrate.

"Let's go get something to eat!" he said.

It was mid-week and close to midnight, but we managed to find a little Italian place, with subtle lighting and red gingham tablecloths. He enthusiastically ordered a big plate of spaghetti and meatballs. I couldn't face anything but a cup of coffee.

As we waited for his food, Greg pulled out a devotional book. It had readings for both the morning and the evening, all of it Scripture, different excerpts grouped together by common themes of subject matter. His practice was to read both portions in the morning, then read them again in the evening. That morning he had only taken time for the morning reading. Now he launched into the evening portion.

"Who is this ... arising as the dawn, fair as the moon, pure as the sun, so utterly captivating?"[1] it began. Well, this was pretty intriguing, right from the get-go, a passage from the Song of Solomon, the lover admiring his beloved. It was followed by a verse instructing husbands: "Show the same kind of love to your wives as Christ showed to the church when he died for her, to make her holy and clean, washed by baptism and God's Word; so that he could have her to himself as a glorious church without a single spot or wrinkle or any other blemish, being holy and without a single fault."[2]

Then came another very relevant passage: "Let us be glad and rejoice and honour him; for the time has come for the wedding banquet of the Lamb, and his bride has prepared herself. She is permitted to wear the cleanest and whitest and finest of linens."[3]

The reading finished with a part of Jesus' prayer to His Father from John 17. At this special moment in our lives, it seemed that He was speaking to the Father directly about us: "I have given them the glory you gave me—the glorious unity of being one, as we are."[4]

Greg was ecstatic. He felt that God was confirming His blessing on our betrothal.

His spaghetti arrived, and he ate with gusto. I leaned against his big shoulder, sipping my coffee intermittently, virtually paralyzed with apprehension. I was so fearful of the finality of this commitment. Nobody had ever suggested that I might feel this way at this wonderful time. Maybe I was the only one who ever *had* felt this way about a marriage proposal. I just leaned on Greg and hung onto God and waited for the worst of this to pass.

By the next morning, I was feeling better already. The relationship once again had that solid sense of inevitability that it had had all along. This was God's will. He wouldn't force me to marry Greg, but I knew that if I chose not to, it would be like veering off from His "Plan A." He would have a "Plan B" for me, and He would still love me and bless me, but I would be missing the best of what He had destined for me. I wasn't about to let that happen. I would choose to be strong and courageous, like Joshua, and go on in to inherit the land of promise.[5]

Greg came over early in the morning. We talked about a wedding date. I had borne in mind all along the date that my sister Polly had suggested: July 31. It would mean we'd say our vows exactly six months from the day we first met. That seemed kind of neat to me. But as we looked at our schedules and our proposed get-togethers that lay between now and then, we couldn't see a time and a way for him to meet my parents before a late-July wedding.

"Why don't we just pray," he suggested, "and then you phone your folks and just see what happens."

So we presented our need to God and then I dialled the old home phone number. "Greg and I were just sitting here talking," I said to Mom (they knew that we were spending this week together in Vancouver). "I'd really like you to meet him sometime, and we were just wondering when it might possibly work out."

"We're already packed," my mom burst out excitedly. They had talked to my sister Ellie and my brother, John, so Mom and Dad knew that the four of us were planning to meet for lunch on Friday. Dad had been trying to talk Mom into jumping into the car, driving the four hundred miles to Vancouver, and showing up for lunch, unannounced. Mom was afraid it might be presumptuous of them, possibly even embarrassing to me. She'd been trying to hold Dad back. But they seriously were half-packed already. So all I had to do was give them the name of the restaurant, right across the street from our conference, where we were already planning to meet the others. Mom and Dad would head out that very afternoon. We felt once again that God was confirming His blessing on our relationship, this time by the ease with which He had dissolved a seeming difficulty.

Late Wednesday afternoon, Greg and I visited the detention centre called "Willingdon," located in Burnaby. We were invited to join the fellows in one cottage for supper. Four of them were kids I knew from Juvie. They seemed so thrilled to meet Greg. I remember one of them shaking Greg's hand, looking down in amazement at the size of the mitt that engulfed his, then looking back up into his face with an awed "Wow!" I could tangibly feel the impression that he made on them: a man's man, and a godly man, in a room full of boys, none of whom had likely ever known a real father-figure. They loved him on sight.

We each picked up a plate of food at the counter, and the boys offered us a place at one of the tables. I picked up my fork and started right into my meal, but the young man across the table from me, who had committed his life to Christ at Juvie a year earlier, interrupted me anxiously: "Hey, don't start eating yet! We say grace around here now."

He called on a fellow across the room, saying, "It's your turn." The young man prayed a fine prayer that left me on the verge of tears.

Another fellow at my table, with whom I'd had some unpleasant scenes the previous summer, confessed proudly to me that he had finally become a Christian just three weeks earlier. "I made the decision all by myself," he said, "and now I'm telling everybody about it. I feel just great inside."

God was showing me some of the fruit of my ministry from the past few years, a nice touch as I saw this phase in my life rapidly drawing to a close. It would be hard to leave all these kids behind, but God was turning the page to a new and exciting chapter in my life.

Friday at noon, as the conference released its registrants for the lunch break, Greg and I hurried out of the coliseum and walked briskly down the street. There was no time to waste; the lunch hour would pass quickly. We soon spotted the restaurant my sister had suggested, across the busy stream of traffic. And we spotted something else: a group of people waiting outside. My family. My mom and dad, my younger sister, my brother, and his girlfriend. Most of them were waving excitedly. My mother completely forgot the dignity of her fifty-six years and began leaping up and down, waving both arms like a cheerleader. My brother was standing a little apart from the group, keeping a large telephone pole between him and the rest of them, declaring loudly to passers-by, "I do not know these people."

We all had a wonderful time over lunch. I did not mention Greg's proposal; I just wanted my family to get to know him a bit.

Bill Gothard sure did a lot of talking about marriage in the conference. "If you're getting married," he said that afternoon, "make sure you know how your future spouse feels about children."

During the next coffee break, Greg and I took our drinks out on the grass and sat down in the sunshine. "How do you feel about kids?" he asked me. This was one of many subjects we hadn't even got close to talking about yet. When it came right down to it, we hardly knew each other.

"I really want to have kids," I answered thoughtfully. "On the other hand, I guess I've always imagined waiting a couple years, just to spend time with my husband and get to know him a bit."

He nodded. "Yeah, that sounds like a good plan. But then," he added after a pause, "I don't know about birth control. I kind of think that family planning should be up to God."

I looked at him calmly, but I could hardly believe what I was hearing. He had to be crazy! Sure, I loved God, and I was sold out to the Lordship of Jesus Christ. I wanted Him to control every area of my life, but it had never, ever occurred to me that I should trust Him to plan my future family.

Greg had thrown me for a loop. All right, I would throw him for a loop also.

"Yeah," I answered slowly, "I think it would make sense to leave that in God's hands. Because—I believe that ideally God brings two people together in marriage only in order to serve Him more effectively, and that ultimately He wants them to be so consumed with Him that they have no desire for sex at all."

I watched my words register on his face. The colour drained out of his cheeks, and his mouth hung open in a rather unbecoming way. He stammered a bit.

"You—you're kidding, right?"

And then I couldn't keep my poker face any longer.

Bill Gothard covered another subject that resounded deeply with both of us: the principle of parental authority. He talked about God's command to honour our parents, about how it is "the first commandment with promise": that God's blessing of a long and happy life is the reward of the one who heeds this counsel. His advice to those considering marriage, even those who have been out on their own for years, was to submit a proposed marriage to the wisdom of their parents. Even in the case of ungodly parents, he assured his audience, God would see to it that those parents gave godly counsel. For those who submit themselves to God's hierarchy of authority, His blessing and protection is promised.

So there am I, thirty years old, having been independent of my parents pretty much for ten years. Even while I was still at home, my father had very little input in my life. And now Greg was telling me that he felt God wanted him to ask my father's permission to marry me before anything was made public. Futhermore, he said, if my dad didn't approve, we should not proceed.

This was radical, but it made perfect Biblical sense. I wanted God's best, so I had better subject myself to His safeguards. I was in full agreement.

We invited my folks to follow us to the Island late Saturday night and join us for church and dinner on Sunday. At the oceanside dining room, looking out on the view, we had a fine meal and amiable conversation. As we lingered after dessert, Greg suddenly stood up, picked up his coffee, and said, "Dr. Fowler, could I talk to you alone for a few minutes?"

Dad jumped up nervously. I remember that his hand shook slightly so that his cup rattled in its saucer as he picked it up. "I guess he wants to talk to me some more about my boat," he said to my mom with a little laugh, comic relief in the face of this sudden seriousness. He trailed Greg out to the lobby.

Greg told me later that he could hardly get his formal request out before Dad was assuring him of his approval. With four unmarried adult kids, I guess Dad wasn't about to discourage anything. Seriously, it was easy to see that both Mom and Dad had been delighted with Greg from the moment they laid eyes on him. There would be no obstacles here.

We said good-bye to Mom and Dad that afternoon. In the evening, after church, Greg and I were scheduled to go out for ice cream with my friends Kent and Dee-Dee. Kent, the one fellow I'd dated who had handled himself in a truly godly way, had married his high-school sweetheart the previous fall. I had set up this double date with Dee-Dee a week earlier, because I really wanted them to have a chance to spend some time with Greg. Before hanging up, I had cautioned Dee-Dee: I was concerned that she or Kent might think it funny to make some playful inquiries about marriage. "This will only be our second date," I had pleaded with her. "I would be absolutely mortified if you guys asked any forward questions."

I should have worried: I had done my share, in the past, of asking premature and leading questions, mostly in the name of humour. Now the shoe was on the other foot, and it was pinching a little.

I had my reasons for wanting to spend some time with Kent and Dee-Dee. Five years younger than I, they both loved God with all their hearts. They had, like I said, got married about six months earlier, and I knew that they had done everything right. By that I mean that they had honoured God in their courtship and in the years before. I knew that both of them had been virgins on their wedding night, a fact that I could hardly fathom but for which I had great respect. I just wanted to be with them, along with the new love of my life.

As we waited to order, the chatter and laughter bubbled up freely. We were having a great time. But Kent was not himself at all. I realize in retrospect that he was excited for me about my new man, and it was making him a bit giddy. A responsible and successful businessman—even back then at the age of twenty-five, normally serious and intelligent in his conversation, that night he was acting like a complete idiot.

Dee-Dee kept rolling her eyes and exchanging looks of mock exasperation with me. Finally, after a particularly silly outburst from her husband, she sighed loudly and said to whomever might be listening, "He's not the man I married."

Then she looked at me, smiled innocently, and said, "But at least he hasn't asked ... *the question!*"

Greg and I picked up the menu we were sharing and covered our faces. We looked at each other, safe in our hiding place, and shared a secret smile before lowering the menu again. Funny, I didn't feel embarrassed at all.

Later that night, as Greg and I said our good-byes before he headed to the place he was to sleep, we talked about our engagement. I had, sometime in the last few days, given him a firm "Yes." Now we were talking about how it didn't quite seem real. Was that all it took? A proposal from him and an acceptance from me? Were we really engaged now?

"A ring!" Greg said suddenly. "We need a ring!"

Right! Somewhere in between the hour that jewellery stores would open in the morning and the time he had to be at the airport, we needed to choose a ring.

We were there before they unlocked the doors. Once we had selected an engagement ring and a matching wedding band, they measured my finger. After making the necessary adjustments, they would send the rings up to Greg. He would give me the engagement ring when I flew up to Wetaskiwin in a month's time.

"But I can't leave you without a ring on your finger," he said. He chose another little ring, one that just fit my left pinkie: a delicate heart with a tiny diamond in the centre. He called it a promise ring. I was sure glad to have it; everything was strangely surreal. I needed something tangible or I might just awaken from this dream.

Then we raced for the airport. He almost missed his plane. I was aware of people watching us as we embraced one last time. I think there must have been a visible glow of love around us, an aura of the blessing of God.

By the time I left the airport, I knew I was going to be late for our 1:00 P.M. YFC staff meeting. I raced my little four-in-the-floor Fiat along the freeway, all the way into the city. A traffic light turned red, interrupting my rather excellent progress. I slowed grudgingly to a stop. The toot of a horn drew my attention to a yellow Volvo on my left. It was Doug Perkins, my boss, scowling in pretended anger, pointing with an exaggerated stabbing motion at the watch on his left wrist. I grinned back blandly, pointing in the same way at the fourth finger of my left hand. His scowl disappeared; his eyebrows shot up and his mouth dropped open. The light turned green and I raced away, revving high, shifting gears. I beat him to the office easily.

Later that afternoon, I ran into Bradley at Juvie. He had remained warm and gentlemanly since our one date the previous fall, even though he had never brought it up again. I had sensed a tiny bit of reserve in him since. I showed him my promise ring. "I'm getting married," I told him.

"Aw, Nancy, I wanted to marry you," he said rather sadly.

I thought he was teasing me. I put my hands on my hips and, feigning exasperation, said, "Oh, yeah, right! You never even asked me out!"

But he looked at me very seriously and said, "I wanted to. But when I asked you to give me a kiss that night, I felt that even that was compromising your commitment to God. And I didn't want to do that to you."

I was so tremendously moved that I didn't know what to say. I was profoundly grateful to Bradley for his integrity. Even more, I was grateful to God for His faithfulness. I could now see so clearly how He had answered my desperate prayers for help after that one date. He knew that I was too weak to go out with this fellow, and so, I believe, He moved directly on Bradley's heart in order to provide a way of escape for me.[6]

A little later I called Dee-Dee. All I said was, "Guess *what!*" She squealed with delight; she knew exactly what I was saying. When she and Kent had got engaged, she had phoned me and announced it with those very words.

Kent was there too. She put him on the line, and I told him my exciting news.

He was much more his usual self than he had been the night before. "Dee-Dee and I have talked about you in the past, Nancy," he said. "We've both felt that there really wasn't anyone around here that was right for you. It seemed it was going to take someone we didn't know yet. New blood. Someone special."

Someone special. Indeed.

Old Things Become New

Greg flew home on the second of May and we went back to writing letters.

Tuesday, May 3
My dear Greg, I love you!

I'm writing this just after getting off the phone with you. Hard to write... I'm lying in bed. You tucked me in here just two nights ago. How precious that was to me, babe. I was so tired and felt just like a sleepy child. I do so look forward to being able to lie in your arms all night. But there's no rush or anxiety or drive... just a great peace that says that this is right for now and the other will come graciously in its own time.

I praise God over and over for how He kept us through the week. I believe that as a result of letting God keep us in purity, He is able to bless us with a light of holiness that is visible to others and that others so <u>badly</u> need to see. Truly a "covenant of the people (of God) and a light of the Gentiles."

Babe, I love you. I love you.

It's a week ago tonight that you told me you wanted me to be your wife. I wish I could have enjoyed that evening more. Still, I guess I had to work through the fears. They seem to be all gone now; also gone is any double-mindedness. I want to give my life to you, to grow and learn with you. I can't picture the details yet, but they don't matter. I am praying for you—of course!—and especially for finances. The closer I draw to the Lord, the less I am intimidated by your debt. But it makes it doubly important that we seek the Lord for His timing and His wisdom during these foundational months.

He had told me during our week together that he had some debts. He would, he said, write them all down and send the list to me, so that I would know where we stood financially.

Greg, is it really true that you're going to be my husband?! God put so much in the package. Even though He had promised, I had trouble imagining Him fulfilling all my needs in one person (outside of Him!). He is doing it in you.

I'm going to sleep now, sweetheart. I love you. Kiss. Hold me, babe.

Continued two days later:

Just had a phone call from a girl I sort of know who said, "I'm getting married July 23, and I want you to sing at my wedding." And I said, "Sorry, but I'm getting married the week after that and I think I'll be too busy." Gee—it gave me a funny feeling to say that.

I had no peace about setting a date till last night on the phone... I wasn't ready. Setting the date seems like an even more final commitment, and now there is a nervousness that's rising up in my throat again, threatening to choke me.

That's just how I feel right now, babe—I'll be okay. Only had time for a few minutes in prayer this morning. I need to press in constantly to the Source of my peace.

If the peace comes back by this evening, I'll call my folks and give them the date. But I'll wait on the peace. Otherwise I won't enjoy talking to them about all the details they will want to talk about.

There sure is a lot to be done. I pray that I can tackle it all with enthusiasm and that the "production" itself won't become a burden. I want to enjoy the whole process.

God has given me grace today to work steadily and accomplish a lot. This will be a daily prayer now, that I can give myself wholly to the work at YFC right to the end of June.

God had confirmed His perfect timing concerning the end of my career as a Youth Guidance worker and the imminence of my marriage. Shortly after I returned from the Bill Gothard conference, Youth for Christ had received word that the director at Juvie, a fine Christian man, who had been instrumental in getting our chaplaincy established there, was being replaced. YFC's involvement there would be terminated as of the first of July. God was dovetailing circumstances. I would be finished work one month before my wedding.

My letter goes on:

When I called Kent and Dee-Dee on Monday afternoon to tell them of our engagement, Kent encouraged us to tie it up quickly. "Give yourselves two or three months to get organized and that's it," he said. We also talked a bit about feelings—he shared briefly some things he and Dee-Dee were feeling a year ago, regarding fears, mixed feelings, etc., as they anticipated their own wedding. "You'll be amazed at some of the feelings you'll go through between now and the wedding day," he told me. A good friend to have around—I might need a pep talk now and then.

In my spirit I don't question a thing. I <u>know</u> that things are closing down here—it's a move of obedience, a time of change—and so much more. It's more vital than ever before that I discern the Lord's voice, each step in this. In my spirit I <u>know</u>—it's just that my soul gets a little rattled now and then.

Today I made some initial contacts for a roller-skating night at Juvie, late June, and a Christian band in early June. Also aiming for a special film and maybe a games night. Going to go out with a bang.

Pray for my back and my crazy, fluctuating emotions. Pray for me to work hard. Pray for me to know God's mind and your mind in the initial wedding arrangements that I need to make. Just pray for me.

I pray for you and I love you.
Nancy

I had hurt my back sometime before, during a wild floor-hockey game at Juvie, and now, for the first time in my life I was seeing a chiropractor. One morning, the day after an adjustment, I awoke with a strange tingling sensation in my arms and fingers. I felt nervous about what it might mean. I fretted about it most of the day at the office, then I finally phoned the chiropractor and described my problem.

"You'd better get in here right away," he said tersely. "You've got some kind of neurological interference happening." I hung up. Now I was terrified. Having no experience with this sort of thing, I was convinced that I was going to end up paralyzed, and just when I was finally getting married! I started to cry; fear was running away with me. I drove to the chiropractor's office, and he got me straightened out in short order.

When I arrived home, I was exhausted from the emotional turmoil. When I went upstairs to check the mail, I noticed a bouquet of fresh flowers on Barb's dining-room table. Taking a closer look, I saw that they were for me—from Greg. Barb must have still been here this morning when the deliveryman came.

The bouquet was huge. There were a dozen lovely red roses and a dozen happy yellow and white daisies, set off by a pile of greenery. Only God could have timed such a wonderful surprise on such a terrible day.

Later that night on the phone, Greg told me that daisies always made him think of friendship. The red roses, of course, represented love. What a special gift from this special man, my best friend, my lover.

May 5
Dear Nancy,

It's been a while since I've written you a letter. It seems somewhat strange to talk to you this way. Nevertheless, since seeing you, I feel as though I can communicate more richly than before, and I find it pure joy to share my thoughts with the dear love of my life. You. You. Thank You, Lord, for my dear Nancy.

I'm doing a double-take. Separating your name and gazing imaginatively upon your face. Don't even try to understand that one. You have to be there.

Thanks for calling last night. A breath of fresh air. I love to hear your voice and through it be able to sense your presence. I'm getting to <u>know</u> you. One spirit. Babe. I want to talk to you all the time. I'm tired. I'm in love. I wanted to call you this morning after I got off work. I want you all the time. Spending the leisurely time last week has left us somewhat deluded. Life has its routine activities that are more the norm than what we have experienced in our time together.

I mentioned that I was getting "cold feet" concerning a wedding date and marriage, because of money concerns. But, oh, Lord, how can we put this off? Nancy, we have to pray. Thank you for sharing with me your feelings concerning finances—and that I ought not feel any pressure to proceed with our wedding so quickly. Babe, this is very important to me, that you have released me from that pressure, which was bearing down on me and all culminating on the wedding date. That you would be willing to wait blesses my heart. Thanks, babe.

Well, babe, I gotta run. Lord, give me time. Settle me down. Keep my love, my dear love, Nancy. Even though we are separated, Lord, give us one mind. We need to know each other. And the many details—give me time to accomplish all the duties. Make me efficient.

Nancy, please find a list of my liabilities. I'm a little embarrassed to share them, because of my mishandling, but I know I must—and I want—to share all of me with you. Even my problems. I want you to help me grow, and I pray that I can help you grow. Let's do it together.

All of my heart,
your guy

In spite of Greg's hesitance at this point about keeping the wedding date as set, and my releasing him from that obligation, the date remained as planned.

May 10
Hi Greg,

I received your letter with your financial info yesterday when I got home from work. I had hysterics when I read it. Praise God for my twisted sense of humour.

I guess the picture is so bad that I can only laugh and thank God for the way He will work it out *and* for the way He will work in us through it.

Looks like your charge cards need to have a little operation—with a pair of scissors. And concerning the debt to income tax: I thank the Lord for my experience in prison ministry. No matter where they lock you away, I should be able to get in to visit you.

May 7
Dear Nancy,

God bless you, my dear! How I miss you. I often think of you, and for some reason I often picture you distressed or perplexed. Babe, don't let the details get you down. Easier said than done?! I hope I don't seem too distant or uninvolved. I pray that we, though separated, can come to that oneness of mind for a moment, right now. Just as you remember it. Let us rest in each other as we rest in God.

I'm somewhat frustrated right now. I haven't slept much, and of course I long for you to be near. Also, I'm not sure of my job right now and how to do it. My financial situation looks shaky, especially when I view it from your vantage point. With you never having been in debt, I'm sure my situation looks overwhelming to you. Rest assured of me and my background: I'm not uncomfortable with my debts, other than the fact that they are debts and must be paid. I've been in worse situations. God is teaching me new ways.

Well, babe, the other night, you mentioned having qualms. The only qualms I have are my own inadequacies, causing me to feel unworthy. I know this is not God talking. I truly am tired. I must stay in the Word. I think I'm about to go through another door. When I find myself at a crossroads or in a situation that leaves no direction, I become uncomfortable. It is then that I must rest in God. He is my sufficiency.

Sometimes I think, "I can't wait three months to get married—let's do it now!" Oh, babe, I want to fulfill your expectations; I want to meet your needs. Lord, make me a godly husband and a blessing to my wife. Sometimes I fear that I am falling short.

I long to pray with you, to build with you, to get _your_ mind on matters.

I gotta go. Babe, I love you.

One night during a phone conversation, Greg made a comment: "Just think, after we've been married a couple of weeks, we'll both be walking around with smug smiles on our faces all the time."

"Yeah," I said.

I knew exactly what he meant. We both had a lot of worldly experience, and once we got into bed with each other, we wouldn't be bumbling and bashful like some Christians I knew.

How God must have groaned to Himself at our attitude! It would be years before I would fully realize how deeply I had been wounded and scarred by my earlier, wanton ways. My past was to become a great hindrance, not a help, in my love life with Greg.

But now, God began to give me new insight in this area. The beginnings of a change in my perspective were revealed in my next letter.

May 7
My dear Greg—my lover:

I love you. Saturday night at 11:00, sitting up in bed writing. I imagine you are sleeping right now—I hope so, if you're getting up to work in three hours. I miss you, babe. (You've been gone five days already.) I want to at least hear your voice on the telephone.

But it's good to discipline ourselves to write letters again. It's like having been blessed in the presence of the Lord—and then having to go through "the desert," having to seek His face in prayer, read His word, and keep going by faith, even when you can't see or feel anything. That's what it's like, writing to you again, after spending a whole long week right with you.

There's something I need to talk to you about, babe. Sex. I don't know where to start. God is doing such a work in me...

The week you were here, I believe I experienced finally what it's like to be free of lust. But with that freedom has come a keener awareness of lust—what it is—and when it's around. I didn't really hate lust before—in fact, I often enjoyed it. I always had trouble separating it from love: they seemed to flow together. Now they seem very distinct.

God seems to be restoring my purity to me in a way I didn't think possible. Let me try to explain.

In the recent past, watching church girlfriends get married (i.e., virgins), I would often think of how they must feel as the wedding night approached. Uncertain. Inexperienced. Inadequate. Just plain scared.

Inwardly I would feel a bit condescending toward them (though I didn't recognize it then). I honestly thought that I had the best of both worlds. Here I was, experienced in loving from the ways of the world. I knew (I thought) how to please my partner, and I enjoyed sex. Now I was saved and sanctified, yet still experienced, so when I got married and

God put His stamp of holiness on it, I could jump right in like an old pro, delight myself and my partner on our first night together and not have to go through an emotionally and physically difficult time of learning.

Oh, dear God, how this is all changing. My dear Greg, as I look ahead toward our wedding night, it's not like I expected. I feel painfully shy of nudity and of you. I'm downright scared of the lovemaking. I feel so naïve and frightened. I feel like a scared young girl. I feel like a virgin.

I mentioned this in part to Barb. She just smiled and said, "Well, 'old thing are passed away; all thing are become new.'"

The reason I'm sharing this with you, babe, is because (in addition to just wanting to share myself with you—in communication), I am hoping you will understand and treat me accordingly.

You know some of my past, and sometimes I'm afraid maybe you take my old nature as a frame of reference in which to relate to me. I'm sure if we'd met "in the world," we would have had many common interests and a mutual attraction. But we must be careful not to relate to that part of each other[1]—but rather to the "new creation."[2]

Sometimes I may perpetrate your relating to me in a less-than-godly way—by my own foolish jesting.[3] Let's seek the Lord concerning sex within marriage and be open to what He wants us to know and experience. I'm sure it will be easier (and better) to start out His way than to make our own presumptions and then try to change later.

I love you, babe, and I'm falling asleep now. Good night. I will be imagining your arms around me again.

May 13
Dear Nancy,

Thanks for your letter, babe. I had to laugh. It was a laugh of joy. I take great pleasure in your newfound innocence. Babe—you are very dear to me. I am pleased to know that you are approaching sexuality from this new direction. I <u>know</u> it is God-given. I have also begun to sense a newness in myself, although it has not manifested itself to the dimensions that it has in you. In fact, I had not even considered this approach—the "virgin" attitude as you described. But, <u>yes</u>.

These elements have been stirring in me as well. I have not given tremendous thought to our wedding night; I have taken a lot of that aspect for granted. I now look forward to that time with a new anticipation. I want the Lord in our bedroom, in our lovemaking. I, also, have been relating to my past when considering our future, almost without conscious thought. The laugh I experienced was one of relief and exhilaration. Babe, thanks for being frank. Thanks for being honest. Thanks for being vulnerable. This shows me your love. How I cherish your love. We must learn sexuality all over, not the act so much as the God-given union in its fullest. I believe we will experience a new dimension and a God-inspired fulfillment such as we never experienced in our pasts. We no longer have to perform. No matter how comfortable we used to be, we still had a sense of pride in our abilities. Ha! What a joke.

God, teach me how to make love to my wife. Never let me violate her, nor use her as an object for my satisfaction. Nancy, may I <u>never</u> hurt you or cause you harm in this area of our life. I will pray for you in this as I hope you are praying for me. Thanks again, babe. I love you. Pray for a new understanding.

You seem so far away. Only two weeks and I can see you again.

Love to you, my dear wife.

With Greg's and my marriage now imminent, Barb bought me a copy of *The Act of Marriage* by Tim and Beverly LaHaye. The flyleaf said that the book was for every person who was married or about to be married.

I understood that proviso as I read the book; it would not have been appropriate reading in my earlier, single state. It stirred up intense desire in me, which is best left sleeping until the right time. As it says in the Song of Solomon, "I adjure you, O daughters of Jerusalem, that you never [again attempt to] stir up or awaken love until it pleases."[4] Passion had been awakened in me way back in my teens, and I had done many things both as an unbeliever and as a Christian to pour fuel on its flames. It had been an ongoing struggle to get that blaze under control, and God had finally accomplished that. Now it was an appropriate time, in His order, to bring up the subject.

There was one particular thought put across in that book that I would never forget. It said that a man's sexual desire for his wife was one of the primary ways for him to demonstrate his love for her.[5] As I read that part, I thought, *Lord, I'm just going to accept* that idea by faith, as a fact—that when Greg desires me sexually, he is expressing his love for me.

I can understand now better than I could then why this quote was so significant to me. I had known a lot of sexual desire from various men in my life, and most of the time their desire had more to do with their love of their own pleasure than their love for me. (To be absolutely fair to the male sex, however, let me also say that, most often, I was guilty of the same thing.) I had no idea how much healing I was going to need in this area.

I knew, back when I "got saved," that according to God's Word, old things had passed away and everything had become new. I couldn't have guessed back then that six years later God would still be busy making everything new, specifically in the area of physical intimacy and especially now that I was entering matrimony. God had cleaned me up a lot, but there were some parts He hadn't been able to get at until they were opened up by my impending marriage.

May 9
My dear Greg,

Writing the date at the top of the page, I realize it's seven years ago today that Derrick's accident happened.

I had, by this time, told Greg about my old boyfriend Derrick and his hang-gliding accident. He had heard, too, about the residual fear, from that trauma, that I'd had to work through back in March.

I usually write his parents this time every year—either now or on his birthday (next month), because I know it's always hardest on them on those dates.
This year I will write to tell them about you: what a different kind of letter it will be. I'll send them a picture of you too. They'll be so pleased:

they've been waiting and watching for seven years to have me meet someone important enough to write "home" about.

As I said on the phone, babe, I think I might send you the part of my old (pre-Christian) journal that I found. I burned some of it—censored other parts [with a big, black felt pen]. Please don't even try to read through the black—it's sick.

I had taken most of my old journal out to the incinerator in Barb's backyard and burned it. It was a strange experience, like once and for all severing myself from a past that, in spite of its ugliness, still held some nostalgic ties. After those many pages of handwriting had been reduced to ashes, I returned to the house and sought out Barb, upstairs.

"Are you all right?" Her question was more like an exclamation. "You look as white as a ghost."

I told her what I had been up to, that yes, I was okay, but that I did feel kind of shaky.

In addition to the journal, I burned some old letters from and pictures of past boyfriends. I felt it was important to make a clean break, to exhibit to all the powers of darkness that I was agreeing with God: my past take on relationships was wrong. I was showing an all-or-nothing commitment, symbolically cleaning the slate, making a fresh start. Was it a loss? Well, yes, in a way. But like Paul said, "I count all things [as] loss ... , and do count them [as] dung."[6] He also said, "Forgetting what lies behind"—both the good and the bad—"and reaching forward to what lies ahead."[7] Nothing in the old life was worth clinging to.

I believe that with my little ritual at the burn barrel that day, something happened on a deeply spiritual level.

The letter continues:

At the Bill Gothard conference, I had resolved to burn the whole journal. Now I don't think I should—at least not this part. It seems harmless. But I'd like your opinion.

I still need to find the ten- or twelve-year-old part—400 pages of it. That will need to be censored more severely.

I also burned the letters I found, to and from Derrick—and some other, strange letters from a fellow... I'm glad I burned them. And I don't want to compromise on this journal issue, but neither do I want to destroy something I shouldn't.

I hope it doesn't bother you when the subject of Derrick comes up now and then. Re-reading some of the journal (that I burned) made me realize what a shambles that relationship really was. I do believe we cared about each other very deeply, but it was such a mess... We had an unspoken agreement to never talk about (or expect) commitment, and now I know (as you know) that commitment is the only ground in which love can flourish.

I always say that I lived with Derrick for two years. That isn't really accurate. I spent so much time running away from him to assert my independence, to prove that I didn't really need him, that I was often absent for two or three months at a time. Yet still, it was the most "committed" relationship I was ever in. Isn't that wild?

I am so looking forward to committing myself to you. Actually, the commitment is already there. It just isn't allowed to fully manifest yet. But you are MY MAN, Greg. I love you; I want to learn to love you more. I know I'm only scratching the surface on what God has in store... I'm excited.

God has taught me much about dying to myself in service to Him (through working with YFC). I have a feeling it was just practising me up to learn to die to myself within marriage. Not simply to submit to the Lord, but to submit to Him through you.

Shortly before our engagement, I'd received a phone call out of the blue from Lucas, whom I'd met at Youth for Christ's School of Ministry in Rockford, Illinois. "Hey, Fowler," he greeted me. "I just phoned to ask you to marry me."

Without even pausing to consider how serious he might really be, I laughed him off. Then I proceeded to tell him all about Greg, how I'd met him, and how God was moving in our relationship. Lucas was not impressed; he thought there were just as many amazing "coincidences" in his and my brief acquaintance. The phone conversation lasted close to two hours.

Now I had received a letter from him enclosing a copy of his phone bill. I think he thought I should pay for at least part of it.

I had a letter from Lucas this morning (friend from Alaska) laying a subtle guilt trip on me for how much his phone call (proposal) cost him: $127.00. He forgets that I clearly turned him down in the first three minutes of the phone call. The letter was like a last-ditch effort (he doesn't yet know that I'm engaged now) and he lamented the things he liked about me the most: my height, my musical abilities, my blue eyes...

BLUE EYES?![8]

So many things to be worked out, Greg. I hope the Lord will confirm soon where we'll be living. If it's Wetaskiwin (as we seem to assume), it will be a serious move, considering my furniture and especially my piano. I would like to be assured that if we're going to all the trouble and expense that we'll be there for quite a while. But then again, in the Lord it's foolish to ask for such assurance. I want us both to be ready to go here or there as the Lord directs. Maybe I need to consider selling my piano and buying another one up there. But I don't want to. We'll see.

Meanwhile, if there are some things you're not worrying about, send down a list and I'll worry them for you.

Wife-in-Waiting

One evening I was puttering around in my suite when the realization hit me: in just a few short months, I really would be married—to this great, big, masculine man. I was suddenly cognisant, alone there in my room, of his huge, powerful physique, and a wave of desire rose up and literally knocked me down. Just like those Jane Austen-type women who were always fluttering and fainting, I swooned into a dizzy heap on the floor.

The remaining ten weeks stretched ahead like a desert that had to be crossed—with just a couple of oases along the way. The waiting seemed to go on forever.

May 14
Dear Greg,

My dear sweetheart, I love you so much. I just keep waiting for the time to creep by until I can see you again. I don't count the days till the wedding: it's too long. I just count the days till I fly up: only thirteen. The time is full, and it will go fast.

I feel really "in love" today, besides loving you. I keep trying to remember how it feels to sit next to you, or across from you—or to feel your arms around me, to imagine your voice. Oh, just to be able to sit and talk and talk and talk.

It will be so good when we're finally married and we don't have to be separated by time and distance anymore.

I know a girl from Idaho; she is married—they are a beautiful couple who I really see as having been put together by God (like us!). But he's a fisherman and is gone for <u>six months</u> out of the year. Dear God, please don't ask anything like that of me. I've done all the waiting I want to do already! Yes, Greg—if you end up building bins, I'd rather work with you. I'm sure not going to wait at home for a week or two at a time!

Speaking of which: that's going to be wild—setting up housekeeping with you. You talk about qualms regarding your inadequacies... it's going to be something else for me to try to be a wife and a keeper of the home. Please be patient—and please be open in your communication. Yes, I've done lots of cooking, but not lately and not for someone I love. Housekeeping is not my greatest gift—this past year living in Barb's suite is the first time I've had to keep up a place on my own, and I've finally realized how much is involved and how little of the load I carried before. No wonder roommates always ended up being so ticked off at me.

A couple of months ago I pulled the ugly carpet out of that little bathroom and decided to clean up the tile. That's the first time in my life I ever waxed a floor! How bad is that?!

I don't think I'm a slob, but I'm no blue ribbon: I've got a lot to learn.

I love you, babe.

I had written a letter to Corinne, the girl with whom I'd roomed in Banff when I'd first met Greg. I wanted to tell her what had transpired and that Greg and I were now engaged. It didn't seem right that she might hear the news via the evangelical grapevine. Now I received a response from her:

> Dear Nancy,
>
> Thank you for your letter. It was so kind of you to write and let me know what has happened between you and Greg. I am not surprised that something happened between you. I must admit I was surprised that it happened so fast!—but when it's right, and God's plan, it doesn't need a lot of time.
>
> I am sorry that the situation was so awkward for you in Banff. You certainly showed a lot of Christian love and understanding. I wasn't really looking past what I wanted. On the "ice-cream-parlour night," I knew Greg wasn't God's plan for me—not that I didn't want it, but I knew it wasn't right, and then I was really sorry I had tried to "push" things (I'm sure you understand). I wanted so much to tell Greg, so that he would understand I didn't expect more, but there just wasn't an opportunity, and

I was feeling very awkward. I was starting to clue in to what was happening between you and Greg (at least that there was an attraction), but I didn't have a chance to let you know that Greg was no way "my territory." I am glad it has all worked out for the best (as God's plans always do), but I am sorry it was so awkward for you (awkward for three of us!).

Thank you again for your letter, and I wish you and Greg all of God's richest blessings. When are you getting married, and where will you be living? Maybe I will see you both again.

God bless.
Love in Christ,
Corinne

May 13
Dear Greg,

Nothing much to say right now. I love you, and I'm so looking forward to everything. It's so right on; there are just no alternatives. The peace grows every day and the confirmations keep coming.
Love and hugs and kisses.

May 17
Dear Greg,

Oh, my dear darling! I love you so much. I can see your picture on my dresser from here at my desk. Oh, babe. Is that really you? Why can't I reach out and feel you, put my arms around you and feel your strong back. Oh, babe, I'm so tired and I wish you were here.

♪ I WANNA PUT MY ARMS AROUND YOU—AND NEVER LET YOU GO—I WANNA TELL YOU ALL THE THINGS I KNOW YOU ALREADY KNOW—AND I'LL TELL YOU ONCE MORE IN A LETTER IF YOU REALLY WANT ME TO—BUT I'D RATHER WAIT TILL YOU ARE HERE TO SAY "I LOVE YOU." ♪

Today I went to Nanaimo to see Kathy and Rod. Spent the afternoon visiting with Kathy, talking about "the marriage bed is undefiled" and related subjects. Praise God. We have lots to talk about when I see you again.

Also, my sweetheart, I can sense you praying repeatedly for God to make us of one heart and one mind. Right?! Something is happening in my heart concerning this birth control issue. I just don't know, babe—it's pretty radical—kind of scary. But I got serious before the Lord about it today and told Him I want to do it His way (and just what His way is I have a sneaky suspicion). I pray for grace and peace and confirmation upon confirmation in this issue—and mostly for a unity of mind between you and me.

I love you, my lover. I'm going to bed now—I'm beat.

Ever since that day sitting on the grass outside the Bill Gothard conference, when Greg and I talked about children and he made that startling statement about family planning being God's department, I had been wondering what God's perspective was on birth control. It made sense that the miraculous process of conception and pregnancy would rest well in God's mighty hands, but the thought of not having any control over the timing of such a blessed event made me feel... well, completely out of control. I, who from the beginning of my walk with God had wanted Him to be completely in charge of my life, who had wanted to be able to yield over to Him any area that He might put His finger on—I had hit a wall.

But to say "No" here would be to say, "Jesus, I want you to be Lord of every area of my life, except for this one." And yet I agreed wholeheartedly with the statement I had once heard: "If Jesus isn't Lord of everything, He's really not Lord at all."

I had begun praying for God to work in my heart concerning this, and already I was sensing that it might be a beautiful thing. Scary, but beautiful.

Eight days before I would fly to Wetaskiwin:

May 18
My dear darling Greg:

I'm at the office—just scanning through a book I bought at the Full Gospel Businessmen's banquet the other night for one of the kids at Juvie. It's <u>The Happiest People on Earth</u>, by Demos Shakarian. I read it some years ago.

As I scanned a few pages, this line jumped out at me: "I had learned...for Rose and me the key to finding God's will was <u>agreement</u>."¹ I <u>know</u> that's a major truth for us, babe—we've seen it work already. And it reminded me of where I finished off writing to you last night, about grace, peace, confirmation upon confirmation, and finally, unity or AGREEMENT.

Praise the Lord.

my dear Greg:

*your mouthwash is sitting
in my bathroom cupboard
your dental floss is still kicking around
on the floor of my car
and I've found a protein tablet for your contacts in the dark reaches of my purse*

*you seem to have invaded
every area of my life—*

and I <u>love</u> it!

♪ *OH, HOW MANY DAYS MUST I KEEP COUNTING?—HOW MANY NIGHTS MUST I FEEL SO ALL ALONE?—MY HEART KEEPS GETTING EMPTIER—MY LONELINESS KEEPS MOUNTING—AND THIS PLACE I LIVE NO LONGER FEELS LIKE HOME!* ♪

Eight days and still counting...

One day Barb gave me a funny card that went like this: "The bathtub was invented in 1850. The telephone was invented in 1875. That means if you'd been living in 1850, you could have sat in the bathtub for 25 years without the phone ringing!"

This card was to commemorate the scene of Greg's phone call the previous night, when I'd come flying out of the bathtub (upstairs), streaming with water, with a towel half-pulled around me. I literally slid across Barb's darkened kitchen, smashed into a chair, which in turn crashed into the table—before I finally got the receiver off the hook.

I forwarded it to Greg, just as Barb had suggested, and enclosed another letter:

Saturday

I guess this will be the last letter till I see you, babe. Especially since the mail won't move on the holiday Monday.

Sometimes, Greg, I feel bad about the amount of time we're spending on the phone. It seems irresponsible. Yet I keep thinking it's only for a while (yeah, right, Nancy—just another couple of months, which could be hundreds and hundreds and HUNDREDS of dollars), and then after we're married we can just start paying it off along with everything else you owe. It's not like me to pass off the self-discipline like this and say, "Oh well, we'll worry about it later." What do <u>you</u> think, babe?

I only know that it feels so good to hear that phone go just after eleven and know that I will hear your voice when I pick it up. And it <u>is</u> hard to hang up again. Maybe for the months of June and July we could set ourselves a limit, i.e., ten or fifteen minutes a night. But I seem to remember suggesting that before.

I'm going to leave this for now—pour another cup of tea and get into the Word for a while. It's a beautiful morning, ten o'clock. I need to clean the house, go downtown—then maybe I'll go sit in the sun somewhere.

I love you, Greg—oh, babe, you're too far away. All you are to me now is a stack of paper letters, a picture on my dresser, and an occasional voice on the telephone. Unreal parts and symbols that make my insides cry out: "But I remember how he felt, to lean against, to hold; he was real, so solid, so real for once, not just a figment of a lonely imagination. Now he's just a memory—a voice, a letter, a picture. But he _is_ real. Oh, God—he _is_, isn't he?

Next day:

I miss you so badly today, babe, that I'm in pain. Maybe God is removing His grace just for a brief time so I can remember to thank Him for His keeping power, His peace, the ability to wait patiently and graciously. My insides are crying out for you. I don't remember feeling this kind of pain before. Maybe I have written a letter like this to you before. Maybe, but I can't remember.

Thank You, my dear Lord, for Greg. Thank You for the love You've put in my heart for him. Thank You that he loves me too. Oh, thank You for that, Lord.

Thank You for the grace You've given me thus far to wait patiently, even as this love I feel for Greg grows deeper and stronger. Father—I need more grace now. I need You to put Your everlasting arms around me and hold me till the time that You give me back to my husband again.

Remind me, Lord, that when I'm lonely, it's _You_ that I need.

The object of my loneliness right now is you, Greg. But loneliness does not need an object to which to attach itself, though it will attach itself to one readily. It exists in and of itself, and it threatens to consume one who refuses, in its early stages, to be driven to God.

Dear Greg—does this make sense to you? Maybe not—it doesn't matter.

I love you, babe.

Things were not going well with Greg's job at the mini-mall. The grocery store there kept pornography on the magazine rack, an issue that caused some disagreement between Greg and the owner. Then there was a fire. Finally Greg gave notice.

May 18
Dear Nancy,

Hi babe! I love you today. Isn't that reassuring? Actually, I'm very much in love with you today. Knowing that we share the same Spirit allows me to rest in confidence in your love. I'm very vulnerable but full of trust. Thanks for loving me.

Well, as of Sunday night, I'm out of work. There are a few things that I'm going to finish, particularly in regards to the fire (insurance claims, etc.) that I will pursue just because nobody else knows anything about what's going on.

I can't use my principles as a lever against them. They must remove the pornography of their own conviction. I talked with the owner again. He knows I'm right. I told him that he can't compromise in any area—not even a little bit. It just leads to bigger issues, which it already has.

God, forgive them according to your tender mercies. Cause them to see the light. Cause me to react not in judgement but in love toward them.

Greg sweetie—

I have to admit that after hearing you're out of work, I now have a "spirit of panic" sitting near my ear, trying to get in. I wish you were here so we could pray together more.

I have to keep my eyes on the Lord and on the EXCITEMENT of this walk—and test—of faith. It's the only thing to do.

I love you, babe.

May 19
Dear Nancy,

Well, babe? Not much news. I'm fed up with waiting around for work. That's a good sign: God is going to do something again. He usually does when I can't see the next move.

God, give me purpose and direction. I feel so useless. Lord, train me up for "the ministry" or let me go to work.

I'm fed up too with waiting to see you again and with waiting to get married. I do so want to get on with it. Babe... babe. I want you. I hunger and thirst for you. I'm lost without you. You are—you have become—so much of my life. Words can't say it.

God be with you.

May 21
Dear Nancy,

It's been a relaxing day. I rode my motorbike for a while, visited friends, and spent three hours in the Word and prayer this morning. Tonight is our organizational meeting for the youth. Six days, babe. Life is certainly full. The future looks tremendous. Beyond my wildest imaginations for sure. How I want you to be my wife! You and me, babe. We'll set 'em on fire. Praise the Lord! This is pure conviction, with the exhilaration only there to spice it up. Thank you, Jesus.

How do you like that? Four topics, one paragraph. Do I buzz or what?

God is beginning to set the groundwork. I can see it "through a glass dimly." Let's get on with it! I'm rarin' to go. It's all coming together so nice. Why me, Lord?!

My little brother, Rollin, is extremely delighted at the prospect of being my best man. I think maybe I will ask John too, then Etienne.

Greg was going to ask my brother, John, to be a groomsman, as well as Etienne, a friend from Holland. He had come to Canada early in '82, stayed with relatives in the Wetaskiwin area, and attended Greg's new church. He and Greg, fast friends, then spent the summer working together out at Circle Square Ranch.

When you come up, we get to pray for God's will in so many things. Where are we going to live? What will we live in? Children, and all that that entails, ministerial direction, what we will be doing for work, the honeymoon. The list goes on. I'm beside myself with excitement.

As I stop to think, sometimes I wonder and ask God what you are praying for, particularly concerning your role in the marriage. I know that you so dearly want to be a good wife in God's and my eyes—the area of housekeeping for example. Your mind is buzzing sometimes concerning cooking, dishes, etc. Babe, I've never taken for granted that you would do the "housework"—that that was your role. As I go on I'm going to realize just what my expectations have been in the past—I pray God. Lord, help me never take anything for granted. I want Your idea. Lord, help Nance and me to meet the area of "roles" head-on, and smooth out the rough areas by Your amazing grace.

How I long to get on with our marriage!

When you arrive, if things happen with you the way they did with me in Victoria, meeting people will be much smoother than anticipated. They are just as excited—and looking forward to it as much—as you. If I don't slow down, we will never be able to stop buzzing when you get here. I may be working too, so there will be a lot happening.

See you soon.

We'll sing, dance, pray, read, share—hallelujah!

Giving Up Control

I remember that plane ride on the twenty-seventh of May. An hour and a half, and I couldn't do anything but sit there and wait. I couldn't do anything but breathe.

I got off the plane to find that it was a scorcher of a day, 30°C. On the way from the airport into Wetaskiwin, Greg stopped his Bronco at a Dairy Queen. As we sat down in a booth with our ice cream, Greg took an ice cube from his water glass and slipped it down the front of my dress. I didn't even react—I just smiled. The feelings inside were so intense, it seemed I could hardly feel the shocking cold on my hot skin.

It was important to both of us that we keep our relationship pure, and for the next ten days we had to keep our wits about us, not sneaking any privileges that did not yet rightfully belong to us. We believed that that would bring the greatest blessing on the intimacy within our soon-coming marriage.

God gave me an amusing reminder about behaving ourselves:

Greg took me for a spin on his big Honda 1100, slaloming down the middle of a secondary highway, out in the country to a friend's place. Jay was a friend of Greg's, an ag-pilot (an aerial crop sprayer). He had recently offered Greg a job, selling farm chemicals. The work would begin shortly after I returned to Victoria. For now, he wanted Jay to meet me.

No one was around.

"We should take his horses down to water while we're waiting," Greg said.

He found a couple of bridles, slipped them on the two horses, and led them through a gate into a pasture on the far side of which a little creek ran. Then we swung on bareback and trotted the horses across the field to the creek.

As we headed once again toward the yard, we saw that a vehicle had pulled in and a man was getting out. We kicked the horses into a canter to cover the remaining ground more quickly. My mount got excited; she dropped her head and started to buck. I hauled up hard on the reins and clung tightly with my legs. I was just getting her under control as this man reached us on the run and grabbed the bridle.

I slid off and found myself looking into the face of a nice-looking middle-aged man with a well-tanned face and worried blue eyes. I guessed that he'd had a bad moment, thinking he was about to see Greg's new fiancée dumped on her head.

The weak muscles in my inner thighs were trembling from the sudden workout, and there was a lot of adrenaline coursing through my veins, but it hadn't really been anything serious, at least not for a proud ex-cowgirl.

"Are you all right?" breathed Jay as he shook my hand and greeted me.

"I'm fine," I assured him. "My legs are just a bit shaky." I rubbed my hands up and down the inside of my thighs. "I haven't ridden in a long time, and you just don't use those muscles for anything else."

Now this fine Christian man suddenly had a naughty twinkle in his eye and a broad smile on his face. "Well," he said, "if you are, you shouldn't be."

Greg still had an apartment in town, above the mini-mall he'd been managing, but we both stayed with friends of his, Karen and Derryl, at night. This couple from Greg's church had made a big difference in his life at the beginning of his Christian walk, a little less than two years earlier. They had invited him out for dinner several times a week, giving him solid and continual fellowship during those first months when his lifestyle was making a radical shift. He had spoken of them to me with the greatest of gratitude. Now once again they opened their home to him, this time to facilitate his courtship.

Karen and Derryl's hospitality meant that our nights were properly chaperoned, and they accommodated us at opposite ends of their big house. This helped to safeguard us against unnecessary temptation during those dreamy, sleep-time hours. But during the days, once or twice we were in Greg's apartment for a bit, and it was difficult to restrain ourselves. It really is good counsel for an unmarried couple to avoid being alone together. We had shared many little kisses on our first date (to my initial consternation) and more serious kisses on the second. On this, our third date, we fell into some extremely passionate embracing, even though all clothing stayed in place and hands behaved themselves. Still, the way we clung to each other sometimes—Greg made a wry comment at one point that it was obvious we were both experienced.

I didn't like him saying that, nor did I like the way the more extreme embracing made me feel afterwards. It threatened to besmirch the new purity that God had been working in our lives. "Stolen bread tastes sweet, but it turns to gravel in the mouth."[1]

Early in the week we made a trip out to Circle Square Ranch. We would be going back out there with Greg's youth group that weekend for a retreat, and so he had some things to arrange. Besides, he was keen for his friends there to meet me. He cautioned me on our way out that the Ranch had strict rules regarding unmarried couples: we mustn't so much as hold hands while we were there. Because this is a ministry to kids and teenagers, they want to set an irreproachable standard of godliness in male/female relationships and to hold marriage in high esteem.

I had no argument with a stance like that; I was only too aware, from personal experience, of the propensity of young, hot-blooded guys and girls to be too easy and too casual about physical contact. "It is good for a man not to touch a woman,"[2] was a Scripture I well understood. Even the affectionate touch of a hand can cause feelings and hormones to skyrocket, regardless of whether marriage is anywhere on the horizon.

In my relationship with Greg, I didn't want to indulge in any pleasures before their rightful time; I didn't want anything to cloud the joy that I knew God had in store for us. Greg was of the same mind.

But there was one time during that weeklong visit that Greg stepped over the line, and ironically, it was on that first drive out to the Ranch, where we were going to be watching our p's and q's even more closely than usual. It was a beautiful day. His Bronco was eating up the miles, speeding down the wide expanse of asphalt, and we were soaking in each other's presence. All at once, Greg reached over and ran his big hand slowly down the front of my blouse. That was all, but it was too much. It gave me a choking mixture of pleasure and guilt. I wished that it hadn't happened. It was the only regret of our courtship.

There was another scene that troubled me, through no fault of Greg's or mine—something more diffuse and subliminal. We had come back to Greg's apartment from the Ranch, all wet and sandy from an impulsive dip in a river on the way back. I took a shower, after which I borrowed a tee shirt of Greg's. There I was, in an oversized and unbecoming tee shirt, wet, stringy hair clinging to my head, no make-up, sitting on Greg's bed and strumming my guitar. I got a glimpse of myself in a mirror, and suddenly I was flashed back to much earlier times. Pre-Christian times. The hippie girl, sitting on a bed in some guy's place, strumming my guitar, wondering who I was and where I belonged.

It was subtle, but it hit me hard. I felt depressed and disoriented. I felt common and unclean. I felt lost.

I see now that the way I had begun to dress and to present myself, as a young Christian woman, had, in a way, offered me a tangible change—a visible covering—from my former misdirected and unhappy identity. This new image had helped me to separate myself from the lifestyle that mocked propriety in everything from dress code to sexual morals. I had now been a Christian for six years, but at this moment, I felt that my new life in God had evaporated, that it was not real and never had been.

Greg sensed the dark mood that had fallen on me, and we talked about it. I don't recall what was said, but I know that he responded with characteristic steadiness and faith, which enabled me to regain my equilibrium before too long.

I believe now that the evil principalities and powers, the spiritual wickedness in high places,[3] were working overtime that day to dissuade me from the sure confidence that my true covering is the blood of Christ. Perhaps my new external image, more feminine and conservative these past few years, had become to me a symbol of the "robe of righteousness"[4] that clothes the nakedness of my soul and hides the sin of my past. Now that my nicer clothes were hanging on the shower rail of Greg's bathroom, the glimpse in the mirror had given me an unpleasant flashback to my heathen years and somehow implicated Greg and our relationship in the process.

More than anything in the world, I wanted my relationship with Greg to be different from what I had known before. As I viewed all of my past liaisons with young men from my present vantage point, whether my experiences from my wild, hedonistic days or those from my supposedly sanctified life of these more recent years, none of them bore any resemblance to what God was offering me in marriage to Greg. At the same time, it seemed that all the hosts of hell were bent this day on superimposing my past on the present, trying to soil and subvert the beauty of holiness.

The night before I was to fly home, I met all of Greg's family. Everyone came out to the old family farmhouse near Kingman. His mom had made strawberry shortcake for an early celebration of Greg's birthday, still three days away. I had met both of Greg's parents earlier in the week; now I had the opportunity of meeting his four siblings, their spouses, and a total of eleven children. They were a wonderfully warm bunch, and they made me feel welcome.

But I felt something else too. I felt overwhelmed by this big family, their possible presumptions and expectations. I felt trapped. I didn't understand what I was feeling or why, and I didn't know how to talk about it.

Later that night, in the hot tub back at Karen and Derryl's, I broached the subject by making a very strange and slightly hostile statement. I was amazed at Greg's objectivity and his maturity, his sensitivity in being able to see past my words and recognize the real issue, which in this case simply boiled down to prenuptial jitters. By the time I wrote again, I was able to clarify my feelings a little better.

June 6
My Greg:

Here we are back to letters again. It doesn't take very long away from you to realize how deeply my life is already joined to yours.

I fell asleep as soon as I got on the plane. Woke up once to look briefly down on a glorious view of snow-capped mountains, white fluffy clouds, and sunshine. Majestic. "The heavens declare the glory of God; and the firmament showeth his handywork."[5] His majesty.

Nodded right out again and didn't know a thing till we were flying over Vancouver with the pilot announcing our descent into Victoria.

I felt so strange greeting Barb. Seemed like I'd been away for months. Didn't feel like I was coming home—it felt like going away from home.

My suite is so empty, babe. I rattle in it. My life is so empty without you. I'm going to have to exert a great deal of discipline, throw myself into these last few weeks of work, bury myself in God—and let this time go by. I need to press in to God anyway: there's too much turbulence in my life right now not to be seeking Him more than ever.

The enemy needs very little encouragement to torment me—I am put to remembrance that he didn't like the idea of you and me from the start.

My dear babe, my Greg—I thank God for you. I'm thankful for the way you stand in the assault of my verbal musing and questioning. I need to get these things out. If I had to be more careful, for fear of your misunderstanding or your feeling that our relationship was threatened, I couldn't vent these things in the same way. Like last night in the whirlpool when I made that whacky statement: "Your family actually seems to think I'm going to go through with this marriage."

My sweetheart, in my heart of hearts there's no doubt that beside you is where I want to be. When I stop and think, there's no question as to God's will in the situation. Even when I'm feeling scared or pressured or doubtful, the only place I want to be is in your arms. Not that I expect your presence to be the ultimate answer to my needs (only God's presence is), but just because that's where I belong. I don't want to withdraw away from you and into myself (though that would always have been my pattern in the past). I want to grow closer to you all the time, through bad times as well as good.

Your incredible patience and understanding has given me the freedom and the desire to draw close to you when I feel most unlovely—i.e., when I'm upset. And because of the freedom I feel with you to express these conflicting emotions, they are finally being stirred up, faced, and, I believe, slowly rooted out. I feel tremendous healing going on inside me, Greg. Even aside from my love for you and the delight I have in you, I'm so excited and grateful at the way I see God using you in my life.

Thank you, Jesus, for this man Greg. Thanks upon thanks for bringing him into my life. Keep him, Jesus; love him for me, Lord. Teach us many things in our absence from each other. Put wings on the next twenty-four days.

I finished the letter with a Scripture that encapsulated for me the long wait for our wedding day, printing it in large block letters across the bottom of the page:

HOPE DEFERRED MAKETH THE HEART SICK; BUT WHEN THE DESIRE COMETH, IT IS A TREE OF LIFE.

Proverbs 13:12, KJV

Plans were taking shape. Greg called one night, excited because he had finally heard from his friend Etienne—a letter from Holland. Yes, he could come, and he would be honoured to be a groomsman.

Greg had burst in on Derryl at work. "Exciting news!" he told him. But as the words came out of his mouth, he remembered that Etienne had made him promise not to tell anyone in Wetaskiwin. Etienne wanted to surprise them. So now Greg was suspended mid-sentence, with Derryl wondering what the news was.

So Greg said the first thing that popped into his mind: "Nancy's pregnant!"

Derryl gulped and said, "Uh, I guess that is pretty exciting, isn't it?"

Hearing this over the phone, I was distraught. I could just imagine that Derryl would be thinking, *And it happened under my roof!*

Greg thought the whole thing was hilarious. Because sleeping with me before our wedding was not even a remote possibility in his mind, he had no qualms about what seemed to him a far-fetched joke.

June 7
My dear darling Nancy,

Too few hours of sleep, lack of direction and inspiration concerning work, and hundreds of miles between us are starting to have their effect on me.

I'm having withdrawal symptoms. One whole week of having you constantly with me and now the shock of your absence is leaving me a little tight-chested and dazed. Where are you, babe?

The sleep has given me energy to bring myself down to earth. The new job and its responsibilities and the desire to have you near—compounded by your sudden absence—makes me want to live life <u>with</u> you all the more. Confirmation. Babe, I need you. These are God-given needs and desires. Thank You, Lord.

Get back here real soon.

From my limited perspective (of one day!) things look good concerning my new work. I would rate it 8.7 on a scale of 10....

He fills in some details on his new job with Jay and then sums up:

Babe! It looks good, but it's too early to prophesy. I've been studying up on the literature and doing some mental gymnastics. Rarin' to go tomorrow. Praise the Lord! Pray that I keep my priorities straight and that I can be effective, redeeming the time. Lord, open my eyes to Your direction.

I turn twenty-seven tomorrow. There's no excitement at all. This is the first time that I've not anticipated my birthday. I must be getting old, or maybe it's just that <u>all</u> my days are so exciting now. Praise the Lord!

I miss you. I know you love me. My heart is with you.

June 9
My dear Greg:

I waited last night for you to call. At midnight I went to bed, forcefully pushing aside the urge to call you and hear your voice.

Today is Thursday, three weeks from the day (I hope, dear God) that you'll fly out again. Back to counting days again, though trying not to—because it seems to slow time down.

I'm slowly going through my files at work, discarding much stuff, compiling some to take with me, sorting the remainder back into the main files. Three weeks from today, I'll clean out my desk, load up the last armful of books and papers, and trudge home like a small schoolgirl at the end of June. School's finally out and the summer holidays stretch deliciously out before me. FREEDOM!

I had been telling friends that now, after ten years in the job force, I was going to get married and take the rest of my life *off*! (I would have plenty of opportunity, in the years ahead, to eat those words again and again.)

My support at YFC had continued to dwindle slowly ever since March, another confirmation that this chapter in my life was ending. My final cheque depleted the small reserves that the organization was holding in my name and left me several hundred dollars short of my usual salary. I couldn't have cared less though: I was looking forward to a whole new adventure, a whole new life. Besides, God had ways of providing for me that I would never have guessed.

Unbeknownst to me, the pastors and board at my church had discussed the idea of giving me a "dowry," an old-fashioned gesture to bless one of their "daughters." So it was that one Sunday morning during the service, I was called up to the front and handed a pretty wicker basket. They explained to the congregation what they had decided to do, and said that anyone who wanted to contribute to my dowry should come up and put it in my basket.

I was deeply moved by the gesture; I felt so very loved, so very much a part of this big family. I stood there with tears running down my cheeks as people flocked forward. Soon the basket overflowed and bills fluttered down to the floor around my feet. When I got home and counted it all, there was over five hundred dollars.

One night on the phone as we were talking about where we might end up living, Greg suddenly said, just kind of off the cuff, "Maybe we should go live at Circle Square Ranch."

I didn't know Greg well enough yet to know that he thinks aloud frequently, muses about possibilities, and dreams verbally—and that his words at this "dream" stage have little to do with what he really wants or what may actually come to pass. Early in our relationship, I responded internally to everything he said as though it were going to happen tomorrow. This particular suggestion put me into an emotional tailspin:

June 14
Dear Greg,

I don't know if I should say anything more about my fears. I wasn't going to because I don't want to alarm you. On the other hand, to talk about them seems to be the only way to disarm them. Also, through communication of my deep (and often irrational) thoughts, I guess you'll come to know me better. And I do want you to know me.

So okay, I'll tell you where my mind was, after talking to you Sunday night.

"Live on the Ranch—in the wintertime? You out and about, working. Nothing for me to do. Trying to housekeep in an ugly, messy, dark room like [I named some friends of Greg's on staff at Circle Square]. *Wearing slobby clothes all the time and feeling like a slob. All my nice clothes hanging in the closet and rotting. Once in a while going in to Stettler for church—big* deal—*I can't wear any of my nice clothes anyway because I'm six months pregnant and I'm not even used to being your wife yet!"*

I was still wrestling with the idea of trusting God with our "family planning." I was sure that if we took this radical route, I would get pregnant immediately. Being married was going to be a huge change, even without factoring in a baby within the first year. I could feel my independent life spinning out of control.

Furthermore, I really knew nothing about pregnancy. I had never been close to any woman who was having a baby, and I had hardly any impressions—and certainly not any favourable ones—about the state of pregnancy. Pregnant women looked fat and awkward—not to mention incredibly dependent—and that's all there was to it. I didn't think it was possible to be pregnant and beautiful at the same time. I was finally going to have a husband to enjoy my slim, athletic body, but that body would be misshapen—ruined—within a few short months.

With regards to where we might live, I realized now that I couldn't just follow my own lead anymore. And I really didn't know if Greg might be quite content living in circumstances not nearly so comfortable and so pleasant as I had become accustomed to. It put a whole new dimension on the Scripture I had blithely embraced earlier in the courtship: "Whither thou goest, I will go."[6] I knew that it was important to submit to my husband. I prided myself on being spiritual, and this was part of the "recipe." But I had never dreamed how much it would tear at my insides to yield over the control to a man, even to a man that I loved and trusted with my whole heart.

Greg was a full three years younger than I (still is!). He was also much younger in the Lord than I—he had not even been saved two years at this point and I had known the Lord now six years. I believed that I was therefore much more spiritually mature than he, and I was concerned, during our courtship, that this might present a problem in our marriage. I mean, I really believed in wifely submission as a scriptural ideal, but how would that play out in real life? What would I do? Just shut my mouth and pretend that I didn't know better than he?

There were so many implications to marriage that I'd never thought of before. I felt panicked sometimes. I had to cling to God and trust Him like I never had before.

I needn't have worried. God soon showed me that spiritual maturity is not directly proportional to earth years, and that He could do a fast work in a man's life when He so chose. And one of the things that made it easy to yield to Greg's leadership was that he was embracing his God-given role. He was ready to take on the responsibility of heading up our home. I had quickly found that, unlike any other guy I'd ever been with, I couldn't push him around or control him or manipulate him. That was one of the things that most endeared him to me. It was actually a great relief to come under his leadership. And God taught me that the trick was to submit to Greg in the same way that I submitted to Him and to trust that as I did so, He would give Greg the necessary wisdom.

My letter continues:

Okay, my sweetheart, does that sound pretty irrational? Do you still love me? I still love you, babe. You know, it feels so good to get that out. Even though you're not here to actually dialogue with, it feels good to put it on paper. I'm crying now—with relief, I guess, partly. Partly too, God's stirring something up in me again, doing more healing.

Dear God! I had no idea I was so complex until you came along, Greg.

Please understand that the scene I've hypothesized about the Ranch, and about being pregnant ("fat and ugly"—I want to be beautiful for you, my babe)—these issues are more between me and the Lord than between you and me. In other words—I'm not saying I even know yet whether I want to live on the Ranch or not, or whether I want to take a chance on getting pregnant right away or not. I think the point is that I'm feeling more and more out of control and I'm just not used to it. I start to think, "Hey—I don't even know Greg. I don't know if maybe he'd be happy out in the boonies living in a dive for the rest of our lives. Just because he looks so excellent and so right in a jacket and tie, I have presumed that living 'nice' (at least sometimes) is important to him. But I don't really know."

Me? Well, I was a slob for so long (before I got saved) and felt like such a fish out of water around girls in dresses and heels that I never thought I'd see the day when I'd talk as though this were so important. Lord, have You taken me to the opposite extreme?

Oh, Lord, my God. Help me to lie still in Your hand. Help me to replace my fear and my rebellion with faith, trust, and obedience. Oh, God, You taught me so much about dying to self in my single life. Now that You're marrying me off, I sense You telling me that death to self has only just begun.

Here I had a mental picture of being on an out-of-control bronc, and I lapsed for a moment into cowboy lingo from my Douglas Lake ranch experience:

Hang on, Nance; lean back, rake 'im high above the shoulder, and LET 'ER RATTLE!

This letter is getting very long, but just one more thing. After dinner with some friends, Sue and Dan, last Friday, Sue wanted to pray for me. As she began to pray, she said, "I feel the Lord saying that you lack confidence in this relationship. The reason is that you've always been in control—you could always be 'successful' because you were only responsible to yourself. Now there's another separate personality involved and it's no longer just up to you. It's a mutual effort, for better or for worse, and therefore it's no longer completely within your grasp and control."

Over dinner, this friend had discerned the turmoil inside me. This was the root of the fear that had first made itself known the night Greg proposed to me and which was still manifesting itself from time to time in my letters. Now I chose to yield up the control of my life in a new way, in whatever way I knew how, to God and to my husband-to-be.

The Final Countdown

In mid-June, Youth for Christ threw a staff-and-board barbeque, a combination school-year-end wind-up for all of us and farewell party for me. After supper, we moved from our hosts' yard into their living room. I was directed to seat myself at one end of a couch.

It was a set-up: the springs in that spot were broken, and as I sat down, it felt like I was falling right through to the floor. I shrieked as my feet flew up around my ears and everyone else roared with laughter.

Once we had all regained our composure and I had been shown to a better seat, I was asked if I would like to say a few words.

How would I rise to this sudden occasion? These dedicated board members and fellow staffers had been a big part of my life in the past three years. They had been a sort of collective calibration point in my ministry and personal growth. I wanted to give a special good-bye.

Handily, I had recently finished penning a funny poem. So, having just been reminded of their love of laughter, I rose from my seat and recited from memory "The Ballad of Nancy and Greg."

There was a young lady who lived for the Lord
(Though on second thought she wasn't that young!)
Who at various times had prayed and implored
That she be blessed with a special some-one

Through many trials and tears, the Lord finally taught her
To keep Him first in her eyes
Then when she least expected, love suddenly caught her
Yes, love caught her quite by surprise

He rode into town on his tractor-steed
With his gumboots all covered with mud
As he swept off the dust, he swept her off her feet
Pulse racing and heart all a-thud

Since he's presently absent, she'll speak in his place
(And we'll just hope she won't make this a habit!)
"He'd heard of laying hold of God's blessings by faith—
Saw this 'blessing' and decided to grab it!"

Together they headed back to Alberter
To the land where the dust clouds blow
He promised to love her and never desert her
She said, "Whither thou goest, I'll go"[1]

Folks said it happened so fast; "But the Lord spoke," she claimed
"With a voice that I couldn't ignore
And if this is His will, well then—praise His Name—
I'll keep suffering for the Lord!"

Greg was planning to fly down to Victoria for a visit in late June. Twelve days before his trip, he wrote a short letter:

Dear Nancy,

Surprise, surprise! I'm actually writing. It's been almost two weeks since the last one.

Well, babe, I love you tonight. I know that I do, in my deepest parts, though you seem far away and almost not really real. Of course I've been preoccupied.

The preoccupation has been work and financial responsibility. Yes, sweetheart, I do want stability. What happens if this job doesn't work out? I've been known to be wrong before, if you can believe it. Then what? I face the embarrassment and pressure at wedding time of being financially strapped. Well, dear God, what next? I have to pursue this line as though heaven-sent. One step at a time.

In one of our phone conversations, Greg had said regarding work and finances that he knew it would all come together before our wedding; otherwise he'd be broke when we got married, "and God would never do that to me."

I said to him, "That sounds a bit to me like pride talking."

"Then go for it, Lord," was his immediate response. On the spot, he was giving God licence to deal with him in the area of work and money and provision—especially where pride was concerned.

I was glad that he was so eager for God to work in his life, but I knew, too, that with a prayer like that, things would probably get a lot rougher before they got smoother.

His letter went on:

Glory to God! I just glanced at my Bible, lying open at Philippians 4: "My God shall supply all your needs, according to his riches in glory by Christ Jesus." Lord, You define that need, of course. Your grace is sufficient for me.

I'm truly enjoying the work and being able to become "wrapped up" to a given degree. When I spend my time in the Word at night, I am enjoying it more. Don't know exactly why yet—and too tired to figure it out.

I love you.

Only twelve days till I see you again!

Who are you?

Who was I? Well, for one thing, I was a young woman who for six years had prided herself on her sold-out stance regarding the Lordship of Jesus Christ in her personal life. And now I was wrestling, still, over the idea of giving the Lord control over the area of family planning. *Jesus, You are Lord of every part of my life, but surely You don't expect me to abstain from using birth control. That wouldn't be about submitting to You; it would be just letting nature take its course. Wouldn't it?*

Did I really believe that God is sovereign, that He has everything under control? That He had a deliberate plan for my life and Greg's, a foreknowledge of the children we might have and when they should be born? Did I believe that it was really He (as He clearly says in His Word) Who opens and closes the womb?[2]

As I continued to try to yield my heart to God in this area,

I began to believe that He was leading me to do what Greg had suggested—leave the family planning up to the Lord.

Greg arrived for our fourth date on the first weekend in July. We drove up to Nanaimo so that I could introduce him to Rod and Kathy.

I was a bit nervous. I was expecting that these dear friends would go over him with a fine-tooth comb, so to speak. And that's exactly what I wanted them to do. So far, I had had nothing but green lights in this relationship. But I still badly wanted approval from this couple who had been strategically involved in my spiritual life. If they had any misgivings upon meeting him, I would be foolish not to pay heed.

We had a great visit with them, but I was aware of the intensity behind the gentle questions that came here and there, mixed in with the amicable conversation.

"I understand you are divorced," Kathy said pleasantly at one point. She said it like a statement, but there was a question hanging in the air.

(Both Kathy and Rod had come through divorce: theirs was a second marriage for both parties.)

"Yes," answered Greg.

"What do you think of divorce?" she asked.

"I hate it and so does God," was Greg's firm and brief answer.

That seemed to satisfy her concerns.

It wasn't until we were driving back to Victoria that Greg realized he had been given the "third degree." He clued in when I made a happy statement: "I think you passed with flying colours."

Also during Greg's visit this time, I made an appointment with Ted Follows for some premarital counselling. It had been only about six months since I had come to see Ted about a very different kind of relationship—the struggle with my attachment to a troubled young man eight years my junior.

Ted was one of several pastors on staff at my church. A couple of the others were more charismatic (in the popular sense), and perhaps it was because of this that the young people tended to seek them out instead. Ted was certainly charismatic in the doctrinal sense; that is, he believed that all of the gifts of the Holy Spirit bestowed at Pentecost were given for all believers for all time. He operated regularly in many of these supernatural gifts. But this mid-fifties British pastor with the dour countenance was sombre in his manner, and he handled the things of God and the Word of God, I felt, with great sobriety. This was what endeared him to me. I had always felt that the Truth was safe in his hands; therefore, I was assured that I would be safe with his counsel.

Not that he didn't have a sense of humour—he certainly did. Sometimes the funniest things came out of his mouth when he preached, but his humour was dry, as it tends to be with the Brits, and he never let on that he knew he was being funny. The whole congregation might crack up, but Ted wouldn't even crack a smile.

Greg and I had a good session with him. Of course, one of the things that was addressed was Greg's divorce: how the marriage, and then the break-up, had come about. Ted talked then about how important it was, now that Greg was marrying again, that he first be completely free, spiritually, from that old tie.

At the end of the session, Ted prayed for us, and he prayed, too, specifically for Greg—that God would sever the bond that had been formed in that earlier marriage.

Then, as he was seeing us out of his office, he suddenly made an offhand and rather personal comment. With never a hint of humour in his face or his voice, Pastor Ted remarked, "It seems that just a couple of weeks ago you were fooling around with boys."

I wasn't sure if he meant to be funny or not, but either way, I felt embarrassed. His words stung. But in my heart I submitted to them humbly: they were true.

His words implied something else, something very precious to me. He was impressed with Greg. He approved of this relationship. It's as though he was saying, "Now this—this is a *man*."

At the end of Greg's visit, when I saw him off at the airport this time, I gave him a cassette tape of the testimony I had given at the Women's Aglow meeting back in March.

July 5
Dear, dear Nancy,

I miss you already this time. Nance, I love you. I listened to part of your tape last night and finished it this morning. It was a pleasure to hear your voice. I could often see your face, and I relished every thought. I love you.

I pray for the day when our understanding and acceptance of each other has come to the point where we are completely free before God and one another, free of sin and guilt—and insecurity (which stems from these), and we can build a wonderful life, together, going on for God. Nancy, I pray again to be as one, in every area of our life.

God, keep us focussed. Our oneness is only in You.

Let's not ever forsake our commitment to God, or to one another, or to our daily devotional studies. Nance, help me to keep these priorities. "He who findeth a wife findeth a good thing, and obtaineth favour from God"—Proverbs 18:22, KJV. Don't be afraid to offer advice. I know that you come in love. I love you. I want to talk lots more; I'm on a roll, but I gotta run. I love you.

Soon, babe!
Greg

July 7
Dearest Nancy,

Good day, my dear. Just a quickie here to tell you that I'm growing fonder of you each moment...

Love and all,
Greg

Barb put on a bridal shower for me at the house. One of the gifts was from a single woman about my age who attended the same church as Barb and I. It is what she wrote in her card that

I remember. She alluded to her own failures and lack of trust in God in the area of relationships. She evidently had no idea of my many stumblings, because she said that my example in this area was an inspiration to her. She quoted from Hebrews 11:6: "God is a rewarder of them that diligently seek Him."

I did indeed feel that I was being richly rewarded, but it could not be for my track record! Happily, what moves God is our continual repentance and our expectation in His goodness. This is what opens the storehouse of His grace.

July 12
My dear darling Greg:

I just finished thirteen thank-you notes for shower gifts, so I thought I'd write you a thank-you note too.
Thank you that you're you.
Thank you that you love me.
Thank you that you're so big and hunky and that you make me feel so feminine and special.
Thank you that you love and trust the Lord.
Thank you that you're perfect—for me.
Thank you that there's nothing more I would or could ask for in a man.
I thank God again tonight for you. I thank Him again that you love me. I love you so much, my babe, my Greg.

I had been warming up to the idea of trusting God with birth control, but now with the wedding date rushing upon us, I felt overwhelmed with the magnitude of all the changes in my life. I talked to Greg about it on the phone one night, told him that I was back-pedalling again. "It's too much," I said, "with everything else going on right now, to trust God with that too."

"That's all right," he said. "And God doesn't hold it against you."

It was a wise thing to say. He must have anticipated that I might easily feel guilt or condemnation for falling short of what I was beginning to see as an ideal.

Twelve days before Greg was to fly out for the wedding, he sent a card. It portrayed a young couple with their backs to the viewer. The picture looked remarkably like him and me. It said, "In everything I do...I want you beside me." And he had written,

You and me, babe.
That's right.
Together!
Uh-huh.
Yep.
xoxo
gc

His enthusiasm and optimism were contagious. And they were comforting to me, so nervous of the commitment and fearful of the future.

There was also a letter enclosed:

Dear Nancy,

Well, babe?! It's definitely true that we are going to experience changes in ourselves as the countdown continues. I am already taking on a "married" state of mind. (Are people really treating me differently or is it just my imagination?)

My feelings are mellowing. After all, could we possibly go on experiencing the emotional anticipation we first experienced, for the full five or six months? We would be utterly exhausted from anticipation. We are fearfully and wonderfully made. Amazing.

I love you! As the card says, "In everything I do...I want you beside me." Some places are hard to conceive of you being with me, only because I know you so very little. I want to learn in these areas with you. I'm truly looking forward to these situations with eager anticipation. It's going to be good. We can discover a new life together. Amen.

When I see married people around me and sense their problems, I find it difficult to imagine that we will have the same problems. If it were to be so, I wouldn't want to get married. Unresolved issues, dissatisfaction—the list goes on. Am I too blind? Am I still too "in love" to see us walking down this same road? Babe, any problem we have, let's take it head-on and resolve it. Still, I don't think we are going to have all these headaches. If I "wake up" on the other side, I will be totally taken by surprise.

Lord, make me to be unselfish.

Yes, we do seem to assume that we will be living in Wetaskiwin. We need to pray for guidance. We must talk about this, babe, and pray together. You said that you just want to be with me, that it doesn't matter where. I interpreted that to mean you would follow wherever?! I felt elated, humbled, and fearful.

Oh, God, give me direction. Let me not assume. Give my wife peace that You are giving me proper direction and that I'm hearing Your voice. Father, cause me to take the responsibility that a husband, guided by God, ought to take. Lord, I need new vision. Lord, I need to be decisive and confident in You.

My dearest, this is to be a marriage of marriages. God, make each of us quick to respond to the guidance given by You through our mate.

I believe the adjustment will be relatively smooth.

No more today. It's 2:30 A.M. Church tomorrow. God bless.

Twelve days! Can't wait to see your face and hold you close.

I love you.
gc

Part 3

Ever After

Photo by Chuck Groot

Is the Honeymoon Over Yet?

I walked up the aisle on my father's arm, in the classic cream-coloured satin gown that my mother had made for her own wedding, thirty-three years earlier. There, up at the altar, was my groom, in a smashing grey pin-striped tux with a white wing-collar shirt and grey paisley cravat. But the real picture of the moment, etched forever in my memory, was the expression on Greg's face as I came toward him. He looked overcome with emotion, a strange mixture of a grimace and a smile on his mouth as he fought to hold back tears.

We had prayed that God would allow us to totally experience and enjoy the whole day, that it would not whisk by in a flurry of confusion, but that He would help us to savour and appreciate every moment so that it would all remain vivid in our memories.

My pastor and counsellor, the Reverend Ted Follows, officiated, and the youth pastor of my church served us communion after the vows. While the youth pastor gave us the bread and wine and, in a hushed voice, delivered to just the two of us a special little sermonette, the congregation listened to a recorded song. I had written it on the day that Greg's first letter arrived, back on Valentine's Day. My brother, John, had come over from the mainland in June, bringing his portable studio and an electric piano, and had spent long hours helping me record the piece.

For me, this was the most personal touch in the service: I wanted to share with all my friends and family this "Love Song."

Lord, if You would, help me write a love song
To tell the world the story from the start

And Lord, If You would, help me sing this love song
To tell everyone the joy that's in my heart

It was a long, long time ago, Lord, You first told me
You were preparing me for someone
As You prepared him just for me
And though I sometimes grew faint-hearted
I never doubted You—oh, I believed you, Lord
Now the fulfilment of that promise I see

You've brought me to the place
Where I'm fulfilled in You and You alone
You've taught me, Lord, to come to You for each and every need
Now You give to me this man to love, to give myself to him alone
Fulfilment on fulfilment: oh, that is joy indeed

The holy state of marriage was ordained from Your Throne
As a picture in the flesh of what we'll share with You eternally
When Christ returns to claim His Bride
Who's kept herself for Him alone
We'll clearly understand what now we only dimly see

Now, Lord, I want to thank You for the love song
You wrote for Your creation, way back at the start
And Lord, I want to sing to you this love song
Just to thank You for the joy that's in my heart

The day was like a dream come true. But then, dreams often take unexpected and uncontrollable twists and turns.

We made our way through the well-wishers and climbed into the back of a big black Cadillac. As our driver pulled away from the church, I settled in next to this precious man who was to be my lover and companion for the rest of my life.

Something was wrong. I glanced up at Greg's face, inwardly checking my feelings for a pulse. The passion was gone; it was completely gone. Yes, I liked this guy. I liked him a lot. But where had the desire gone? This was unhappily reminiscent of our experience at the hot springs in Banff on our first date. Greg just seemed like "the boy next door" again.

I felt something else. I felt vaguely fearful. I was no longer my own. I knew what the Scriptures say, that the married woman does not have authority over her own body; rather, her husband does. And the married man does not have authority over his body; it now belongs to his wife.[1]

I didn't care about the latter part of the equation right now; I suddenly wasn't sure that I really wanted this man's body anyway. What concerned me was that, according to the Word of God, my body now belonged to my husband. Taken to its natural conclusion, this meant that any old time he wanted sex, he had a godly right to it. Why did this knowledge suddenly fill me with dread? Where was this subtle, creeping fear coming from?

My past had been colourful, to put it mildly. I have been known to make this caustic qualification regarding my pre-Christian lifestyle: "I wasn't really promiscuous; I only slept with guys that I really wanted to."

Translate that this way: I had been in control; I was the one in charge. Nobody ever got anything from me that I didn't want to give. A couple of times I had got myself into situations with hormonally charged young men where I had been in danger of things going where I didn't want to go, but quick thinking had rescued me.

I had been smart and resourceful, but I had also been, without realizing it, very lucky. Many young women have not got out of such predicaments unscathed. But now here I was in a whole different kind of situation: I was married, and I was suddenly feeling trapped, in a way that stirred ugly memories from the past. It seemed strange to drag these kinds of gut-sick feelings across the fresh, clean page of my brand-new marriage. But I couldn't help it: I was who I was and I had been where I had been.

The things we have done and the places we have gone remain a part of who we are forever. They are simply "there," and they will pop up whenever they please. God can and will completely forgive and cleanse, and then use the past for His purposes, but this healing, this restoration, had not yet been accomplished in this area of my life. There was so much buried in me that had not yet been exposed; God would use my marriage to bring these wounds to the light. And he was going to start immediately, within a half an hour of my saying my vows.

I realized that, before God, I had now relinquished, to my husband, control over my body, simply by saying my vows. Perhaps many women do not truly enter into marriage in this respect; either they don't understand the significance of yielding on this level or they're not willing to do so. But I understood, and I had pledged myself willingly.

Willingly? Yes, absolutely. I wanted my body to belong to my husband. I wanted his to belong to me. It's just that this part of me, this part that was used to being in control regarding sex, that *needed* to be in control, was beginning to cry out. Other fears had made themselves manifest during our courtship, and I had brought them to God and continually worked at opening and yielding myself to Him and to Greg. But this need for control in the area of my sexuality, with the exception of a couple of little murmurs, had remained silent throughout the courtship. Now it was finding itself trapped in unfamiliar territory, and it was frightened. And it manifested its discomfort by turning off the passion switch.

The reception at the historic Oak Bay Beach Hotel was a stand-up affair, waiters circulating with trays of fancy hors d'oeuvres. Greg and I were kept busy, first with photos out in the hotel's sprawling gardens, then with a formal receiving line, less-formal circulating with guests, and finally the program. We were so busy that we hardly got to taste any of the fine food. In fact, the afternoon got quite long and breakfast became a distant memory.

My friend Kent was the master of ceremonies. It was fitting that this young man, who had exhibited to me such spiritual consecration in dating, courtship, and marriage, should preside over this celebration.

Doug Perkins, my boss from Youth for Christ, gave the toast to the bride. I'll always remember how he ended it, with that well-known verse from Proverbs 31: "Favour is deceitful, and beauty is fleeting; but a woman who fears the Lord, she shall be praised."[2]

Pretty young bride, never mind your beauty. It will fade before long. And don't set your heart on the attention and favour you receive from family and friends on this special day. It is temporal. Lock in to your relationship with God. It will last forever, and it will sustain and breathe life into every day that follows after the wedding. The woman who fears the Lord, she'll not only be praised, she'll be blessed.

If I would stay in reverential fear, holy awe, of God, believing His Word and living accordingly, I'd be able to meet any challenge that marriage might bring my way. His grace would be sufficient for me. But of course, no bride can begin to guess how much grace and faith it will take or in what areas of her life it will be needed.

It was finally time to throw my bouquet; then we made our getaway, this time occupying the front seat of the black Caddy. But here a logistical oversight made itself known: we had booked a suite in the same hotel, just for the wedding night (unbeknown to our friends, of course), and we now would have to wait till all our guests were gone before we could sneak back to our room unobserved. Initially that didn't seem like a big deal; we went for a drive down to the ocean and parked for a while. No passion—there was plenty of time for that later, and besides, I was still feeling strangely detached emotionally. We just talked, and after a bit we drove back to the hotel. The parking lot was still full of familiar cars. We continued to drive around, occasionally looping back to the vicinity of the hotel, then racing past furtively lest we be spotted by any friends who might have practical joking on their minds.

It appeared that our guests were having a wonderful time, even without us. No one was leaving in a hurry. It actually got quite late, and we were very tired and hungry. We considered at one point finding a restaurant where we could have a cup of coffee and a bite to eat, but we felt very conspicuous (an understatement!) in our wedding clothes. Talk about being all dressed up and no place to go!

Finally we were able to retire to our room. God may have had serious work in mind for Monday morning, but for now, our wedding night, He gave us a very pleasant time. We prayed first, asking God to bless our time together.

Greg talked to God about something we had touched on a couple of times during our courtship. "Lord, we want Your idea of marriage. We want You to bring us into everything You intended marriage to be. Do the work in us to make us fit to experience Your design."

Then I prayed out what was on my heart, the family-planning thing: "Lord, I feel that You ideally would have liked me to trust You in this area, but You know that I just felt it was too much to deal with all at once. But Lord, even though we are using birth control, if You have a better plan in mind—if for some reason You want us to start a family right away, then I would ask You to override our precautions. Then I would know for sure that it was You, that it was Your will, and not just 'nature taking its course.'"

I had a hard time finding the feelings that were supposed to be there, but I was able to go through the motions physically, and Greg's presence, his love, and his confidence in God made a comforting haven in which to hide myself.

But it was strange, too, to be lying in bed with a man. For six years now, as a Christian, I had battled to keep myself out of situations like this. During those years, "sex" had been synonymous with "sin." It had been by far my greatest struggle, the fight for personal purity, and it was hard to just suddenly switch gears and feel that this was really all right. I found myself glancing over and over again at the rings on my left hand, silently reassuring myself, *It's okay, Nance, it's okay; you're married now.*

It was midnight when we realized again how hungry we were. But room service was closed now until 7:00 A.M., and furthermore, on Sunday night in Victoria back then, you couldn't find a single food establishment that was open, at least not one that would deliver. We were out of luck until morning.

Breakfast was huge and very welcome. We sat out on the private balcony, and I wore the flowing negligee and gown, a gift from a bunch of lady friends, that I hadn't got around to putting on the night before.

I tied in to my sausage and eggs, smiling at Greg, thinking that I hardly knew this wonderful man. And sure enough, I didn't.

"There's something I feel I should tell you," he said, looking suddenly very sombre.

My goodness, this sounded serious. "What's that?" I answered calmly, drawing him out.

"I think you need to know that I am responsible for my nephew Shawn."

All I could think was that he was confessing that he had had an affair with his brother's wife and that he was really the father of their child. I nearly lost my eggs and sausage. I knew that in this crazy, sin-sick world, people end up doing some terrible things; I had done quite a few myself. I knew that God could, certainly does, forgive absolutely anything through the blood of Jesus, anything that we truly repent of. I knew that I would get through this, somehow, with God's help. It's just that right now it was such an awful shock.

"What do you mean?" I managed to say.

"They've asked me to be his guardian if anything should ever happen to them. Are you feeling all right?"

The shock and then the relief were almost too much for me. Then I started to laugh. I told him what I had thought he meant. He was taken aback at the miscommunication and shocked at even the thought of such a possibility.

There is a proverb that says, "[She] who answers a matter before [she] hears it [all], it is folly and shame to [her]."[3] In other words, if we respond to a matter before hearing the whole story, we will sometimes jump to some very foolish conclusions.

Late in the morning we packed up, checked out, and headed up Vancouver Island in my little red Fiat. I had made arrangements to rent a place on a secluded island, a short ride on a tiny ferry from Nanaimo. Never mind exotic cruises and foreign destinations—we didn't need or want sights and sounds and stimulation. We wanted quiet and solitude and each other. We wanted some time to get acquainted.

We bought some groceries in Nanaimo then rode the ferry and followed the directions to a small mobile home, set by itself in the bush and overlooking the ocean. We settled in, and that evening I cooked supper for Greg for the first time.

Over the meal he said to me, "I'm really looking forward to spending the next fifty years of my life with you." Again I was amazed at his confidence—and I was grateful. The commitment to love "until death do us part" still loomed huge and formidable in my mind. There was so much unknown territory ahead: who knew what kind of struggles might come against us to test the mettle of our love?

There was something else that I rested in, in addition to Greg's assurance: a promise that God had given to me during the courtship. I thought about it often, especially at first: "He is able to keep that which I have committed unto Him."[4] There were two things I was very sure of: that I had committed this marriage into God's care—and that He was able to keep it safe.

It was a good thing that I had that confidence, because there was some rough sailing just ahead. After giving us a nice wedding night, God was ready to get down to the business that we had requested of Him: to make this marriage everything that He ever intended marriage to be. It's kind of like renovating a house. If you want to make a run-down place into a beautiful home, you must first expose and tear out what is rotten, smelly, or unsound, and then you have to build with good materials, working from a well-thought-out plan.

It was Day One of our honeymoon, and I was already finding it difficult to respond to Greg's intimate advances. I found that I wanted to wear a nightie to bed and keep it on; Greg would have preferred to see me and to hold me in the buff.

The thought of not putting on a nightie brought dark shadows over my soul, subliminal memories of my hedonistic younger years when I was casual and irreverent about nudity and sex. And my reticence now was triggering painful things in Greg. He told me, during one of our very long and very frequent dialogues—during times when anyone would have thought that newlyweds would have been making love with carefree abandon—that when his first wife began to wear a nightie to bed, this had signalled the beginning of the end of their marriage.

"Forced" into marriage by an unexpected pregnancy, Greg had shouldered his responsibility and committed his life to this young woman, choosing to love her. And after three years together, he had grown to truly love her. But their communication was not good, and he was young and naïve and didn't understand the warning signs when they came. One evening she announced that she was finished, and the next morning she packed up and left. That was the end of it.

He was devastated by the loss and the rejection. At different times over our years together, he has tried to describe to me the pain of trying to reach out and touch someone who is no longer there. Some good things came of it, however. He learned to communicate: he needed to vent his pain—to whomever would listen, and in the process he learned to express his emotions (which, as he says now, most men do not know how to do). Getting in touch with the deeper parts of himself opened him up to God. He consciously turned to the Lord in the fall of 1981, a little less than three years after the break-up. As he grew in the Faith, he began to think that perhaps God might want to bring healing and reconciliation in his broken marriage. Given this, and knowing too well the folly of playing with emotions and hormones, he had not so much as held a girl's hand from then until the time he met me, almost a year and a half later.

Just a couple of weeks before travelling to Banff for the conference where he and I were destined to meet, he received a letter from his ex-mother-in-law, telling him that her daughter had remarried. He didn't recognize the full implication of this at the time, nor did he think of it when he met me, but as he returned from Banff, he began to realize the significance of the timing of this happening: he was now a free man. Free to marry again.

Now, back to the present, he was remarried—and his new wife wanted to wear a nightie when she snuggled up to him. His issue with rejection came out of the closet and paraded around the room, demanding almost as much attention as did my uneasy feelings from the uncleanness of my past. There was a whole lot going on in the bedroom, and it wasn't what you'd expect from newlyweds.

But even though our emotional hang-ups were causing a clamour in soul and spirit, our own voices stayed quiet and reasonable. We talked and we talked, with patience, with understanding, and with faith. We began immediately to trust that this had not caught God by surprise and that He had a plan to walk us through this.

All we had to do was hang on to Him and to each other. But it was hard.

God never wastes anything; especially He never wastes our pain. He used my inability to respond to Greg to trigger his own deep feelings of rejection. This heightened his need to reach out to me for reassurance and love; this in turn increased my fear, my feeling of being trapped, which caused me, even more, to withdraw sexually. In this way God flushed both of these hang-ups out into the open where we could see them and start to deal with them. We knew that God was at work, for our higher good, and we drew comfort from the knowledge of His involvement.

I also drew comfort from the fact that I wasn't the only one with a problem. Misery loves company. Faith loves company also.

There was a humorous little incident that, in my mind, forever sums up our honeymoon: On a sunny morning in the middle of the week, Greg had got up early to go for a jog on the little-used trails through the bush around our hideaway. When he got back, he settled himself on the porch steps in the sunshine. I came out with a cup of coffee for him. Setting the coffee down, I knelt behind him, putting my arms around his neck and leaning over his shoulder. He had nothing on but his runners and a pair of navy shorts. As I leaned forward, I saw a bunch of fuzzy grey stuff all over the front of his shorts.

"What's that?" I asked.

"Oh, it's just cobwebs," he answered, trying to brush off the clingy stuff with a big hand.

"Well," I responded, "it's a sorry state of affairs when you've got cobwebs growing in your crotch on your honeymoon."

(I once tried to sell that little anecdote to Reader's Digest. They didn't choose to print it; I guess it was a bit too risqué for their magazine. I have thought, ever since, that it was their loss. They could have called it *Webbed Bliss*.)

Friday night, we took a trip over to Nanaimo. There was a family camp happening a short distance out of the city, and my friends Rod and Kathy were involved in the organization of it. Greg and I sat down to a spaghetti dinner in the busy dining room across a long trestle table from Kathy and had a welcome visit. Time slipped by and the room slowly emptied. When Greg got up to see if he could find seconds on dessert, Kathy leaned across the table with a twinkle in her eye and whispered, "How's the honeymoon going?"

I sighed. "You know how when the world says, 'Well, I guess the honeymoon's over,' they mean the good part's over, the easy part is over? Well, when this honeymoon is over, I'll just say, 'Praise the Lord!'"

She laughed, and I knew that she knew exactly what I was saying. She hadn't expected anything different. She knew that, contrary to the idea that the world likes to portray, the honeymoon is not a period of uninterrupted bliss so much as a time of adjustment. I had thought that we wouldn't need much settling, that the physical dimension of our relationship would immediately be up and running smoothly, thanks to our rather extensive past experience. After all, we were not shy, bumbling puritans.

But it was exactly because of these pre-Christian experiences that the adjustments necessary, particularly in the emotional department, were huge. It was not our purity that was causing awkwardness; it was the lack of it.

In Biblical times it was customary—no, it was *commanded*, by God—that the husband would not go off to war for a whole year after marrying, neither was he to be burdened with any business, but he was to be free at home to "cheer up" his wife.[5] (This quaint phrase, "cheer up" in the King James, is rendered this way in the *Abingdon's Strong's Hebrew Dictionary*: "to brighten up, to make blithe or gleesome, to make glad, to make joyful, to make merry, to rejoice.") Those who are just married need time to learn about themselves and each other: to learn about the art of lovemaking. Those who have a sexual past (like Greg and I did) also need time to *un*learn some things.

Those who are without God and therefore without a strict sense of sexual morality have probably been sleeping together long before they ever take their vows. They won't need the honeymoon as a period of adjustment. In this case, it's not really even a honeymoon—it's just a vacation.

I couldn't say that our honeymoon was a holiday—a lot of it was hard work. It was painful—like surgery. But surgery, sometimes, is a necessary prelude to healing. And the honeymoon, though painful in places, was good in its own way; it was special; and it was just what the Great Physician ordered.

What Is Wrong With Me?

At the end of our week alone, we returned to Victoria, packed everything we could into my little Fiat, piled the rest of the stuff into Barb's spare room until a future time, and made the long drive back through the mountains to Wetaskiwin, Alberta.

Greg found a bit of work building some granaries, but he couldn't find anyone to help him. So I began working with him, almost immediately. We went on the road together, building on co-op sites and in farmyards. I loved the physical work, but I wasn't in the best of shape after my YFC job, so I was always exhausted at the day's end. Around the time that I should have been getting hardened up to the job, I conceived (although I didn't realize it at the time) and began to feel weaker and sicker every day.

All in all, when bedtime came, I wasn't up for much more than cuddling, and this gave a handy excuse for my emotional hang-ups to procrastinate their dealings. Sometimes, by God's grace, we were able to make love quite readily, but most of the time Greg's advances triggered a sick feeling of dread in me.

This became the pattern for years, sometimes a little better, sometimes a little worse. I ached to be able to give to Greg freely what he wanted, whenever, but so often I would start to feel violated, and I could not accommodate him without betraying that deeply wounded part of me.

Through it all, Greg maintained great patience and a very unselfish attitude. At times he struggled with his feelings of rejection. He also sometimes became resentful that he was being denied the most basic "right" of marriage. But he never allowed himself to stay long in that attitude. He didn't believe that, in the Lord, he could demand his rights, and he was always quick to yield his frustration to God. He would say that there are no rights in marriage, only privileges, and he cultivated gratitude for those privileges.

"Regardless," he told me on more than one occasion, "I am committed to you. I am committed to loving you, and I *do* love you." There even came a time when he verbally gave up to God the right to ever have sex again. He knew that even in this area, he must die to himself, to figuratively lay down his life. After all, this is part of how the enemy is overcome, by God's people "[loving] not their lives unto the death."[1] Greg's making this declaration became, I believe, a strategic counteroffensive against Satan's attack on our marriage.

As I write this, I have asked Greg to expand a bit on the stance he took back then.

"Whatever the future holds for me, regarding personal sexual satisfaction, is irrelevant," he says. "I hold fast to that which is true, that is, to what God says. I believe that God has designed great things for marriage, even if *I* might never experience them. The heroes of the Faith, in the eleventh chapter of Hebrews, *believed*—though they never saw the fruition of the promise.[2] They died not having received it. Shadrach, Meshach, and Abednego said, 'He is able to deliver us, but even if He doesn't, we *will not* bow down.'"[3] Greg was refusing, back then, to bow to the idol of self-gratification. That spirit, he says, is the direct antithesis of the Spirit of God.

He continues: "The world says, 'I was designed for my needs to be met. My needs are not being met, so I'm leaving.' But God declares, 'You were designed to bring glory to Me. Hold fast to that which I say is true. What I say about marriage is true, even if you may not be experiencing it at this moment. Trust Me. Honour Me. And then—and only then—will you find your deepest needs being met.'

"Only as we cleave to God," Greg concludes, "will we give an opportunity for the fulfillment to come. We will never really find fulfillment otherwise."

We must trust God in the long haul. Through faith *and patience* we inherit God's promises.[4]

Hearing Greg submit his physical needs to God and confirm his commitment to me helped to free me from the fear that sometimes tried to taunt me: *You'd better come across or he'll get fed up with you, get angry—maybe even leave.* It freed me from the compulsion to sometimes ride roughshod over my own feelings, my own traumatized reticence, in order to give him, at all costs, what I felt he wanted and needed and deserved. That was all right sometimes— to lay down my life for him, but in general, it only exacerbated my problem, because it forced my pain into silence again; buried it in a sense of obligation. Greg was not satisfied, anyway, to have sex without my full emotional involvement. "The physical release itself is very shallow," he would say, "if I don't get the emotional release that comes when I know you really want me."

When Greg told the Lord that he was yielding up his "right" to ever have sex again for the rest of his life, I didn't think for a moment that this would be required of him. But I did believe that Greg was covering a very important spiritual base. To enjoy God's fullest blessing, we must submit everything we are, everything we have, and everything we want, to Him—even pleasure and fulfilment in sex.

Throughout it all, both of us maintained an attitude of faith. That doesn't mean that we didn't each have some very low moments, but we never seemed to have those moments at the same time. One of us always had enough God-given faith to encourage the other. We were convinced, and we were determined to stand fast in the assurance, that God had great plans for our marriage; that He really wanted, just as we had prayed, to show us everything He designed marriage to be.

Perhaps it would have been an easier road if we had not made that request of God. Many people who have entered marriage, as damaged or more damaged than we, have slipped into an okay sort of status quo. But we wanted, from the outset, for God to pull out the stops and make us fit to receive what we believed He wanted to show us and give us. We sensed, when we first prayed this way, that things could get tough. Of course, we didn't know just *how* tough, but that was providential too: God knows that sometimes it's not good to give us too much information ahead of time. He doesn't want to scare us off, to cause our hearts to fail with fear or discouragement. Sufficient unto each day are its challenges.[5]

One night in the wee small hours, after a particularly long and frustrating session of starts and stops and dialogues, I fled from the bedroom, grabbing the afghan from the end of the bed as I left, wrapping myself in it as I crawled behind a big chair in the living room. I really didn't want to be dramatic; I just felt naked and ashamed. I wanted to cover myself, pull away, hide—just as Adam and Eve did in their relationship with God, after their transgression damaged their ability to be intimate with the One who loved them.

I don't really know whether or not I wanted Greg to come looking for me, but of course he did. I remember weeping in his arms and saying, "I just want to be a sex goddess for you, and I can't."

I didn't mean anything weird in an idolatrous sense; neither was I talking about wanting an inordinate emphasis on sex in our marriage: I just wanted both of us, especially Greg, to have a full and satisfying love life. I wanted to be available to him, to satisfy him, to fill his cup to the brim whenever he had a desire. I loved him so much, so I wanted the very best for him. I wanted to *be* the very best for him.

I could not understand why I could not respond to him. It helped to talk, and we always did, when I couldn't reciprocate his advances. Sometimes after talking for an hour or two, a wee little spark of desire would ignite in my heart. If Greg took care to fan that spark ever so carefully, it would grow to a flame, but often, in his eagerness, he only served to extinguish it.

Do you know what it reminded me of? We had a very old travel trailer with a propane heater in it. Once in a while, in cool weather, I had to try to fire up that heater. I'd get a good supply of matches; I'd turn the knob to "pilot"; I'd push in the red button and hold it. Then I'd light a match and stick it over the pilot. There'd be a little "pop," and then a small blue flame would appear. But that flame was kind of a false alarm—it wasn't really "lit" yet. I'd have to hold that button in, for a long time, till the pilot got hot enough to keep burning by itself.

It was always cold when I'd be trying to do this, so my fingers would soon be numb. And I'd be down on my knees and twisted sideways to boot, and the lighting would invariably be poor.

The button wasn't very large, and furthermore it was very stiff, so I'd have to exert a lot of pressure on it. It'd be okay for ten or fifteen seconds, but that wasn't nearly enough to do the job. I'd hold it for a minute or two, until my numb fingers couldn't stand it anymore, then I'd give up and release the button. If the pilot wasn't warm enough yet, the flame would just disappear, like it was never there. All that effort—for nothing. Then I'd light another match and start all over again.

That's what it was like, so many times in the first ten years of our marriage, for Greg to try to coax desire out of me. My pilot light had gone out, and it was hard to get it lit. After a lot of wooing, he would think he had a bit of a flame started, then one false move and—nothing. Starting all over again.

It was such a paradox that on the one hand I was full of lust in my single years and yet now, within marriage, was repelled by sex. When I was young, living wild and reckless with no rules but my own, Satan encouraged me, it seems, to plumb the experiences of sex to the depths, whispering that it was good and right and natural, all the while gloating secretly that I was wandering far away from God's parameters and slowly rendering myself unable to enjoy this blessed experience within marriage. Then, once I was resting under the blessing of God in the covenant of a lifelong commitment, the enemy continually tried to whisper to me that it was shameful and wrong. It shouldn't be surprising: half-truths are one of his favourite means of deception. When I was single, what he told me about sex was true—for married women. And the thoughts and feelings with which he tormented me within marriage would have been appropriate if I were still single. Satan is always changing his tune to suit his tactics, and he is always lying. "He is a liar, and the father of it."[6]

In the fall of 1985, there was a Christian businessmen's convention in Calgary. Rod and Kathy would be there. We drove down Friday for a weekend away and some fellowship with these dear friends.

Saturday there was a women's luncheon, with the meal followed by a speaker. I don't remember what the woman spoke about or whether it touched at all on my difficulties, but they were certainly weighing heavily on my mind. At the close of the meeting, I responded to the altar call. As I stood in the prayer line-up, I began to weep and I could not stop. Kathy had left her place at the head table and was helping with the ministry when she spotted me and came to pray for me.

I poured out my heart, as tactfully as I could, feeling a little shy about my troubles. I explained that I sometimes found myself unable to respond to Greg. She addressed selfishness and tiredness, which are, of course, two very typical weaknesses of the human condition. "Even if it's the middle of the night, try to put his needs ahead of your own. Just yield. Just yield," she encouraged me gently. Then she prayed for me.

As I headed back to the room to look for Greg, my heart was far from relief of any kind. Yes, I understood what Kathy was talking about: I certainly had had to learn to lay down my life for my husband. I was as selfish and as wilful as the next person.

I was also chronically exhausted. It seemed that God had honoured the prayer on our wedding night, when we had invited Him to overrule our birth control measures if He so chose, because amazingly, our first baby had been conceived just three weeks later. And so by now, I had a wee toddler, Benjamin, to chase and also another baby already on the way.

Assuredly, in addition to dealing with my natural selfishness, I was extremely tired—all the time. But I knew that there was something else, something much bigger, much darker, than these natural weaknesses.

I found Greg in the room. I tried to talk with him about all I was feeling but could do little more than lie in his arms and weep. I was overcome with love for him and with sorrow that I could not be a responsive lover.

It was late afternoon, and it was time to get ready for the huge banquet of fifteen hundred people. But we ended up crawling under the covers and having a very tender time of lovemaking.

It was like that all through the early years of our marriage—just a few good times sprinkled in with all the hard times, just enough to keep us encouraged that God would make everything beautiful in His time.[7]

I remember one special morning in particular, back before our first baby was born. It was Saturday, and the bright blue sky threw a happy light through the bedroom window in the basement of our duplex. There was no need to get up and go anywhere: oh, the relief of a lazy Saturday morning! We stayed in bed several hours, enjoying each other's presence.

Our love on that particular morning was characterized by hilarity. Everything was so funny. Everything I said made him laugh, and everything he said and did made me think of something else funny that I could say to make him laugh some more. We both laughed ourselves silly. What a wonderful tonic! "A merry heart doeth good like a medicine."⁸ It was late in the morning when we finally climbed the stairs to the kitchen to make some breakfast. We were still laughing as we climbed. Greg was being so silly that I suddenly thought of Kent and Dee-Dee on that date that we'd had with them at the time of our engagement, how Kent was being so silly, and how Dee-Dee had used that classic line. I decided to use it on Greg:

"You're not the man I married," I told him with pseudo exasperation.

"Well, then," he replied without missing a beat, "you've got no business sleeping with me."

Most of the time, though, our love life was nothing to laugh about. I spent a lot of time thinking about what the source of my difficulties might be. There is a stereotype in the world that suggests that religion breeds revulsion of sex. Perhaps religiosity does, but not true religion. Holiness does not bring uptightness and frigidity to marriage; to the contrary, I have always believed that for those who are truly godly, who love the Lord and who are letting Him have His way with them, sex can be and should be a delight like no other. After all, God created sex, and He designed it to be a blessing, so it follows naturally that those who live closest to Him would most likely experience this mystery in its greatest fullness. No, holiness was not in any way my problem; rather, it would be my solution.

I believed that the root of my difficulties lay back in the time when I did not know God and did not want to know Him: I believed that I was feeling guilt from my past. Not guilt *for* my past—I knew that Christ had paid the penalty for that and had forgiven me. Rather, I think that somehow I was now experiencing the guilt that was *connected to sex* because of my past.

I had never felt guilty while I was "sinning" in my pre-Christian days. Here's why: Even as an unbeliever, I didn't want to go against my conscience, so I would not do anything that I believed was wrong—I had refused to. However, at university and thereafter, I found myself surrounded by very intelligent and very fine people who were also very "liberated." I came to believe (however wrongly) that I had been raised with an obsolete value system and that my conscience was misguided and needed to be realigned. As the values from my upbringing were challenged, I was careful to rationalize and then, intellectually, to fully accept any previously forbidden behaviour—before I partook. Over the period of a couple of years, I carefully re-programmed my sense of right and wrong.

As a teen, I thought that "purity" meant technical virginity—that is, abstinence from intercourse—and that no other sexual behaviour was wrong. By the time I was in my early twenties, after wrestling and finally agreeing with the values of the world around me, I had laid aside virginity as well. I came to believe that anything and everything between consenting adults was right and good—not just for the sake of "love," but even for lust, for the pleasure of the moment, for friendship, or whatever.

My conscience had been silent for years, beaten into submission by rationalization. This would explain why, when I first came to know the Lord, I didn't believe that I had ever sinned. The night of my conversion, when I had my first real heart-to-heart talk with God, I actually told Him, "I know I've never done anything wrong."

Nevertheless, I was guilty. I had at many times, in many ways, transgressed God's laws. But because of the godless philosophies I had embraced, I did not understand that I was guilty in the absolute sense of the word. I knew neither God nor His precepts. Still, that did not alter the fact that He had been there all along, that His kindly laws had been in effect, and that I had transgressed them. My guilt was an absolute fact.

Let me illustrate the idea with a story: When I was sixteen years old and was studying the driver's manual in preparation for my learner's test, I remember being forever sobered by one little warning: Ignorance would be no excuse. That is, just because I might fail to acquaint myself with some of the laws, I would still in no way be absolved from the consequences if I unknowingly violated them.

It's the same principle. There is an absolute law in effect, and for the same cause as the driving laws are legislated and enforced: God's law is for the highest good of the individual and of society. The fact that I was unfamiliar with His law in my younger years did not absolve me from the guilt, nor from the repercussions, of my behaviour.

I am not saying that I *felt* guilty about sex in my past and that it became a conditioned reflex. I was not conscious of guilt back in my pre-Christian days. I did not recognize its bitter edge in the intense sweetness of the pleasure of early sexual experimentation. It was just a strange aftertaste of uneasiness that lingered on my tongue after the pleasure was all gone. I came to accept this sad, sick feeling as part of the pleasure; and the headiness of the pleasure was far too powerful for me to be turned away by a bitter feeling afterward in my belly.

I am saying that guilt, as an absolute fact, was present every time I experienced premarital sexual pleasure.

Now, if every time I taste pleasure, I also partake of guilt; if every time I swallow a little pleasure, I also swallow some guilt, the two become inexorably linked in my soul and I cannot then enjoy one without experiencing the other.

Picture it this way: Sexual Pleasure is a beautiful woman, clothed in diaphanous veils, having a demure and innocent countenance, wearing a garland of leaves and springtime flowers in her upswept hair. But what's this? A host of ugly little demons have attached themselves to her, silently, parasitically, all over. Here is a little one called Uncleanness; one called Masturbation; another called Fantasy. Here is Fornication, and there is Adultery, and Lasciviousness, and Lust, and Licentiousness. Over all of these repulsive beings, there presides a large and intimidating bully named Guilt. He is reclining across the shoulders of this beautiful woman, an evil leer on his face. One hand is wrapped around her forehead, oppressing her mind; the other is clasping her breast, holding her heart captive.

There were some ugly things in my past. Now I was born anew, made pure and righteous by the blood of Christ—and married, covenanted to my husband under the great blessing of God. But whenever I opened the door to welcome Pleasure, a host of ugly, unwanted guests slipped right on in with her. It would still be years before those parasites would be disentangled from beautiful, godly Sexual Pleasure.

"We must through much tribulation enter into the kingdom of God," says the Scripture.[9] Greg and I wanted the fullness of God's design in our marriage, so the difficulties should have come as no surprise. Great trials give us wonderful opportunities to cultivate a desperate need of God. This reaching out to God inevitably ushers His kingdom into our lives. "Blessed are the poor in spirit [those who recognize their spiritual need]: for theirs is the kingdom of heaven."[10]

> I know that all things work together for the good
> And for a long time now I've understood
> That the good being done
> Is to conform me to the image of Your Son[11]

When the heart is tenderized with pain, God is more easily able to impress on it the indelible image of His Son.

Babies and Kisses

The years slipped by and the babies came.

Benjamin, as I said, was first. A month before he was due, I started having false labour, and it kept happening off and on for a week. I was concerned: I wanted to carry this baby full term. Of course, that would be healthiest for both the baby and me, but my main concern was this: I could just imagine people at church counting on their fingers and wagging their tongues if this baby showed up too soon. It had been very important to both of us that we restrain ourselves from sex until we were married. How ironic it would be if our first baby arrived a month early!

Fortunately on all counts, Baby Benjamin waited all the way to his due date and then deliberated casually for an extra six days after that. He arrived nine months and three weeks after our wedding.

Because Ben had made his appearance so directly, even in spite of our using birth control, we were convinced that God had sovereignly chosen for us to begin our family immediately. In the strength of that confidence, we now chose to leave the rest of the family planning completely in His hands. Our second son, Lindsay, arrived twenty-two months later; Melissa was born another two years after that.

I had thought I was busy with one baby; now, with three, I was stretched awfully thin. Still, both Greg and I wanted to let God have His way in giving us the children He wanted, when He wanted. When we chose to trust God in this area, that meant that we gave no consideration to times and dates and temperatures. It's not that we were using natural means of birth control: we simply were not trying to prevent pregnancy. It was God's business completely. He showed us, with the conception of the first three, that it wouldn't necessarily happen when medical science said I was fertile, and it might happen when it shouldn't.

When Melissa's second birthday came and went with no sign of another baby on the way, Greg and I began to wonder if there were going to be any more. We felt a sad sense of loss to think that this might be the end of it. We were thrilled when later that summer we found that I was pregnant again. Rachel was born a few weeks after Melissa turned three.

It was a tremendous blessing to both of us to have learned to let God plan our family. I often had opportunity to share our convictions on the matter with other women. But there was a harsh edge coming into this subject: I had begun to feel that this way was the only way and that couples who would not or could not put birth control into God's hands were not only missing a blessing, but also they were less spiritual than we were.

Six months after Rachel's birth, I suffered a complete collapse, mental, emotional, physical, and spiritual. I had driven myself to exhaustion, and I would be a long time coming back to full health. Greg was away more than he was home, and there was no family close by to help. The care of the children fell almost entirely to me. Throughout Rachel's first year, I lived in fear of getting pregnant again; there was no way I could handle another child. I was too ill to properly look after the four babies I already had. And yet I felt bound and obligated to retain my conviction about trusting God with the family planning.

Greg finally addressed this issue one evening. "This isn't faith," he said. Once I thought about it, I had to agree: I was no longer "trusting God" in this area, yielded to whatever He might bring my way; I was hoping desperately that I would not get pregnant. The conviction that had been such a blessing had turned into a curse that was tormenting me.

"It's like God is over here," I said to Greg, "loving me and wanting me to live in peace, and over here is this conviction, totally separate from God now, beating me with a big stick."

I began to see that because of my lack of compassion and understanding and tolerance for believers who did not hold the same position on this subject—because I had allowed pride to come in and puff me up—God had allowed this conviction, a blessing that had originally come from Him, to now oppress me and humble me. I made plans to have my tubes tied.

Providentially, just the day before I was to have this little surgery, I was chatting with a woman friend and mentioned my intent. She knew that I had been struggling with anxiety and depression for a year and that I was on medication, and she gasped: "Don't you know what happens to some women when they have that done?"

I didn't, and I told her so.

"Because of the hormonal implications," she explained, "many women have severe problems with depression afterwards."

I couldn't understand why my doctor had not volunteered any such information. I phoned Greg to apprise him of this turn of affairs. He told me to cancel the surgery immediately: he would get a vasectomy instead.

The fear of another pregnancy had done nothing to help my receptivity to Greg's advances, and it was a relief to lay those concerns to rest. But even though four babies in seven years may have made it look like our love life was thriving, it was still full of hang-ups and struggles, with or without the pregnancy issue.

I had discovered not very far into our marriage that I usually didn't even enjoy kissing Greg. I put it down to the way he actually kissed, as opposed to any neurosis of mine. But also, whenever he came home from work and folded me up in a big hug and gave me a casual kiss—or even as he just happened by me in the house and caught me up in an impulsive embrace, something stiffened inside of me. I loved him with all of my heart, and I loved and appreciated the fact that he loved me, but I couldn't help but feel, when he expressed his love spontaneously in the middle of the day, that he was buttering me up for the evening—that he had hopes and expectations for what might happen that night when we climbed into bed.

Sometimes I tried to express to him how his embraces made me feel, because I earnestly wanted to get to the bottom of it all. But it was hurtful to him; he didn't like to think that his expressions of love were interpreted as calculated advances. And my rational mind did not think that of him either; it was just a very deep feeling of uneasiness that I couldn't shake.

As far as the actual way he kissed, I couldn't bear to tell him that it turned me off. I was sure it would hurt him, so I went on putting it off, thinking that probably I would have to put it off forever.

When we had been married seven years—*seven whole years*—I finally took the plunge one night. "I'm uncomfortable with the way you kiss me," I told him gently. "Your kisses are too wet."

He was quite matter-of-fact. "Oh," he said. "I thought women liked wet kisses. I thought sloppy was sexy."

"No," I told him.

We spent a long time talking about the whole kissing thing that night. Greg thought my distaste ran deeper than personal preference, that it wasn't really about the way he kissed. "Maybe you need to forgive all the guys who ever kissed you," he suggested, "to forgive them for taking from you what they had no God-given right to take."

I considered this briefly; then I had to disagree. "I don't think so. I don't see how any guy ever really wronged me. Nobody ever got anything from me that I didn't want to give."

He was thoughtful. "Maybe you need to forgive them for taking from you what you had no right to give."

Something in this rang a bell. Yes, I would try doing that. (You see, it isn't just a question of whether a sexual act is perpetuated on a woman against her will that determines whether emotional damage is done: if it's against God's will, even if the woman is quite willing, something is blighted.)

The next morning, after Greg had gone to work, I got a blank sheet of paper and a pen. I sat down at the kitchen table and began to write down names, beginning with the ones with whom I had exchanged both simple and serious kisses, continuing on with the ones with whom I'd got a little more involved—and a lot more involved, working up to the ones with whom I had actually had intercourse.

It was tough going; it made me feel sick. I filled up the first side, two columns, and then the list spilled over onto the other side. I'm ashamed to say that in a couple of cases concerning kissing and "making out," I had to jot down a situation instead of a name, because I hadn't even known the name of the fellow involved. Such in the party scene sometimes.

I would never have guessed back then—in my teens and early twenties—that in my future some of these faces, any of these faces, might at any time suddenly leer out of the bedroom shadows when I was trying to make love to my husband. What was done in darkness, I thought back then, was between just me and that guy. Consenting adults. Nobody else knew; it might just as well have never happened. I didn't understand then that these people were becoming a permanent part of my personal history, and that they could never be removed except by the grace of God. Now here I was, coming to terms with all of these men on this piece of paper.

It's not that I had never repented of these situations; I certainly had—as many as I had remembered, whenever I had remembered. In some cases I had repented multiple times for just one ugly scene. But now it seemed that the Lord wanted me to take a good hard look at all of them, all together. And I did. I faced all of my sexual sin, clearly and squarely, and asked God to forgive me for giving away what was not right to give at the time. I received His forgiveness, based on 1 John 1:9, "If we confess our sins, He is faithful and just to forgive us our sins, and to cleanse us from all unrighteousness." I believed His Word, accepting it at face value.

And then in Jesus' name, I forgave the whole bunch of young men represented by the names on my paper. I forgave them, as my wise husband had suggested, for taking from me what I had no godly right to give. Then I crumpled up the paper, grabbed a little book of matches out of the drawer, stepped out on the deck, and burned that vile list in the fire pit.

(A note to the reader: Please don't look here for a method to release you from your own traumas and difficulties: look to the Lord. Sometimes someone else's experience can give us an idea of how God might want us to proceed, but as in anything else, this is about our own relationship with God and how He leads us personally, out of bondage and into freedom.)

I can't say that I felt any great, cosmic rushes of healing that day, although I did feel rather relieved about it all. But amazingly, I never, ever had a problem again with my husband kissing me. Forever after, it has filled me with a sense of loving and being loved. Yes, I think he toned down on the "wet" after our conversation, but that all seemed to be beside the point now. His kisses simply fill me with delight that he is who he is and he loves me.

The new freedom in the area of kissing gave me renewed faith that God would completely heal the intimate part of our life. Meanwhile, I wondered how and when I would broach the facts of life with my children. I longed for them to grow up unscathed in their sexuality and enter into marriage without inhibitions. I was convinced that godly instruction was key.

My own sex education was almost non-existent; my instruction regarding morals, implicit rather than explicit. "Nice girls don't" was the way one might have summed it up, and even though it was never really stated, I understood it that way. And I accepted it, until I moved away from home at the age of eighteen and began to discover a whole lot of nice girls—and guys—who, indeed, "did."

I knew now, raising my own kids, that the facts of life needed to be spelled out clearly to them, along with an unapologetic mandate of right and wrong. But even that wouldn't be enough. I needed to do my best to nurture in them love and reverence for God. Principles alone become powerless as children mature and go out on their own into the real world—unless they are founded on a relationship with the Principle-Maker Himself. I was a case in point: I'd been raised with "good morals," yet with no understanding of why right was right and wrong was wrong. That is, I did not know God and so I could not understand, much less accept, the absolute nature of Truth. Furthermore, I did not have, until the age of twenty-four, an indwelling Saviour to give me power over my own sin nature, even if I had been inclined to maintain a stand against immorality.

How would I approach this part of the children's education?

I heard Dr. James Dobson comment on the subject one time, something to this effect: "You need to talk to your children about sex when they're young. If you wait until adolescence, you'll lose them to embarrassment."

I agreed that "when they're young" is a good time, but I wasn't sure precisely what time would be right.

As it happened, I would not have to choose the time: the time would present itself. Meanwhile, I took whatever opportunity came along with a teachable moment. For instance, there was the time that Benjamin, at the tender age of four, climbed out of the bath and raced into the kitchen, stark naked. "Mom, look!" he cried. He had just discovered his testicles and didn't know whether to be excited or alarmed. He was looking to my response to decide which emotion was appropriate.

"Yes, dear," I replied calmly, "those are your testicles, and when you're older, you'll get little things inside them called 'sperm.' And when you get married, God will take one of those sperms and put it together with an egg from your wife, and He'll make a baby."

Ben had wonder written all over his face as he looked down at his parts again and back up at me. "Amazin'!" he breathed incredulously. This moment had definitely reached him before the embarrassment stage.

But that was just one little bit of information, given to one of my kids, on one occasion. I knew there would have to be a time to give a more complete picture to all of my kids.

As I say, the time presented itself. The kids and I had driven down to the Lethbridge area to camp for a week, close to where Greg was working. On our last morning there, the three older kids had found other children to play with in the campground and were busy off by themselves while one-year-old Rachel slept and I was getting things packed up. Melissa, four years old, came crying to the trailer. "Mom, the boys are playing in the fort and they won't let me come in."

"Well, I'll tell you what—let's see if we can bribe our way in with some cookies."

I took the cookie tin in one hand, and with the other hand I held her small one. She led me to this "fort," a ramshackle construction of boards and sticks. As we crept up quietly, we could hear the voice of a boy who was a couple of years older than Ben.

"...and then they had sex."

"Uh," chirped Lindsay's little six-year-old voice, "what kind of sex?"

As far as I knew, Lindsay had never even heard the word "sex" before; I believe his question actually meant, "What is sex?"

"You know," answered the older voice, and then he proceeded to describe the sex act using words in crude, locker room vernacular.

I was horrified. Grasping Melissa's hand more tightly and still moving quietly—though now at three times our original speed, I hustled back to the trailer. I didn't want the boys to know I had overheard. I lifted Melissa ahead of me into the trailer, then turned in the open doorway, cookie tin still in hand, and called in a high voice, "Boys! Oh, bo-oys! Time for a snack!"

Ben and Lindsay came running, and I made sure that they stayed within my sight and out of the company of those nasty older boys until it was time to leave.

Finally I hooked up the trailer and loaded the kids. Greg still had at least a week's work here; it was just the kids and I heading home. As I drove, I thought: *The boys are still very young to be taught about sex. But they've just had their first lesson, and from the wrong teacher and from a very wrong angle. Ready or not, it's time.*

Melissa was even younger to be hearing "the facts of life." But a year earlier, she had been molested by a babysitter. The world was not going to sit back and let my children grow up in innocence. I didn't dare sit back either. Sadly, I had not been able to prevent their innocence being stolen, but I could and I would teach them about purity—and trust God to seal it on their hearts.

I took a deep breath and gently launched in. I told the boys that Melissa and I had overheard the conversation in the fort, that we had heard them talking about sex. "But the way that boy was talking about it was wrong. How did it make you feel, what he said?"

The boys, aged six and eight, were quick to acknowledge that it had made them feel yucky and kind of guilty.

"That's not the way sex is supposed to be," I told them. "God made sex to be good and beautiful."

I went on to talk to them about the love of a man and woman within marriage and about the sex act itself, using the correct anatomical terms, explaining that the words the boy had used were rude and vulgar. I told them that the devil likes to taint anything that God has made, and that the more special God has made something to be, the harder the enemy works to ruin it and make it ugly.

When I had done with the initial explanation and reassurance,

I told them that if there was ever anything else they wanted to know about sex, they should come and ask Mommy and Daddy.

"You're going to hear kids talking about it, just like you boys did today, and you're going to hear mention of it in movies and stuff, but a lot of what you're going to hear will be from the wrong perspective. We want you to understand about sex from a godly perspective, so please feel free anytime to ask us anything."

I asked them if they had any questions right then, and they did, so the conversation went on and on. Finally Ben summarized the conversation in the administrative way that he was born with, saying in a large, grown-up sort of voice, "I think it's been good for us to have this talk, and I think that when we get home, we should all have our baths and get our pyjamas on, then we should go sit on Mom's bed and talk about this a little bit more."

Still the subject continued to come up, off and on, throughout the remainder of the journey, as it was a five-hour trip in all. I was responding to yet another question from one of the kids as we rounded a certain corner in the country near our home, and to this day, every time I drive by that corner, I remember the statement I made and I remember the internal reaction to my own statement, even though it is now many years ago:

"Yes, sex is a beautiful thing. God made it to be that way. It's a wonderful blessing between a man and his wife."

Hypocrite, I thought immediately. *You don't really believe that. You don't even enjoy sex, most of the time.* But then I took that devilish thought captive with my next one: *I am not a hypocrite. What I am telling the children is the truth, the Truth according to God—which is the only truth there is. It may be that my mind and heart cannot yet fully embrace this particular truth, but I still believe it, and furthermore, God will bring me to the place where it is true to me personally.*

Healing Finally Comes

Early in June of 1993, I began seeing a wonderful counsellor, Jim Robertson. I had heard good things about this man and the gift that God has given him to help people break through in difficult areas of their lives. When I first went to see him, I had no thought of talking about my marriage. I suppose I went just because seeing Jim was the "happening" thing in my little Christian community and I wanted a piece of it too.

When I filled out the patient-history form, it asked me the primary reason I was seeking help. I wrote down that I needed counsel regarding my anger toward my kids. This certainly was the most pressing concern in my emotional life. With four kids and a nervous breakdown under my belt, I was perpetually one raw nerve looking for a reason to lose control again. As the counselling sessions came and went, though, we plumbed the gamut of subjects, so it wasn't long before my unhappy love life lay naked on the table.

By now I had come to accept that my past behaviour had left me with a lot of baggage, and I was trusting that God would, in His time, wipe all the guilt away. I knew His Son had paid the price for the things I had done in my ignorance and unbelief. Jesus' blood also covered the mistakes I had made in the "Christian dating" scene.

But there was something deeper than the guilt: it was fear. Why was it that I sometimes felt and acted as if I didn't trust my husband, even though I surely did? Why was it that deep down I felt as though his sexuality were a savage beast from which I needed to protect myself?

As Jim drew out my attitude toward sex, I could see he suspected that I had been sexually abused in the past. I told him at one point that my feelings regarding sex could be summed up in two words: fear and revulsion. These were certainly classic symptoms of abuse.

Some experts believe that as many as three out of four women have been molested in some way, or have at least been interfered with sexually.[1] Yet of those three out of the four, only one will have conscious recollection of the traumatic happenings.[2] Jim, too, was quick to assure me of this: the fact that I remembered nothing out of the ordinary was no guarantee that some such thing had not transpired. Still, all his gentle prodding and questioning brought nothing out of the realm of the subconscious. However, it did bring to attention a couple of things in my conscious memory.

At the age of thirteen, I still knew nothing about the sex act, nor did I have any clear idea of where babies come from. During the Easter holiday that spring, my best friend and I went for a four-day stay at a horseback-riding place. It was there that we inadvertently witnessed a stallion breeding a mare, a fearful and revolting sight to our virgin eyes. Late that night, hiding in the safety of our sleeping bags, we talked and giggled and wondered if *this* was what parents do. Intuitively we knew that it was so, and although it went without saying that the human act would be a little more refined, it still all seemed so barbarically bestial.

Oxford: bestial / *adj.* 1 brutish, cruel, savage. 2 sexually depraved; lustful. 3 of or like a beast.

Precisely. I couldn't have said it better myself.

Of course, as I got a little older, I became more interested in this naughty business. This stuff had some good trade-offs. As I mentioned earlier in this book, I found strong affirmation for my shaky self-image in the attentions of my male friends. Stirrings of desire came too, an awakening that increased with each new experience, so I was the more drawn to this unfamiliar pleasure.

But deep down, there was a repulsive feeling about the whole thing. Why was this? Why did it all seem so smirchy? Yes, the object lesson by the stallion and the mare had been a shocking display. But there was something uglier, dimmer, much farther back.

I was seven or eight years old, walking to school. As I so often was, I was running late. My older sister was long gone; the streets were empty. It was a little over a half a mile to the school. As I came over the top of the Big Hill (as we called it) and headed down the other side, I could see clear past the school and on up the other hill beyond. Over that hill now came an old car. It came slowly, ominously. It came on forever, it seemed. Finally it was abreast of me, cruising slowly by. I can still picture it: yellow and white with big rust patches on it. (I can identify it now as an early-fifties Chevy.) It was driven by a man. I can see him yet, with his dark-rimmed glasses and expressionless, staring eyes. As he passed me, he raised up his pelvis, using the steering wheel for leverage, looking at me all the while. Then he was gone.

A few days later it happened again. Then again. I have no idea how many times it happened, but every day now, I walked to school with a sick feeling of dread. I knew nothing about sex. I had never even heard the word. We didn't have TV back then. And the only movies I had seen were *Bambi* and *Lady and the Tramp*. But even without ever having heard the word, "sex" was communicated to me as a concept, a very negative one. I could feel it, right in the area of my own genitals, though I had no consciousness of my genitals as such.

I don't recall ever having experienced fear and vulnerability before that point in my life. I didn't dream of telling anyone, so it seemed that I was doomed to carry this frightening, shameful, ongoing secret alone.

Then one day I saw the car coming yet again, slow and sinister, but this time was different. This time as he passed by and thrust his pelvis upward, I saw, as I glanced at him with sick dread, that he had exposed himself.

That night, embarrassed and ashamed, but too frightened to keep silence any longer, I approached my mother, eyes downcast, speaking barely above a whisper:

"Sometimes when I'm walking to school, this guy drives by, and when he goes by, he stands up and sticks his thing out."

"You'd better start leaving for school on time," my mother told me, rather sharply. I think she was embarrassed. Perhaps she didn't really believe me. Regardless, I don't think she wanted to deal with it.

Fortunately, it never happened again after that day. Maybe I got serious about leaving on time and had the safety of the presence of other children making their way along the road. But for years afterward, as I walked to school each day, I watched that far hill with fear and dread.

As I talked these things over with my counsellor, he brought them to God in prayer. That was how he closed each session.

I always thought that Jim was able to offer the best of both worlds, secular and Christian. Whereas a secular psychologist or psychiatrist might be very gifted at uncovering the root of a problem, once he does, the means of dealing with it are often limited. But as a Christian with the best of secular training, once Jim uncovered something painful, this dear man would carry it to the throne room in prayer, sensitive to the Holy Spirit's leading and full of faith that God would work His healing wonders in the Name of His Son. After all, it was the promised Messiah Who was called "Wonderful Counsellor."

During the time in between appointments (sometimes two weeks, sometimes four), I continued to ponder these shadowy experiences that seemed to have instilled a fear of male sexuality. They had also left me with a quiet but abiding revulsion of the male anatomy. Were there other things that had contributed to these dark feelings?

In my single years, I always managed to maintain the upper hand with young men. If anything wild was going to happen, it was going to be at my whim and no one else's. But there had been two incidents in my late teens and early twenties where, for a few frightening moments, it seemed I was to become a victim to testosterone. Once, as a naïve young (pre-Christian) university student, I accepted an invitation to go up to a young man's dorm. I took a book along; I assumed we'd probably read and listen to some music. I was wrong. This guy had in mind some passionate kissing and who knows what else. He pulled me onto his bed without so much as breaking the ice and pressed his lips hard on mine. I was not strong enough to prevent what he was doing, so I waited for an opportune moment and then bit him. He said some bad words, and I left quickly while he was preoccupied with his pain and surprise.

Another time, about five years later, during my ski-bum years, I found myself in a compromising situation with a very tall, strong young man who was high on acid. He simply would not believe that I meant it when I said "No!"

"If you're not playing, then play it for real," he said, the drug making riddles of his words.

Okay, I would play for real. There happened to be a heavy bar glass within reach, the kind that has about an inch of solid glass in the bottom. I grabbed it and whacked him over the head with it. Once again, I broke up the "party" in a big hurry.

I was lucky to get out of both situations physically unscathed, but they certainly left an ugly gash on my psyche regarding the selfish and bull-headed sex drive of the male gender. Had experiences like these marred me more deeply than I knew? Was I now unable to really trust any man, even my dear, loving husband? I would tell him that I trusted him with all of my heart, but so many times when I stiffened and pulled away from his embraces, it was hard for him to believe that I did. And that hurt him.

As I struggled with the sick feelings that so often rose up in the face of my husband's advances, I frequently remembered the reassurance in Tim and Bev LaHaye's *The Act of Marriage*, that a man's sexual desire for his wife was one of the primary ways for him to demonstrate his love for her.[3] I often felt that God had given me these words as a sort of "true north" to set my compass to, when the confusion of emotional storms confounded my sense of direction. I chose to believe the LaHayes' statement, all through those difficult years, embracing it with my mind and my will, the way I choose to believe the Word of God. In my spirit I knew that this was right, and that this was what God wanted me to believe.

So this helped to appease, on one level, the fear of being used selfishly by my husband simply for his sexual pleasure. But choosing to trust my husband's love still did not really lay my heart to rest. Deep inside, it still felt sad and sick and silent. Why did my heart feel so wounded and out of touch? As I waited for God to make His Truth real to my feelings, I examined my past more fully.

In addition to a few traumatic experiences with male sexuality, a whole lot of "positive" sexual experiences had taken their toll. During my wild years, I got physically involved with whomever I chose. Some of those men cared for me; some of them even loved me; some were just toying with me. But even if some may have desired to make a lifelong commitment to me, I was not interested in any such thing at that point in time. I only wanted what I wanted "right now," with no thought for the future. But I believe that deep inside, my heart was crying out, "I was not created for such behaviour and treatment as this!"

During these encounters, my heart, longing as it was to be cherished and made forever secure, knew the sad truth: this sexual act—or the kissing and making out—was rarely born of love, never of a lasting love, and all too often of a selfish desire for sexual pleasure, sexual release—on both sides.

My heart had been violated, not just by selfish men, but by selfish *me*. To be entirely truthful, and to be fair to the men in my past, I must confess that I also was guilty of the selfishness of which I accuse them. Although my needs were perhaps different from those of the young men (the need to feel cherished was always primary for me), I used them, the way they used me, to get what I wanted.

It seems perhaps that I am throwing the idea of selfishness around loosely, when, after all, we are speaking here of consenting adults seeking mutual pleasure. I suppose, to clarify, that I am speaking of selfishness as an objective absolute. In the final analysis, the life that is not centred on Christ is centred on oneself. The degree to which we are not centred on and submitted to Christ is the degree to which we are "selfish"; and I've come to believe that to that same degree, unhappiness will hound both us and those with whom we're involved.

In making impulsive, short-sighted, self-centred choices, I lost touch with the deepest needs and desires of my own heart, leaving it wounded and withdrawn.

In early November of 1993, I had a dream. I was with the young man to whom (in real life) I had given my virginity at the age of twenty. In the dream I was wearing a short cotton nightie. I was aware that the thin, clingy knit was very provocative. I was also aware that this was intentional on my part: I wanted to make this young man desire me, *enough that he would affirm me by his desire, but not so much that I would have to deal with his sexuality.*

The dream shifted, as dreams do. I was now outside my parents' home (where they lived when I was growing up). I was being chased by a huge grizzly bear. He was so big and powerful. His muscles rippled under his fur as he moved; the fur was thick and glossy, shimmering in the light. He was beautiful—and he was absolutely terrifying.

I was almost paralyzed with fear. I could hardly breathe. I couldn't seem to run fast enough, and the bear was close behind. I raced from door to door around the house, trying each doorknob in turn. They were all locked. I was cornered. I couldn't get away.

When I awoke from the dream, heart pounding, I knew exactly what it was about. That bear was male sexuality, in all its beauty and terror.

A week later I had another appointment with my counsellor. As it happened, Greg was in town that day, and his schedule was quite flexible.

"Why don't you come along to my counselling appointment," I suggested, "so that you can see how this guy works. He's really great."

So we went together. I was pleased and proud to introduce the two men to one another. We chatted lightly for a few minutes, then Jim asked me:

"What would you like to talk about today?"

I just said the first thing that came to mind. "I want you to fix Greg."

"Oh? And what's wrong with Greg?"

"He's over-sexed."

Then we all laughed, because we all knew that I didn't really think that was the problem.

"Actually, I want to tell you about a dream I had," I continued as we got more serious. I related it to Jim, and when I was done, I said, "You don't have to tell me what it means. But I don't know what to do with it."

Jim began to talk about the passage in the ninth chapter of Isaiah where it describes what it will be like when God's kingdom fully comes: "The wolf also shall dwell with the lamb, and the leopard will lie down with the kid; and the calf and the young lion and the fatling together; ... and the cow and the bear shall [graze]; their young shall lie down together; and the lion shall eat straw like the ox.... They shall not hurt or destroy in all My holy mountain: for the earth will be full of the knowledge of the Lord...."[4]

I had always been intrigued with my discovery in Genesis that God originally did not create animals to prey upon one another—that rather, He made both man and beast to live exclusively off fruits and green plants.[5] It was only after the flood that God allowed man to eat meat and some of the animals to prey upon others.[6]

The point implicit in Jim's use of the Isaiah quote was that, similarly, God never intended for men to prey upon women—or women upon men, as they sometimes do, to consume each another upon their lusts[7]—their emotional and physical needs. Many relationships, sadly, are like a couple of leeches attached to one another, sucking the life out of each other. "'Give! Give!' they cry."[8]

In God's original design, He never intended that women would feel preyed upon, fearful of masculine strength and the demands of testosterone. God was reassuring me that as His kingdom had its way in our lives, my fears would be swept away.

The prey always fears the predator, whether we're talking lambs and lions or women and men. But God's plan and purpose was not for a world where fear ruled; his sceptre is one of love. "Perfect love drives out fear."[9] "The one who fears is not made perfect in love."[10]

When God's kingdom comes on our earth, formerly antagonistic animals will live happily side by each, without fear. What this symbolized in my situation was this: when God's kingdom fully came in my marriage, all fear and apprehension would be disenfranchised.

When Jim addressed my dream by bringing up the Scripture in Isaiah, my attention was riveted by the mention of the bear. The bear is, of course, a predator, one of the animals to be feared in an imperfect world, a world where the knowledge of the Lord does not yet prevail. But under God's full dominion, that fearsome animal will dwell benignly and peaceably beside the one that it used to prey upon.

When our session ended that day, Jim, as always, prayed for

me. All I remember him saying is this: "Lord, show Nancy how to embrace her bear without being destroyed."

That was all. But I felt the Word of God pierce my heart with its sharp, two-edged sword. I knew it had found its mark; I knew the work was done.

Nothing changed immediately. I still struggled, most of the time, to yield myself fully and happily to Greg's advances. But now it was different: I knew that God had touched me; He had "sent His word and healed my dis-ease."[11] It was just a matter of resting in Him with faith and patience until I experienced the full manifestation.

About six months went by. I climbed into bed one night and Greg reached out and pulled me into his arms. I had the strangest feeling: I felt like I was being held in the embrace of a huge, friendly bear. Not a teddy-bear thing; nothing childish or silly or immature about it. It was the embrace of a powerful beast, yet it was entirely benevolent and loving: the creation of God in all its glory.

Greg loved me then, and I felt peaceful and content and very much cherished. Several times I felt the uneasiness and dread and revulsion begin to rush in, like water through a breach in a dyke. And when it did, I found myself softly whispering, "I can trust my bear. I can trust my bear." And the torrent would be dammed again; the torment would be stayed.

When it was over this time, I knew it was finally over. It was finished.[12] We were soon coming upon our eleventh anniversary, and God had finally caused us to triumph in Christ.[13]

Happy Ever After

Sex became a new joy. Now, where there was once a pervasive uneasiness regarding my husband's male parts, there was a warm affection for his whole body, head to toe and everything in between. Whereas foreplay used to remind me of the struggle to light the propane heater in our beat-up old trailer, my frozen libido was frozen no more.

My "pilot light" stays on by itself now, all the time. Once in a while it's a little sluggish to burst into full flame. As in the healthiest of relationships, fatigue, busyness, distractions, or worries can crud up the flow a little—or a lot. But that's the exception now, not the rule. Most of the time, that little flame will burst ablaze at the slightest encouragement, and sometimes when Greg is sleepy and just as happy to let it die down, we have a wildfire on our hands. But he never minds. I just tell him I'm trying to make up for all those earlier times, when he so often got left out in the cold.

It is a spiritual principle, however, that areas in which God has given us victory may have to be reclaimed from time to time. Once in a while, a very long while, when we are loving each other, I will suddenly find those uneasy feelings trickling into my heart again, like a sick suspicion that sex is naughty and dirty after all. It's like there's a leak in the dyke.

I will pause and hold very still. Greg will say, "Are you all right?" because he knows what's happening.

"Yes," I will say, and I just quietly wait a moment.

Sometimes that's all it takes. Other times, the assault is stronger and the pause doesn't seem to help. I'll say to Greg, "Just a minute." And then, under my breath, I tell Satan to shut his lying mouth. At this point Greg will enter into prayer with me, agreeing, standing with me in the battle. I confess aloud what I know to be true about sex from God's perspective: that He created it, that it is good and beautiful, that He made it for a husband and wife to enjoy. I invite God's presence, and then I glorify Him and thank and praise Him in whatever way occurs to me at the time. Then I quietly wait for God to make the Truth manifest. It only takes a moment, or sometimes maybe a couple of minutes. And it's like God sticks His finger in the hole in the dyke. The enemy retreats, and the peace and the passion return.

Why did we have to go through such deep waters in the area of intimacy? Not everyone does, even though it is probably more common than not for people to have some sexual history from the years before marriage.

I believe that God took us at our word when we prayed on our wedding night and asked Him to give us everything in our marriage that He designed matrimony to be. He had to tear out the old foundation and build it right. Wrong ideas, wrong experiences—they all had to be exposed and disenfranchised so God could build what we'd asked for—and what he desires every husband and wife to enjoy: a marriage *Made In Heaven.*

As this book was nearing completion, I received an invitation to speak at a youth gathering in Victoria. The topic: "Sexuality and Intimacy from a Biblical Perspective."

About a month before the event, I went through a period, a week or ten days, of intense spiritual oppression. I felt depressed and anxious and mentally unstable, and as if that weren't difficult enough, a coolness and distance came into Greg's and my relationship.

He and I prayed against the oppression daily; I asked different friends to remember us in prayer; and finally at church I had another friend pray for me. It was a couple of days after that that the heaviness and darkness suddenly lifted, and it did not return again in the weeks leading up to our event.

However, the perceived wall between Greg and me was still there; intimacy seemed impossible. Not only did this make me sad and frustrated, but I began to feel like it was going to be hypocritical to talk to these young people, ages ranging from thirteen to twenty-six, about our "great" marriage relationship. I could imagine myself speaking to them, and I could hear a nasty voice in my mind hissing, "Liar!"

I talked to Greg, about both my sadness regarding our relationship and my feeling of being unfit for the task at hand. First he reassured me that he felt no differently toward me. "It's just something we have to go through. This is our reality right now," he said, "but reality is not necessarily the truth. God's Truth is much bigger than our present reality."

This was immensely reassuring. We had gone through some difficult years early in our marriage, to be sure, but God's Truth was that He had always intended to resolve the difficulties, and He most assuredly had. We had enjoyed the fruit of that healing for well over a decade, and the occasional "blip on the screen" (as Greg called it), the present one included, did not negate the wonderful freedom of those years, nor could it overshadow God's intent and ability to bring us through once again. I took a firm stance of faith and patience, trusting that God would bring us delightful intimacy once again in His own good time.

A speaking engagement often feels to me like a pregnancy, the conception happening at the time of the invitation and the burden of the "blessed event" growing and growing within until it's almost too heavy to bear. And as any woman who has borne a child can vouch, intimacy often becomes difficult and completely undesirable in the final stages. Best to patiently wait.

We flew to Victoria early on a Friday morning. That whole day was like waiting for the onset of labour: I was so full of the burden I had been carrying for three months, full of anticipation to get on with it and get it over with.

I was exhausted when the first evening was over but full of joy also for the way my message had been received. Just like the Word says: "When a woman is in labour, she has sorrow, because her time is come: but as soon as she delivers, she remembers the anguish no more, because of the joy of new life being brought into the world."[1]

Greg and I went back to our hotel, and I had a long and restorative sleep.

I awoke in the morning, heavy and groggy. Greg was gone; he had obviously awoken earlier and slipped out quietly. The phone rang: it was our host, reporting in on some of the feedback from the night before. Everyone seemed very pleased and excited with how it was going.

By the time I got off the phone, I was absolutely starving. But what a pity to go down to the lovely dining room alone. Oh well, no matter. I wrote a note for Greg and headed down. To my surprise and pleasure, I found him sitting reading in the huge lobby.

"Have you eaten?" I asked.

"No," he said. "I didn't want to eat without you."

"Oh, how nice of you! Thank you!"

"I headed out for a walk," he continued, "but I didn't want to walk without you either." His eyes were warm and tender, and they warmed my heart.

"Well," I said, "let's have breakfast and then go for a long walk."

We lingered over our meal, talking up a storm, as we love to do. Then we headed out into the windy sunshine. We'd been accommodated at a luxurious resort overlooking the Inner Harbour. Our host had urged us to check out the two-and-a-half-kilometre walkway that wound along the shore. As we walked, I was moved to exclaim again and again at the wonders around us. My senses were all fully and amazingly alive.

The gulls cawed and wheeled overhead, and the breeze carried the ocean's scent. Spring was springing up everywhere, even though back home we were still in the grip of winter. A gull landed on the rocks below us, surveying his domain.

"Look!" I said to Greg. "Look at the colour. He doesn't even look real; he looks like he was painted by a child."

"He was," said Greg. This gave me a mental image of God seated with an easel and palette, full of childlike delight and creativity, choosing colours and applying them with His brush to this common bird.

The gull's feathers were white-white; its wings flat grey; its beak a clean, startling yellow; and its feet as pink as pink can be. I felt like I'd never really seen a gull before.

We walked slowly and chatted; we walked fast and let our muscles wake up and stretch; we paused to look at things; leaned on a railing to take in the scenery. We reached the end and turned around and started back; stopped and sat on a comfortable bench, close together, looking at the ocean through the arbutus trees.

The sun poured down so warmly, I had to remove my coat and sweater, basking in bare arms. A rest and relaxation came over me that was so deep; every trace of tension drained out of my entire being. My body, soul, and spirit entered into complete peace. Friday night was behind; Saturday night and Sunday morning now felt like a foregone conclusion. It would be fine; it would be easy. I could relax in God and just trust Him to carry me the rest of the way through the weekend.

Relief, that the "birth" was over. Joy, that God was working in the lives of these kids to whom we had come to speak. Creation around me so full of the glory and the love of God. Fullness and fulfillment rose up from my very toes, flooding my being, filling my heart to the bursting. Greg had his arm around my shoulders. With his other hand he softly stroked my face and gazed at me, pouring all his love and attention on me. My eyes brimmed over and tears coursed down my cheeks. Greg wiped them off one at a time with his big fingers.

How can life be so full? Lord God, I know You want it to be this way—life abundant.[2] *But it's elusive for so many people, so much of the time. God, You are so good. If people only knew...*

At length we left our secluded bench and finished the walk back to our hotel. We intended to take a nap, but God had something much more special in mind...

The day had such an anointing of joy and romance on it, and we carried that anointing with us into the evening meeting. I know that the kids could see it on us.

I spoke, and Greg joined me on several songs. We came to our final piece, taken from the Song of Solomon, the Bridegroom and the Bride singing to each other. Greg was standing beside the piano, facing both me and the audience. I was deeply into the song, concentrating on the piano part and my voice, but I happened to glance up at Greg and found that he was singing directly to me, his eyes full of love. It was so powerful that it startled me, and I almost lost my composure and focus.

We heard later that a whole row of girls, some of the older ones, had wept their way through that whole song. One of them later wrote to me, and in part, said this:

> You have a gift and a way to express your thoughts and experiences that young people can relate to.... I was greatly impacted.... I felt like that night God removed the chains of temptation (sexually), and though I know that doesn't mean the struggle disappears, I know He has taken off a great load and I feel it every day. I am very grateful that you two made the journey out here, so thank you.
>
> It was also really powerful to see how in love Greg and you are (especially when you sang together). You look like you just met and fell in love, and that is so wonderful to see, because society tells us that getting hitched is a drag and it's boring once you get old. You both have a fresh spark in your eyes.
>
> God bless you both.

There is nothing that thrills me more than to help direct a young person—no, *any*one of *any* age—into a deeper grasp of God's intent for them in the area of love and sex and marriage. How much more our own children. My husband and I have had two deep desires for our children ever since they were born: that each one should find the rich love and life of Christ Jesus and that each should find God's choice of a life-mate so that they can all enjoy the kind of marriage their father and I have shared.

A relationship with the Lord is primary. As our kids establish that and, in so doing, learn how richly God rewards those who seek Him, they will be keen to yield to Him in every area of life. And as they get to know His voice, He will direct them surely on their way. Without a relationship with God first, finding the right partner is at best a crapshoot, an uncertain gamble, and even with a partner who starts out being suitable, marriage is a scary proposition without daily doses of grace and faith. God, in His love, is willing to step in at any point and right a wrong situation; but how much better to start out with everything possible in one's favour.

As a young mom, I assumed that my kids would all grow up knowing God, all the way. They had that advantage over me, I thought, being raised by parents who were fervent and open in their pursuit of God. It has been a gradual revelation that I could not make any of my kids see the Truth of God. I have been able to do many things that I'm sure have helped, but I am equally sure that I have done many things that have hindered.

It always comes back to trusting in God's grace—what a relief! I have a dear friend whom God told years ago that it would be her very failings as a mother that He would use to draw her children to Him. I believe that that promise is for any parent who has ears to hear it.

In addition to being open and real with our kids about our relationship with God, so we have been candid with them about our own relationship as well as the many stumblings in both of our pasts. We believe that honesty and openness are the best teachers.

One day I received a phone call from our son Ben, then twenty-three years old, from a ship in the Caribbean where he had hired on as a musician. It came as a surprise to me when, in the course of the conversation, he thanked me for my transparency during his formative years. He said that he remembers once asking a very personal question about my past, and that my forthright answer has given him a lot of moral strength over the years since. Some weeks later, I e-mailed him, asking if he would write out the details of that occasion and explain how it has impacted him. He e-mailed back a short while after:

> There seem to be two schools of thought on how parents should deal with kids on sensitive issues including general sexuality, sexual drive, masturbation, and

specifically in this case, the sexual sins and pasts of the parents.

I firmly believe that my parents' way of approaching it was by far the most effective, and I say so because I firmly believe that the consequences of deception concerning sexual history are far more destructive when passed from generation to generation.

Let me explain.

I distinctly remember being ten or eleven years old, standing by the fridge in the kitchen one night. My mother happened to be in there, probably busying herself getting the kitchen cleaned up. She was tired, exhausted, and anxious to get to bed. Out of nowhere, I suddenly had the urge to ask her about her past. "Mom, did you ever have sex with anybody except for Dad?"

This is probably a parent's worst nightmare. I can only imagine what ran through her mind in the first few nanoseconds.

The most important part of that uncomfortable moment was my mother taking a breath, looking me in the face, and replying, "Yes, dear."

She went on to explain some of the implications and a little bit of the pain she had endured in the marriage because of her actions.

To this day, I gain an incredible amount of strength from knowing what both of my parents endured as a result of their sin, the time it took to heal, and the result of eventually living a sexual lifestyle that was pleasing to God. In situations where I might normally be compromised, God has blessed me through the honesty and sincerity of my parents.

For kids growing up under the deceptive illusion of parents with perfect pasts, I can only begin to imagine the confusion and pain they endure from hearing one story and having to live another. I will say from a few circumstances with friends that not being able to approach their parents in the confidence of being able to just discuss hard things, this may be the most detrimental thing a teen can face. Parents need to be able to lay down their self-righteousness and their fear of their children's future mistakes and trust that God will protect them from the traps and snares of this world.

They must also continue to believe, regardless of circumstance, that God will grant the grace to bring teens and young adults through the mistakes they've already made. The less honest parents are with their kids, the less transparent their kids will be with themselves. And the worst thing anyone can be is dishonest with oneself.

I have heard, I have read, and I really do believe that one of the greatest gifts parents can give to their children is to love their spouse—openly, continually, and unconditionally. Free exchanges of affection, like kisses and hugs, give children of all ages a sense of security, because they speak of stability and permanence on the home front. And this builds a sense of hope and anticipation concerning their own marriages in the future, faith that God wants to give them the same enduring joy.

When our children were younger and they witnessed a display of tenderness between their dad and me, their faces would light up with a knowing, happy grin. As teenagers they were sometimes a little embarrassed; there might be comments of "That's gross!" or even "Get a room!" But the little smiles playing on the corners of the frowns told me that they were still happy to see the strength of our love and commitment.

Of course, anything beyond hugs and kisses belongs behind closed doors, when teenage children are absent or asleep. Our boys' bedrooms are in the basement, so they are a long way from our room. But our girls are on the second floor with us. The proximity of their bedrooms to ours might create a problem; however, we have a perfect set-up. There is a separate furnace upstairs with a very powerful fan that makes a whooshing sound in all the ducts and registers. It makes a terrific sound baffle. It's a simple matter to open the bedroom door, reach out to the thermostat, and just quietly switch on the fan. This gives us a little cocoon of privacy; we might as well be in a separate house. Or so I always thought.

One summer night when Melissa was fifteen, she had spent the whole evening working on a house plan. (We have some architecture software on the computer that fascinates her; she spends hours designing homes.) At bedtime she came into my room to say her good-nights, flopping her long, leggy frame onto the bed beside me where I lay reading. Greg was out of town.

"I just love designing houses," she enthused. "I can't wait to design my own house." She paused and then continued. "Especially the bedroom. I'm going to make sure that it has soundproof walls and a bed that doesn't squeak."

I looked at her, aghast, my mouth hanging open and my face beginning to flush. She had a big grin on her face, a sweet blend of sass and innocence. I couldn't believe what she had just said. But she wasn't finished yet.

"I always know when you guys are doing it, 'cause someone comes out and turns on the fan... then after, the fan shuts off and I hear someone using the bathroom."

I was absolutely mortified. And she was obviously enjoying my reaction. Still smiling broadly; just letting me know what she knew. Probably giving me a "heads-up" so that we could change our strategy. Likely she didn't really want to know what was going on and when.

I don't recall where the conversation went after that, but we talked for a long time, very comfortably in the end, before she finally gave me a hug and a kiss and went off to bed.

So much of what kids view inadvertently in the world around them today concerning love and romance—via movies, magazines, and media—is really about fornication. Because God's laws of right and wrong are written on every heart,[3] the spirit of fornication necessarily carries with it a sense of unrighteousness, especially as it impacts pure, young hearts. Their perceptions of sexuality become tainted at a tender age. Then it confuses their emotions when they see Mom and Dad, who are "good," expressing or hinting at these "bad" passions. Often kids have to be clearly and boldly told that this is God's design, and that, just like everything else He's created, it is *good*. This is what I had to do with my young children when I overheard them being given the facts of life in crude street vernacular. The enemy continually tries to sully this beautiful gift from God, leaving dark cobwebs of wrongness, uneasiness, shame, and guilt clinging to the subject. Truth, vigorously applied, should clean things up.

Teenagers need to know that their mother and father love each other, that the marriage will endure, that their home is stable. If a teenage girl (or boy) can be secure in her parents' love for each other, she feels more confident in the constancy of their love for her, and ultimately it reflects on how much she can trust the love of God. Her parents' love or lack thereof, for each other and for her, will teach her much, rightly or wrongly, about the father-heart of God and the husband-heart of Christ.

It's Saturday morning. I drift slowly into consciousness. My body feels like it weighs a thousand pounds, the pleasant feeling of a heavy and rejuvenating sleep after several exhausting days.

I open my eyes. I can see Greg's profile inches away, and an open eye staring straight ahead. Obviously he's lost in thought. He's lying very quietly, trying to let me sleep as long as I might. I want to say "Good morning," to let him know that I've awakened, but for the moment my brain and my voice are not in gear. Instead I drape one leg over his.

He turns his head slightly and sees me peering at him. "You're gorgeous," he says.

"You're crazy," I answer. *Gorgeous!* I think, *I must look a complete sight. Thank You, Lord, for a husband that loves me so much. It's so wonderful to be loved.*

I snuggle closer, laying my head in the crook of his shoulder. I am slowly remembering what I was just dreaming about. Something about a guy at the Co-op calculating aloud how many bushels of grain-storage he would need to plan for a customer, and what size tanks they would need to build. Not exactly my kind of dream.

"Hey," I ask Greg aloud, "were you just lying here doing mental calculations about one of your jobs?"

"Yeah, partly—I guess I was."

"I think I picked up on it in the dream I was just having." I tell him what it was about.

"Hmm. That's strange, isn't it? I wonder..." he muses. He is silent for a few moments; then he speaks again. "What was it I was dreaming about?" He thinks, trying to bring it back. "Oh—it was so amazing! These cows were praising God. Wow! It was so amazing. It's not like they were singing or anything, they were just mooing, but they were praising God. It was awesome."

He is silent again, and then he begins to demonstrate: a loud, rather plaintive bellow that could only be so duly delivered by someone who grew up with cattle. The noise comes abruptly, startling and ridiculous, shattering the peaceful quiet in the house this early morning.

"Hush," I rebuke him. "Melissa will think we're having sex again," and then we both go into gales of laughter.

Thank You, Lord. How wonderful to be able to talk and laugh like this.

The mention of cows praising God has drawn my attention to the Scriptures. I think I know where the Word says something about that. I roll over and reach for the little New Testament and Psalms at my bedside. I flip it open to Psalm 148 and survey the text. What a glorious paean of praise! I want to read it aloud and let the words frame our day, this beautiful Saturday morning. But my voice is so sleepy and croaky, after forty-eight hours of seemingly non-stop cheering at the basketball tournament the high school was hosting.

"Here." I pass it over to Greg. "Read this one aloud." He does, but we keep interrupting the reading to talk about the thoughts and insights that spring up, plump and ripe for the picking. He gets to the part that says, "Praise the Lord from the earth,... all cattle,"[4] and he stops again, lost in wonderment at what he saw and felt in his dream.

I tell him how I've been thinking and writing lately about this subject, particularly this psalm, and how it's interesting to note that all of creation, animate and inanimate, offers praise to God and obeys His voice, with the notable exception of man. Man is the only one who has a choice in the matter. "And yet," I conclude, "the Word says that the day is coming when every knee shall bow and every tongue confess that Jesus Christ is Lord, to the honour and glory of God the Father."[5]

How wonderful, Lord, to be able to talk between ourselves about You like this, to share our love for You and Your Word, to share our thoughts and insights, to allow You to bring inspiration and revelation even as we lie here barely awake. Thank You, God, for our marriage. How rich and full and enduring it is.

Aloud I say, "How can we be so rich, so blessed, to enjoy the marriage we have! Oh, God, we want to give these riches away. As with monetary riches, You give this wealth to be shared with others."

I think of my book, waiting patiently for real life to slow down once again long enough for me to work on it. Will I ever get it finished? Of course I will. It is God's project, and He has His perfect timing. I only need be obedient to Him, every day, and it will happen in His good time.

Greg is still thinking about the psalm, how all of creation glorifies God. He begins to pray for each one of our kids, asking God to receive His glory from each of their lives. What a neat thought.

"Receive Your glory, Lord, in their lives," he says again.

Then he goes on, praying for our children's various friends, name after name, with me adding in others as we go.

Help them all to know You, Lord, so that they can delight in the riches that we enjoy. Give us opportunity to share with hungry hearts of all ages the wonderful things that You have prepared for those that love You.[6] Thank You for our wonderful marriage. You've been able to give such a relationship to us because we believe You; we love You and we hold You in the highest reverence. We are committed to letting You have Your way with us; we are convinced that You have our highest good and richest blessing in mind; we believe that You not only know what is best, but that You also have the power to pull it off.

We count not ourselves to have apprehended or laid hold:[7] we have not "arrived." Our marriage presents daily challenges along with all of its joys. The challenges and the growth will go on until the day we die, and we can trust You, Lord, with each new day as it comes, just as we have trusted You in the past. You have proven Yourself faithful, and You will continue to be faithful, because that is Your very nature.

And now this one thing we do: Forgetting the things that lie behind us—being neither discouraged by our failures nor caught up in our victories—we press on toward the goal of the high calling of God,[8] *allowing Him to flesh out in us the beautiful design that He originally* Made In Heaven.

Photo by Rachel Christenson, 2006

Endnotes

Dedication (p. 9)
1. Ephesians 3:19, NAS

A Note from the Author (p. 19-23)
1. Matthew 19:6, NKJV
2. MSN Encarta
3. Wiktionary

Part 1: Chasing Mr. Wrong
Paperback Romance (p. 27-36)
1. Mom was actually married at twenty-three—my mistake. Couldn't change it once she straightened me out; it needed to rhyme.
2. Carole Chatt and I had shared an apartment way up north in Fort McMurray one winter—and she frequently had to lend a listening ear to my troubles concerning my romantic escapades.

The Search for Love and Acceptance (p. 37-44)
1. Betty Robison on *Life Today*, November 26, 2003
2. Nancy Christenson, from a poem, "To Ben," written for her son.

Dream or Delusion? (p. 45-53)
1. Source unknown
2. 1 Thessalonians 5:22, KJV
3. Romans 2:24, KJV
4. Titus 2:4–5, KJV

The Young and the Restless (p. 55-64)
1. Matthew 26:41, KJV

2. Luke 17:26–27
3. Joel 2:31; Acts 2:20; Revelation 6:12
4. Judges 16:4–21
5. Ephesians 4:30, KJV
6. Hebrews 6:6, KJV
7. Philippians 3:14, KJV
8. Nancy Christenson, from a poem, "Sweet Wine."
9. "Create in Me a Clean Heart," composer unknown.
10. 2 Timothy 2:13, NAS.
11. 1 Corinthians 10:13, KJV
12. 1 Corinthians 6:18, NIV
13. Proverbs 7:22, KJV—check out the context of this one!
14. cf. Galatians 5:17
15. cf. James 1:14, KJV
16. John 20:23, KJV
17. cf. 1 John 1:7
18. 1 Corinthians 10:13, KJV
19. cf. James 4:8
20. 1 John 1:9, KJV
21. cf. 1 Corinthians 6:19
22. cf. Ephesians 4:30, KJV
23. cf. 1 Corinthians 6:18

Fleeing Youthful Lusts (p. 65-71)
1. Genesis 2:7, KJV
2. John 20:22, KJV
3. cf. Isaiah 55:9
4. 1 Peter 1:6–7
5. cf. 1 Corinthians 13:12, KJV
6. Romans 6:4; Philippians 3:10; Colossians 2:12
7. Matthew 3:11
8. Comment made by my friend Laurel Stevens when she read this part of the manuscript.
9. cf. Hebrews 6:12, KJV
10. cf. 2 Corinthians 12:9, KJV

A Flame and a Funeral (p. 73-77)
1. Galatians 5:22
2. Exodus 12:13, 23; Revelation 1:5, 5:9

    3. James 4:6; 1 Peter 5:5
    4. Isaiah 55:11, KJV
    5. 2 Corinthians 6:2
    6. Acts 2:21; Romans 10:13
    7. Psalm 51:12
    8. John 14:27
    9. cf. Ephesians 2:4; Psalm 145:8

Re-Enter the Doctor (p. 79-86)
    1. Numbers 11:4–34
    2. Numbers 11:33, NIV
    3. Numbers 11:20, NIV
    4. Psalm 106:15, KJV, emphasis added
    5. Psalm 106:15, MSG
    6. Isaiah 55:2, KJV; TAB
    7. 2 Corinthians 6:14, KJV
    8. Good-bye: Origin: 1565–75; contraction of *God be with ye*—Dictionary.com Unabridged (v 1.1)
    9. 1 Samuel 16:7, KJV
    10. 1 Corinthians 2:9, author's paraphrase

Go East, Young Woman (p. 87-92)
    1. Galatians 5:24, KJV
    2. 1 John 1:8–9, KJV
    3. Hebrews 11:25, KJV

Delightful Delinquent (p. 93-99)
    1. 1 Corinthians 2:2, NAS
    2. 2 Corinthians 5:17, NIV
    3. Titus 2:3, TAB
    4. Titus 2:4, TAB, emphasis added
    5. cf. Romans 14:21
    6. cf. Romans 14:23, TAB
    7. cf. 2 Corinthians 12:9

Charming a Snake (p. 101-111)
    1. 1 Corinthians 13:7, NAS
    2. 2 Corinthians 6:14, NIV
    3. 1 Corinthians 6:18, NIV

4. 1 Corinthians 10:13, King James Version, w/ Study Bible margin notes
5. Mark 4:19, KJV; Hebrews 3:13, KJV
6. cf. James 4:14
7. James 1:14–15, KJV

Progress of a Pilgrim (p. 113-122)
1. cf. 1 Kings 18:21; James 1:8, KJV
2. KJV uses "lust" here instead of "coveting."
3. Romans 7:7, 8, NAS
4. NLT
5. Strong's Exhaustive Concordance of the Bible, Dictionary of the Words in the Greek Testament, emphasis added
6. cf. Proverbs 16:7, KJV
7. Proverbs 29:1, KJV
8. TAB
9. Galatians 6:7–8, KJV
10. Psalm 91:3, KJV

Letting Go (p. 123-128)
1. Micah 2:7, KJV
2. Micah 2:7, NLT
3. Matthew 21:44, KJV
4. cf. Hebrews 10:29
5. Hebrews 10:31, KJV
6. cf. 1 Samuel 15:22
7. Hebrews 4:15, KJV
8. John 15:15
9. Isaiah 64:6, KJV
10. cf. Romans 5:20
11. Lamentations 3:22, KJV
12. Ibid.
13. Lamentations 3:23, KJV
14. Ibid.

Part 2: Finding Mr. Right
God Has Some Fun (p. 145-152)
1. 2 Corinthians 10:5, KJV

A Valentine's Letter (p. 153-159)
1. Ann Kiemel Anderson, *I Gave God Time* (Tyndale House, 1982), page 31
2. Ibid., p. 38
3. Ibid., p. 50
4. Ibid., p. 46
5. Ibid., p. 82
6. Ibid., p. 41
7. Ibid., p. 47
8. Ibid., p. 59

The First Date (p. 161-169)
1. Song of Solomon 2:7, MSG
2. cf. 2 Timothy 1:12
3. William Cowper, *Olney Hymns*, 1779, "Light Shining out of Darkness"

Lots of Letters (p. 183-197)
1. cf. Philippians 4:6, KJV, NIV
2. cf. Jeremiah 17:9, KJV
3. Colossians 3:5, KJV
4. cf. Job 13:15, KJV
5. cf. 2 Corinthians 5:17
6. Psalm 103:12, KJV

Needs and Expectations (p. 199-205)
1. Hannah Hurnard, *Hinds' Feet on High Places* (Kingsway Publications, 1957) pp. 185–187, emphasis added. By permission.
2. cf. Deuteronomy 23:21

The Breakaway Letters (p. 207-214)
1. The correct reference is actually 1 Samuel 16:7, KJV.
2. The germ of this thought comes from listening to a series of lectures by Arthur Burk, entitled *Nurturing Your Spirit*, www.plumblineministries.com.
3. Ephesians 2:1, 5; Colossians 2:13; esp. NIV
4. Proverbs 18:14, KJV
5. Mark 12:11, KJV

6. cf. Psalm 25:3, KJV: According to Strong's Hebrew Dictionary, the word "ashamed" (as it's usually translated in this verse) also includes the sense of being disappointed or delayed.

Home Again (p. 215-221)
1. 1 Thessalonians 5:22, KJV
2. Galatians 5:13, KJV
3. cf. Psalm 51:12
4. cf. 2 Corinthians 12:9
5. cf. Ephesians 6:13, KJV
6. cf. 2 Corinthians 2:11, KJV

The Second Date (p. 223-235)
1. Living Light: Daily Light in Today's Language from the Living Bible (Tyndale House Publishers, 1976), April 26 evening reading, Song of Solomon 6:10
2. Ibid., Ephesians 5:25–27
3. Ibid., Revelation 19:7
4. Ibid., John 17:22
5. Deuteronomy 31:17, 23; Joshua 1:6, 9; KJV
6. cf. 1 Corinthians 10:13, KJV

Old Things Become New (p. 247-249)
1. 2 Corinthians 5:16, KJV and NIV
2. 2 Corinthians 5:17, NIV
3. Ephesians 5:4, KJV
4. Song of Solomon 8:4, TAB
5. Tim and Beverly LaHaye, *The Act of Marriage* (Bantam Books, 1978, by arrangement with The Zondervan Corporation). I have been unable to find the actual quote.
6. Philippians 3:8, KJV
7. Philippians 3:13, NAS
8. I have *green* eyes.

Wife-in-Waiting (p. 251-260)
1. Demos Shakarian, as told to John and Elizabeth Sherrill, *The Happiest People on Earth* (Chosen Books, 1975), p. 76, emphasis added.

Giving Up Control (p. 261-273)
1. Proverbs 20:17, NLT
2. 1 Corinthians 7:1, KJV
3. cf. Ephesians 6:12, KJV
4. Isaiah 61:10, KJV
5. Psalm 19:1, KJV
6. Ruth 1:16, KJV

The Final Countdown (p. 275-283)
1. cf. Ruth 1:16, KJV
2. Genesis 20:18; 30:22

Part 3: Ever After
Is the Honeymoon Over Yet? (p. 287-298)
1. cf. 1 Corinthians 7:4
2. Proverbs 31:30, KJV and NIV
3. Proverbs 18:13, NKJV
4. 2 Timothy 1:12, KJV
5. Deuteronomy 24:5, KJV

What Is Wrong With Me? (p. 299-308)
1. Revelation 12:11, KJV
2. Hebrews 11:13
3. Daniel 3:17–18, Greg Christenson's paraphrase
4. cf. Hebrews 6:12, KJV
5. cf. Matthew 6:34
6. John 8:44, KJV
7. cf. Ecclesiates 3:11
8. Proverbs 17:22, KJV
9. Acts 14:22, KJV
10. Matthew 5:3, KJV
11. Nancy Christenson, from the song "When My Heart Is Full," this verse based on Romans 8:28–29

Babies and Kisses (p. 309-317)
1. cf. 2 Corinthians 10:5

Healing Finally Comes (p. 319-327)
1. From a lecture by Fred Littauer, author of *The Promise of Restoration*

2. Ibid.
3. I have been unable to find the actual quote.
4. Isaiah 11:6–9, KJV Study Bible, "graze" from margin notes
5. Genesis 1:29–30.
6. Genesis 9:1–3
7. cf. James 4:3, KJV
8. Proverbs 30:15, NIV
9. 1 John 4:18, NIV
10. Ibid.
11. Psalm 107:20, Psalm 103:3, KJV; hyphenation added
12. John 19:30
13. cf. 2 Corinthians 2:14, KJV

Happy Ever After (p. 329-342)
1. John 16:21, author's paraphrase
2. cf. John 10:10
3. cf. Romans 2:15
4. Psalm 148:7–10, NIV
5. cf. Philippians 2:10–11
6. cf. 1 Corinthians 2:9
7. cf. Philippians 3:13a, KJV & NIV
8. Philippians 3:13b, author's paraphrase

Other Works by the Author

In September of 1975, a self-described hippie went to work as a camp cook at Douglas Lake Cattle Company in the British Columbia interior. Little did she know that what started as a short-term diversion following a summer of disenchantment would not only transform her into a cowgirl but change her life forever.

Douglas Lake, the largest ranch in Canada, offered up a host of wonderful characters and a landscape that could soothe a restless soul. For a young woman floundering amid the confused values of the seventies, it was a place for healing, for introspection, and for song-writing. It was a place where she would come to know a God Who would give her a frame of reference where she could hang her hat.

From spring branding through to fall round-up, the author spent four seasons swept up in a panorama of adventures and cowboy tradition. It was a tradition that had scarcely changed in a hundred years, a lifestyle now fast disappearing, a heritage of which this retired cowgirl now says it was an unspeakable privilege to be a part.

Christenson delivers a humorous and warm-hearted story.
Order the book at **www.cowgirlstory.com**

For other works by Nancy Christenson or to contact the author:
www.ogdenfish.com or Box 6834, Wetaskiwin, AB, T9A 2G5, CANADA
Visit the website for information on
the **CD of the songs from** *Made in Heaven, Fleshed Out on Earth*

listen|imagine|view|experience

AUDIO BOOK DOWNLOAD INCLUDED WITH THIS BOOK!

In your hands you hold a complete digital entertainment package. Besides purchasing the paper version of this book, this book includes a free download of the audio version of this book. Simply use the code listed below when visiting our website. Once downloaded to your computer, you can listen to the book through your computer's speakers, burn it to an audio CD or save the file to your portable music device (such as Apple's popular iPod) and listen on the go!

How to get your free audio book digital download:

1. Visit www.tatepublishing.com and click on the e|LIVE logo on the home page.
2. Enter the following coupon code:
   7fde-8e9b-61f2-9878-f53f-bd84-98c6-d9a7
3. Download the audio book from your e|LIVE digital locker and begin enjoying your new digital entertainment package today!